ESCAPING THE БЕДЯ

BOOK FIVE OF THE GEOPOLITICAL TECHNO-THRILLER SERIES
ANDREW B. LOUIS

A Russian oligarch wants a new life outside of Russia, helping Mossad and Shadow Experts with his cyber warfare experience.

This is a work of fiction. All characters, organizations, and events portrayed in this novel are either products of the author's imagination or are used fictitiously.

Copyright © 2023 by Andrew B. Louis

All rights reserved. No part of this publication may be reproduced in whole or in part, or stored in a retrieval system, or transmitted in any form or by any means, electronic, mechanical, photocopying, recording, or otherwise, without written permission of the author, except for the inclusion of brief quotations in a review.

For information regarding permission, please write to:
info@barringerpublishing.com
Barringer Publishing, Naples, Florida
www.barringerpublishing.com

Cover, graphics, and layout by Linda S. Duider
Cape Coral, Florida

ISBN: 978-1-954396-40-1
Library of Congress Cataloging-in-Publication Data
Escaping the Bear / Andrew B. Louis

Printed in U.S.A.

DEDICATION

To those friends and family members who have kept pushing me to write and helped me get better. They know who they are, and I thank them from the bottom of my heart.

A special hello to my French confrere, Pat Cartier.

OTHER BOOKS BY THE AUTHOR

Other novels by Andrew B. Louis include:

Operation Kovesh, The Shadow Experts, Below the Surface, The Crypto Trap, Glitter and Smoke (Coming 2023), *Seven Miracles to Save the World, A Crooked Few* and *Tough Choices* available at Amazon.com.

www.AndrewBLouis.com

ACKNOWLEDGMENTS

Though all the writing and errors are solely my own doing, a number of people contributed to the creation of the text. I would like to thank the numerous friends and family members who were kind enough to comment on various drafts and led me to make material changes for the better. A special mention is reserved for my wife who labored through so many versions that I am certain she has lost count.

SYNOPSIS

Mossad accidentally learns that a Russian oligarch is looking for safety for himself and his family. They invite the family to Israel and discover that his fortune was in part the result of his being the founder, head, and majority owner of a cybersecurity company in St. Petersburg. Though a recognized world leader in cybersecurity, Israel is very keen to benefit from the gentleman's expertise. With the help of "The Shadow Experts," the group headed by Countess Renate, *Mossad* works to capitalize on the insights they can gain into Visla Cybersecurity all the while trying to postpone as much as possible any Russian discovery that the oligarch has indeed effectively defected.

However, a couple of details in the biography and history of the oligarch suggest that he may not be a defector, but a Russian plant. If he was, his goal would have to be to learn as much as possible on the latest techniques and any cyber tools developed in Israel. Yet, *Mossad* cannot officially doubt the credentials of this individual as the opportunity to sabotage the Russian systems exported to Syria or Iran is potentially too attractive. Furthermore, the onset of the Russian attack on Ukraine does not allow the time which one would need to evaluate the situation in as much depth as desired. Thus, will *Mossad* be able to protect the oligarch against what appear to be assassination attempts? If those attempts are real, who are the spies in his entourage? On the other hand, if he is a spy, how will *Mossad* avoid providing too much information to the enemy? Will they solve that riddle early enough?

Preface: All the parties to this story are totally fictitious and if there was some resemblance with individuals or institutions, it would be purely coincidental.

PROLOGUE

ST. PETERSBURG, RUSSIA, ZURICH, SWITZERLAND AND TEL AVIV, ISRAEL

Adolf Edelblume was the managing partner of one of the most secret private banks in Zurich, though certainly not considered the best or most widely known. It was a classical, excellent firm which catered only to billionaires. While all of its financial services were certainly as good as most in Switzerland, the quality that it was mostly appreciated for had to be its utmost discretion. On that count, it was at the very top of the leagues.

The personal cellphone which he always kept on his desk when at the office suddenly rang. Adolf Edelblume picked it up and looked at the screen. It indicated a number which he immediately recognized. The bank, Zurick Private Verein, had developed a clever system which allowed it help those clients who needed the utmost secrecy. The account number was paired with a cellphone which was given to the client for his personal use on matters related to the bank. This phone number was listed as one of the several lines of the bank. Therefore, to anyone intercepting the call, it would appear to have come from the bank to itself; in other words, an internal phone call, though the client might be calling from anywhere in the world.

Upon finding out that Dimitri Godunov was on the line, Adolf immediately realized that it had to be a very important issue. After all, he did not often call him directly, though he always used the "special phone" when he did. Adolf Ederblume wondered why Dimitri Godunov might be calling him. He probably ought to have guessed as the geopolitical environment had taken a decided turn for the worse when Russia started a campaign of indirect and then direct threats to invade Ukraine. Though not reported by the press, or if reported, burried in the back pages, the threat of the invasion was dividing the ruling classes in Russia. "Ruling classes" here might be somewhat of an exaggeration: there was indeed one ruling party, on the surface at least totally in the camp of President Konstantin Yushin. Somehow associated with the ruling party, there were a number of people, generally known under the monicker of "oligarchs" that had made massive fortunes owing mostly, if not totally, to their connections to political leaders. Adolf had already received quite a few calls from individuals such as these; they were worried for their fortunes when not even for their lives. However, Dimitri Godunov was not really one of those. He had led his life somewhat differently, though, on financial criteria alone and owing to his Russian origin, he would qualify as an oligarch.

After the first few words uttered by Dimitri, Adolf made a mental note that his voice seemed a bit different than usual. But the difference was not in the tone of his voice: it was the same relatively but not excessively low voice with clear elocution and speaking in German. It was more in the way Dimitri was speaking; he was making no attempt to be friendly or charming in marked contrast to his usual style. His conversation was just a series of short instructions rattled off a bit like the shots from an automatic rifle.

Dimitri had indeed simply said:

"Sell all securities in the account. Buy gold and investment grade diamonds with the proceeds. Two thirds of the funds should be

allocated to diamonds and the balance to gold. Diamonds should be D or E color, internally flawless and in sizes ranging from one to three carats. Gold should be in one kilo bars."

Adolf had only asked:

"How quickly do you need that done?"

"As quickly as possible."

Dimitri paused for a second and then added:

"By the way, something else: I want at least $250 million to be made available mostly in diamonds in Tel Aviv in a week or less. Keep the bulk of the gold bars and the rest of the diamonds in your custody."

"Tel Aviv?"

"Yes, I am going there and may need the money. Do you have an Israeli custodian bank correspondent I can trust?"

Adolf was quite surprised. First, all these trades and the request for money were surely not in character for Dimitri. He had always tried to maintain some balance to his portfolio and certainly never asked for any significant amount of money to be transferred outside of Switzerland, other than for specific purchases but nothing in the range of $250 million. Adolf asked a few discreet questions just to make as certain as he could that it was really Dimitri talking on the phone and even if it was he that Dimitri was not talking under any pressure. Surprised but as satisfied as he could be, he replied to the question of a potential correspondent bank in Israel:

"We have at least a couple, but this is a lot of money."

Returning to the need to raise the funds and buy the required diamonds, he argued that the depth of the gold market would allow him to execute virtually any trade. However, such was not the case for diamonds. Adolf therefore added:

"I'm not sure it can be done in such a short while, particularly if you don't want your name to come out . . ."

"Do the best you can. I'm sure gold is not an issue, right?"

"Clearly not, all the more as you want me to keep most of it here. The real potential problem has to do with the diamonds."

"Wait. I don't understand. What does that mean?"

"Just normal caution. The diamond market depends on whatever is available or in demand at the time. We can be lucky and do it all in one or two trades or it could take a while. You don't want to pay retail. Correct?"

Almost mechanically, Dimitri replied:

"Probably not. What's the difference?"

"Investment grade diamonds might go for four or five thousand dollars per carat in one carat sizes at wholesale. Retail prices would be twice that, may be even more."

Dimitri thought for a few seconds and then, matter-of-factly, asked:

"I see. Clearly, I'd rather not pay retail. Do your best. But I am prepared to pay what I must pay, at least for the first lot of diamonds. For the rest, park the money in gold if needed. Anyway, could you deliver the $250 million yourself at Ben Gurion Airport?"

Dimitri had spoken almost mechanically, without thinking the whole thing fully through. Suddenly, thinking a bit further, he asked:

"Wait a minute. Back to the diamonds, don't we own quite a few diamonds already?"

"You do. Sure, you do. Actually, almost enough to give you the quantity you say you currently need . . ."

Adolf paused for a second and continued:

"If you're prepared to have me dip into that reserve, the trade becomes much easier to execute. I thought you meant for me only to deliver new purchases—that's why I was worried."

"Sorry for the confusion. Let me try to help. I really want two things. First, I want to liquidate as much of the financial securities portfolio as you can; I don't want to park the proceeds in cash, I want to use the proceeds to buy gold and investment grade diamonds.

Second, I need you to deliver $250 million, with at least 90% of the total in diamonds and the rest in gold in Tel Aviv. For the balance of the funds, I'd like the same mix of diamonds and gold as for the delivery to Tel Aviv, but we can get there in stages as the diamonds are available. Is that clearer?"

"Totally, thank you. I'll do the best we can and I'm certain you'll have what you need when you get to Israel."

Adolf, who was used to somewhat unpredictable requests from his clients, went back to Dimitri's question as to the desired delivery at Ben Gurion Airport. He pointed out that it would not be a problem if the meeting was to take place before going through customs and immigration. Nevertheless, he immediately added he could not deliver the diamonds after customs and immigration because he could not bring that much in diamonds and gold into the country without declaring it, adding:

"That would be totally illegal. You understand?"

Dimitri's mind was racing, and he simply replied:

"Of course. Plan on our meeting prior to customs and immigration. Let me call you back with more precise delivery instructions. By the way, you should know I plan on declaring the shipment when I take it into Israel . . ."

Shifting back to the current issue, Dimitri added:

"May I assume that you can take the funds out of Switzerland?"

Though Dimitri could not see Adolf's face, he imagined a discreet, confident smile when Adolf simply answered:

"We have ways . . ."

■ ■ ■ ■ ■

David Heller, the head of the *Disruption* department of *Mossad* was quietly winding down a day which had been pretty routine when his phone rang:

"David?"

He had immediately recognized the voice of Mark Levi, his deputy:

"Just got a call from Switzerland. Do you have a minute?"

"You bet. Come right in."

■ ■ ■ ■ ■

Mark had rapidly risen in the ranks after he captained a very difficult but in the end extremely successful operation that had involved him impersonating a terrorist.[1] During the mission, he had been able to locate and deactivate a series of explosive devices that were paired to small glass containers filled with biological agents. The virus which the vial contained could have easily caused a much greater havoc than Covid 19 which was still debited with a large number of deaths and an important global economic slowdown. The unexpected promotion of David to run the *Disruption* unit, was itself caused by the unexpected retirement of the legendary head of *Mossad*, General Ariel Landau, and the appointment of his protégé, Simon Rabinowitz, to take his place.[2] It had created the vacancy that Mark was only too happy and honored to fill.

■ ■ ■ ■ ■

"So, what's up, my friend?"

David's greeting was quite normal for an individual who was known to have a great deal of charm and empathy for his troops, though who never seemed to want to waste any time. Mark understood the context and accepted the implicit offer to take a seat on the cream leather sofa in the corner of the David's office.

"Coffee? Scotch?"

---

[1] See "The Shadow Experts" by the same author, published by Barringer Publishing 2021
[2] See "Glitter and Smoke" by the same author, to be published by Barringer Publishing 2023

"No thanks, David, but a glass of sparkling water would be great."

David asked Joan, his assistant, for the glass of sparkling water for Mark and an iced coffee for himself. He then went straight to the matching armchair at a right angle to the sofa. Mark took his cue to begin his explanation:

"Got a call from *Mossad* in Bern. They were contacted by someone whom they described as an industrial leader in Russia. Bottom line: he is looking for protection."

"Wait a minute. You can freely move into or out of Russia today, can't you? Been able to do that for years. What does this mean?"

"Seems there is a bit more than meets the eye here. The individual is quite wealthy and is trying to bring some of his wealth here, though he must be very discreet."

"Could he be an oligarch trying to escape Yushin's reach?"

"Unsaid, but exactly what I thought."

"What does he want?"

"He wants permission for a Swiss connection to bring $250 million principally in diamonds with some in gold to him at Ben Gurion Airport, in the duty-free zone, . . ."

David was about to interrupt, but Mark did not let him, finishing his own sentence:

"He asks to be allowed into the country, deposit the wealth in a local bank and be given protective custody for himself and his family."

"Sounds terribly fishy my friend . . ."

"I know. At the same time, it's also totally plausible. So, here's what I've done. I asked him and he has agreed to meet me in Tallinn, the capital of Estonia. That's the good news. The bad news is that he wants very rapid answers. *Mossad* Bern was pretty clear in their view that he is in a hurry. A great hurry."

"You know my rule: never accept to make a decision with a gun to your head. You'll always regret it."

David paused for a second and with a wry smile added:

"However, I don't see what would be wrong with you flying to Tallinn to meet him. At most a wasted day. Be careful and do not promise anything that we can't walk away from if things don't turn out the way we expect."

"Of course. Thank you, sir."

CHAPTER.01

PROVENCE, FRANCE AND TEL AVIV, ISRAEL

The next phone call Dimitri placed right after hanging up with Adolf Edelblume was to his wife, Irina. She was in their property in the south of France, enjoying a considerably warmer early February than the very cold environment which Dimitri was experiencing in St. Petersburg. He surprised her with a voice that seemed much more determined than usual.

■ ■ ■ ■

Irina Godunova was with her two children in her property in the southeast of France. She and her husband, knowing how challenging winters can be in Zurich, had indeed a few years earlier decided that their winters would have to be spent away from their Swiss home. They had hired a private tutor for the children and had built one of the two largest houses in the Domaine des Terres D'Azur, an exclusive gated community providing exceptional personal security and offering at the same time unparalleled amenities without any form of ostentation. It had two championship golf courses and a suite-only hotel on the property. It offered privileged guests the ability to fly by helicopter to the closest airports, Cannes-Mandelieu for those who used private

transportation and Nice Cote D'Azur for those who wanted a larger airport capable of dealing with larger planes, private or commercial. The Godunovs were well liked among the membership of the golf club, perceived as they were as very discreet individuals who asked few questions, but were always smiling. In that, they seemed different from a few of the other Russian owners who appeared a bit rougher.

Though the Domaine des Terres D'Azur was known to have been chosen as a place of residence by a number of very rich Russians, only a couple of them were suspected to be really close to the government, and as such potentially to be oligarchs. One family bore the same name as a former president of Russia and a story circulated that Konstantin Yushin, the current Russian president, had been known to visit them; it was generally assumed that they had to be closely allied to the regime. The other was somewhat more difficult to pin down, as the gentleman did have connections to St. Petersburg and was known to have ample means; however, no one had ever traced a direct link that would justify assuming that he was an oligarch. After all, being wealthy and at times spending money in a way that may be considered a bit ostentatious surely does not or at least should not suffice for anyone to be labelled a Russian oligarch.

■ ■ ■ ■ ■

Dimitri did not seem ready even to countenance any disagreement in his conversation with his wife. He seemed to be in a hurry and, even possibly fearful:

"Honey, dear, you need to book yourself a private flight from Nice to Tel Aviv. When you get there book yourself at The Drisco Hotel on Auerbach street. It's the nicest hotel there. I'll meet you there in three days!"

Irina stuttered:

"Why, Dimitri? Why?"

"I can't explain at this point. You must trust me. I'm doing this to protect all four of us. Don't bring the tutor. Let her stay at Terres D'Azur. We should soon know better which way the wind is really blowing. I love you, but I must hang up now."

He did not even give her time to react.

■ ■ ■ ■ ■

Irina was anything but a trophy wife, though she could certainly have been a model. Everything about her oozed class, and she could point to an exceptional educational cursus. She had briefly worked as a lawyer but became a stay-at-home wife as soon as she and Dimitri tied the knot. They were both quite adamant they wanted children quite soon and were lucky to welcome a boy and a girl in somewhat of a rapid succession. As she often put it with a smile "I don't get paid for what I do," and she surely was willing, able, and ready to assist Dimitri on legal matters, usually prior to him discussing them with his lawyers; she was an excellent "bouncing board."

She was fully aware of the kind of business which her husband was conducting. Though she was proud to know that he was probably one of the least corrupt of those young entrepreneurs who had become nearly overnight billionaires, she also knew that he depended fully on the powers-that-be to keep his wealth. She had supported fully her husband's decision to stash money away and had been careful to be sufficiently involved that if anything should happen to him she would know what was where and officially belonging to whom.

Like most Russians leaving outside of Russia, she had heard the propaganda battle which had played in the press between the western and Ukrainian politicians on the one hand and their Russian counterparts on the other. Russia had been conducting complex and sizeable military maneuvers both to the east of Ukraine and in concert with their Belarusian neighbors to the north. Though President Yushin kept arguing that the maneuvers were just that,

maneuvers, she had heard discussions in the Western press suggesting that Russia was preparing to invade Ukraine. Russia's vehement denials notwithstanding, she could not help worrying what any form of confrontation might yield, though, in fairness, there was no doubt in her mind that Russia would come out on top. After all, wasn't the country one of the two global superpowers, maybe three, if China is included?

■ ■ ■ ■ ■

Though she was surprised, the worries which had been welling up in her led her to follow her husband's instructions without hesitating. She was thinking that he had to have just found out something which she did not know. She did not feel any more comfortable but accepted that there were times when one must act. She immediately called "Privatefly," a service offered out of Nice Cote D'Azur Airport to secure a private flight in the immediate future. She was surprised that jet availability was less than she would have expected, given that there was no major event currently going on anywhere on the French Riviera. There was little choice and the only plane that was available would be smaller than she would have wanted. She made a tentative reservation but indicated that she would only confirm it within an hour at most. Disappointed, she then called CentralJets at Cannes-Mandelieu Airport and was delighted that a flight to Tel Aviv could be arranged the next day, and with the kind of plane and amenities she wanted. She booked it on her black American Express card and cancelled the earlier Nice reservations.

She proceeded to pack what she would need, and then some as Dimitri had not told her how long she should expect to be away from Terres D'Azur. The degree of care and discretion she put into these preparations was illustrated by the fact that she did not call any of their neighbors to let them know she would be away. The Domaine indeed had a number of Russian homeowners, and the Russian

community was known to socialize among themselves, although people supposedly in the know argued that it was not really one but two groups: one tended to be viewed as close to the president, while the other would have been perceived as less supportive. However, truth be told, only they, these Russian families, knew who stood on what side; and even there, were they always right in their assessments? There did not seem to be a lot of political conversations in the community.

■ ■ ■ ■ ■

The next day, Irina and the two children boarded a Falcon 200 at Cannes-Mandelieu. She had left the house three hours before their loosely scheduled flight time, using a car service that was in no way related to either the Domaine or the Hotel at the center of the property. This was part and parcel of the strategy of having as few people as possible in the know. She realized that words travel fast and that the comings and goings of the wealthy property owners in the region are not very hard to monitor; after all, there were not that many of them to start with. Nonetheless, at the very minimum, her precautions would slow any enterprising potential follower. She had told the children's tutor that they were going on a trip to Greece where they would be joined by her husband.

She was feeling very odd as she settled into one of the nine brown leather seats available onboard. On the one hand, the prospect of seeing her husband earlier than she had planned was certainly a strong positive that was shared by the children. On the other, this was very much a step into the unknown. Why did Dimitri ask her to leave Provence in a hurry, why Israel, why all the secrecy? So many questions. No answers. Yet, she had to maintain a composure that did not betray her state of mind, as the last thing she needed or wanted was for the children to feel awkward. At that point, they indeed only focused on "going to a different place" and "see Daddy." The fact that

the tutor would not be on the trip was to them an indication that this was just another holiday.

The four-hour flight was totally uneventful. The children were used to private travel and indeed seemed to know what to expect. The plane she had selected was a bit more expensive than certain alternatives, but, in addition to the standard two-pilot setup, it also included a flight attendant. Irina had ordered lunch for the family and wanted help serving it. It was not so much that she expected to be hungry, but she saw lunchtime as an opportunity for the children to be occupied; it also increased her chances to have them take a nap before landing in Tel Aviv, as the onset of digestion pulled more blood toward their stomachs and away from their brains.

The plane landed in a private area of Ben Gurion Airport, but the family and their luggage were brought to the normal customs and immigrations channels by a chauffeur-driven black Mercedes Benz. Irina and the children went through immigration using their current Swiss passports. They showed documents demonstrating that they had the financial means to secure their return trip to France or to Switzerland, though they conceded that they had not up until then booked that flight. The fact that they had flown in by private aircraft made the assertion quite easy to accept. Irina explained that she expected to meet her husband who was traveling to Israel on business a couple of days hence. She readily allowed custom officers to check, however cursorily, their luggage, answered a few more general questions and stepped into the limousine which the Drisco Hotel had sent for them. Though traffic was relatively light, it still took them almost a half hour to travel the fourteen odd miles on Route 1 from the airport to the center of Tel Aviv. As they walked into the lobby, they were greeted by the general manager of the hotel who took them personally to their suite, indicating that the forms they would need to sign would be "completed upstairs," as he put it.

■ ■ ■ ■ ■

A Russian man arrived in Tel Aviv by private jet. He was immediately whisked away by the Israeli authorities. They brought him to a salon where a Swiss individual was waiting for him. They exchanged a smile after which the Swiss gentleman produced a piece of paper which the Russian man signed. He returned the duly signed paper to the Swiss gentleman and had shown the required identification, though this should not have been necessary as the two men knew each other. Still, procedures are procedures. Seemingly happy that everything was in order, the Swiss gentleman pointed to a briefcase and a small wooden crate. The man opened the briefcase; $220 million worth of diamonds glittered in the light. He was told there were 20,574 carats in investment grade diamonds averaging about 2 carats a piece, in a range of 1 to 3 carats. He allowed himself a wry smile, mentally computing that he had paid about $11,000 per carat, for flawless diamonds in D or E color. As he turned his attention to the relatively small crate, the Swiss gentleman said:

"Be careful, it is very heavy! Nearly a half a ton."

The crate indeed contained 430 one-kilo gold bars. A short mental computation later, the man was satisfied that the crate contained indeed the correct amount of money. A particularly perspicacious insider might have noted the minor disbelief that crossed the faces of the Israeli officers: they might well never have seen that much gold in one place. At any rate, they probably could not believe that a crate that was barely 1.5 cubic feet could hold that much value.

The Swiss gentleman, after having introduced another gentleman, excused himself and returned to the private departure area where he would board his return flight. The new gentleman was an Israeli banker representing an institution with which Zurick Private Verein did business. He had been briefed on what he needed to do. He took custody of the crate and of the briefcase after having written

and signed a receipt which he handed to the Russian man. Adolf Edelblume had taken care of all the necessary paperwork earlier so that the account opened for the Russian man and his family were all already properly documented.

The Israeli authorities then drove the Russian man to the Drisco Hotel downtown.

■ ■ ■ ■ ■

Dimitri was overjoyed to meet with his wife and two children who had arrived two days earlier. Tears were shed, followed by hearty laughter. After having been allowed a solid hour of private time together, the whole family was then driven to an official building where they were given a new identity and the appropriate official papers issued in that new name. The family was offered the use of a large penthouse in Park Tzameret, arguably the most desirable neighborhood in Tel Aviv.

The apartment surely did not match the kind of luxury to which the family was accustomed, but it was still a great place by almost any definition. Most important for *Mossad* was the fact that it enjoyed the use of a dedicated elevator, which made providing round-the-clock surveillance considerably easier. All domestic employees provided with the house were *Mossad*-hired and approved, ensuring almost total peace of mind while inside. The only material risk that Mark had identified was the fact that, being the highest point of one of the highest buildings in the neighborhood, the apartment windows were vulnerable to an outside attack. Such an attack could come from a helicopter, flying drone or even a high-powered rifle operated from a neighboring building. He had therefore organized special surveillance to ensure that these risks were appropriately covered.

At the same time, though a very nice prison, the apartment still felt a bit like a prison because of the limitations it imposed on the family's freedom to move around. Whenever they wanted to go

anywhere in the Tel Aviv area, and that would have included the beach, they had to accept a chauffeur-driven ride and the presence of security officers around them. Thankfully, the building was one of the first to offer a private terrace and pool area just for the penthouse. This made it easier for the parents to manage attacks of cabin fever in their two children, who did not seem to mind, or even notice, the two security guards who were permanently monitoring the surroundings of the building. Nonetheless, in the end, everyone knew very well that the situation could likely not be maintained indefinitely.

CHAPTER.02

ST. PETERSBURG, RUSSIA AND TEL AVIV, ISRAEL

Oleg Nichakov had made his fortune very much in the same way as most other oligarchs, starting when Russia privatized its economy in the wake of the fall of the Soviet Union on December 26, 1991, while Boris Yeltsin was president. These oligarchs emerged as well-connected entrepreneurs who were ready to take advantage of the corrupt nature of many Russian government officials, as the country's leadership was taking steps to move from a communist to a capitalist system. There did not seem to be any limit to the ingenuity of every twist that was conceived and executed to allow a few to make a lot of money at the expense of the many. Equally relevant is the fact that these newly minted billionaires who were pillaging the wealth of the country were keen to repay the ruling politicians regally, although not often in a manner that would have been visible. In many ways, practicing what has been dubbed "bandit capitalism," they simply shifted an earlier strategy of vying for more power which meant more privileges to acquiring more wealth, which in the end would buy them similar or better privileges. They were the first to use the tax havens which were so frequently cited as horrors created for the benefit of capitalists.

One of the most profitable avenues toward massive wealth had involved the voucher privatization program. This program was designed to transfer the ownership of companies from the all-powerful state to each and every individual Russian citizen. Citizens were given potential shares in state-owned companies as the first step in the move from communism to capitalism. They would buy the vouchers at very low prices, though they truly had no concept what they owned, or of what its real value might be. So, they often eventually quickly sold these vouchers at a handsome profit, but for a fraction of their value: any extra money which these generally poor people could get would be very much welcome. Was it going to alleviate in their views the shortages and lack of means to which they had become accustomed?

Though it was not always the case, many of newly privatized companies had preferred shares which provided substantially higher dividends than the ordinary alternatives. Yet, often, whatever one might call "the market" did not seem to see a difference between the two instruments and therefore vastly under-priced these higher-yielding preferred shares which traded at a fraction of their real value. Oligarchs and the odd hedge fund manager—frequently from the West—accumulated many of these highly discounted instruments. They were as such able to capitalize on massive market moves, when prices went straight up, at times by a factor of nearly 100. In short, perversely, the wealth of the state, rather than being transferred to the majority of Russian citizens, thus ended up accruing to the accounts of a few well-placed oligarchs.

In another trick, these entrepreneurs were able to arbitrage the difference between old domestic prices for Russian commodities (such as natural gas and oil) and the prices prevailing on the world market. Domestic prices had been kept low so that a poor citizenry could afford to live with the meager incomes they received from the state. The opening up of the economy to the world allowed a few to buy commodities at controlled domestic prices and resell them

at floating real market prices abroad. One can only surmise that a few government officials received some share of these profits, as they ostensibly turned a blind eye to an activity which if not strictly prohibited by the letter of the law was surely totally against its spirit. The wealth of the oligarchs eventually grew even further as they were allowed to take leading ownership and management positions in the business ventures which the regime wanted to foster.

Oleg Nichakov, though unmarried and without the usual reputation of craving female company, was somewhat different from many of his contemporaries. Conscious of the need to maintain the appropriate image, he would occasionally allow his picture to be taken with some model or actress; however, no one needed to know it was all for show. His flowing blond hair, youthful face and athletic body had at times led many people to think he moonlighted as a movie actor. The dark tortoise shell glasses he wore had become almost a trademark as he never went without them. Certain people said that he really did not see much without them, though nobody could point to any hard source for that information. Many people would observe that he did not seem as wealthy as several of the other oligarchs, although his name came up as frequently as others when one spoke of influence. He did not live the life of the average Russian, and surely had a few visible assets ranging from the ubiquitous fancy cars to a yacht that had been photographed in many places, ranging from the Baltic Sea, the Black Sea or the usual Mediterranean or Caribbean playgrounds for the jet set. He just did not seem to have as much as the others.

Oleg's ancestry could be traced back in part to the Cossacks of Ukraine; his family had suffered greatly at the hands of the Bolsheviks after the communist revolution of 1917. Many died, others went from some wealth to being the same paupers as the average Russian farmer. He carefully made absolutely certain that nobody that mattered knew his connections to the Cossacks. What's more, he went as far as

moving from Kiev to St. Petersburg to put as much distance as he could between the new Oleg and his old roots. He even added a "v" at the end of his original name, Nichako to make it Nichakov, which sounded more Russian. However he, himself, had not forgotten, and so harbored quite a strong measure of suspicion vis-à-vis the regime.

This led him to park quite a few of his assets outside of Russia and explained why he did not seem to live the same extravagance as all of his peers. He could not stash assets away and live the same extravagant lifestyle. Hence, though on the surface a typical oligarch, Oleg was in truth quite different. He knew he needed for some of his wealth to be visible; people would not have understood if he seemed not to have it. At the same time, his strategy involved assuring that enough of his wealth, accruing through income or appreciation of assets was squirreled away beyond the reach of the government. In short, if he ever had to leave in a hurry, he might not be as wealthy as he was, but he would still have more money than he realistically needed. He would accordingly be ready to liquidate some of his holdings before they had fully appreciated or move rapidly and surreptitiously extra savings out of the country. Nevertheless, he always kept enough assets "in the sun" so that nobody questioned his loyalty or worse yet would entertain the idea of digging a bit deeper into his affairs, particularly into his nest egg hidden away in Switzerland.

So, while potentially less ostensibly wealthy than his peers, Oleg's reputation among them was that he had to be one of the smartest if not the smartest. He always seemed to think of great ideas before anybody else. People, both within and outside of government liked him and respected his thoughts because he had a knack for identifying the one trend that others had missed. Perversely, though those peers might look down on the fact that he "had to have bad habits that had eaten into his wealth" they were always asking to be included as partners in several of his ventures; it seemed that any Oleg Nichakov venture was an almost guaranteed ticket to significant profits. This is

how one of his major ventures related to cybersecurity had led him to help the government develop extremely powerful cyber warfare tools; he was kind of the Russian cyber king!.

■ ■ ■ ■ ■

"So, should I call you Dimitri or Oleg?"

David had invited the Russian man to his office to further their conversation on what he expected *Mossad* to do for him and his family and what he was willing to offer in exchange. With David was his second-in-command, Mark Levi, who had actually handled the first conversation, in Tallinn.

"Oleg's the real name, but I'm hoping I can shed it and become Dimitri for good as soon as possible."

Though not totally unexpected, Dimitri's reply led David to raise his eyebrows in a sign of surprise. Dimitri continued explaining that he had decided to create a second persona when he married Irina. He did not want anything ever to happen to her and the children they both hoped to have soon. So, the couple established themselves in Zurich and appeared to their neighbors as quite "normal" individuals, of Russian descent. He also started then to move some of his money abroad, that is from Russia to Switzerland. He enjoyed the success which he was ostensibly having, but the way he was achieving some of it was not "right" in his own words. He argued:

"At one point, early in the privatization program, the government decided to give away thirty percent of all corporate Russia to every Russian citizen. Around 150 million people then. Most of these people had no idea what they should do with those, or what they were worth. So, a number of enterprising individuals took advantage of them. I was a consolidator in the St. Petersburg area, and I took full advantage of the scheme; buying vouchers for less than $10 when they were worth nearly $50. Then, you had all the funny dealings as these vouchers were exchanged for the shares of the companies; another opportunity

to make money off unsuspecting people. I hate to say this, but that's how I made my first fortune."

Mark had to ask:

"If you did not like it, why didn't you stop?"

"Totally fair question. The point is, frankly, that at that time I did not realize either the extent of the scheme or even of the money that could be made. It only hit me when I realized that I had made so much money . . ."

Oleg paused for a second and added:

"That's when two things happened. First, I stopped participating in the scheme and second I opened my first account in Switzerland."

"So that's when you changed name . . ."

"Exactly David. Though, in fairness, I did not change my name. I just got the account set up under a different name, Dimitri Godunov. Then, I bribed a junior official in St. Petersburg to issue papers, including a passport to me in that new name."

"How about your wife?"

"We weren't married at that time. We were about to be married. So, she never was Mrs. Nichakov. She did know me initially as Oleg Nichakov. That's the name I had when we met. But quickly, I realized that we shared a deep love, and also a measure of discomfort at what was happening in Russia. At the same time, we both knew that my finger was stuck in the wheel and that pulling out could just as easily lead me or her or both of to be "eliminated" as people say with the usual understatement."

He paused with a trace of a tear in his eye. He continued:

"Frankly, we probably wouldn't have been the first or the last to meet that fate."

He wiped the small tear from the corner of his right eye and kept going on his brief autobiographical presentation:

"We got married in Zurich, where we were able to get all the appropriate papers. I had my "fake" Dimitri Godunov passport, and

she had her own totally official Russian passport in her maiden name. So, once we were married, she naturally applied for and got a Russian passport in the name of Irina Godunova. The odd bit is that once you had one fake identity and the appropriate papers, all the other documents you get in that name are totally genuine."

"Weren't the Russian authorities surprised that your wife did not have the same name as you?"

"Again, David, it's all a question of timing. Initially, they had no reason to be; we were not married when we left Russia. Then, when she asked for Russian papers in the name of Godunova, she could point to her husband's name being Dimitri Godunov, a Swiss resident."

David nodded in recognition that Oleg/Dimitri's assessment was, however crazily, totally rational in the world of bureaucratic practices. Oleg added:

"Now the issue is moot because ever since our daughter Tatiana was born, we became official residents and then actual Swiss citizens in Zurich. I commuted between Zurich and St. Petersburg, changing name as I went from one country to the other. Not fun, but not too different from what many people do when they have two nationalities. The twist here is that each nationality came with a different name . . . But the money was such that I could spend all weekends with her and the children. And when I say I commuted between these two places, I am implicitly forgetting the many trips I naturally had to take both within Russia and even outside, including in the Middle East. In truth, though I've honestly never checked, I bet you that only a very small number of trips were actually between Zurich and St. Petersburg."

He paused again and mischievously added:

"I had a bit of a reputation as a ladies' man before I met Irina. But some of it was way exaggerated."

Seeing David raise an eyebrow, he immediately corrected his statement:

"Irina knew it by the way, and it all stopped once we started dating seriously. So, I have kept cultivating that image in Russia, except that my "dates" always somehow appear to live outside of Russia. By the way, that fits quite well with the image of the oligarch sharing the life of the jet set."

David realized that the topic could take a lot of their time without shedding much more light on the actual issue. He elected to move the discussion back to the real agenda item: what did Dimitri want and what was he prepared to offer? Dimitri explained that he was worried that all the discussion about maneuvers and war in the Ukraine region were potentially quite serious. He added that he saw the situation in the same light as the Crimea takeover eight years earlier, arguing:

"Yushin wants to have total control over the whole of the northern coast of the Black Sea, probably the whole of it eventually. Clearly, he can't go for the whole thing in one fell swoop, but he'll keep trying. So, while I hope he won't, I am betting that he will indeed go to war."

He paused and then continued, making the point that this was likely to be costly in terms of both money and people. He conceded:

"I have no idea how the Ukrainians will fight, but I can tell you that they are a fiercely independent people. My bet is that they won't take it lying down. Also, I've no idea how the West will react. But Ukraine is a much bigger nut than Crimea."

"How does that play into your own life decisions, Oleg?"

"I suspect that there will be some real internal opposition within the elites. All of those who, like me, have made money are not in this for the power but for the money. So, anything which the West does that could appear to threaten our ability to keep making money and living the life we live today will be taken as a signal that we need to take care of ourselves."

Again, he paused and with a sad look on his face added:

"However, that's where the real danger lies. Yushin will not hesitate to eliminate anyone whom he thinks is not 100% behind him. I have no idea when he might think I am not 100% his friend, but there's bound be to a time when he stops seeing me as an unconditional ally. Add to that the idea that other oligarchs might begin to jockey for position. You know, there is a lot of denunciation going on in Russia. That was one of the bases of security under the communist regime. So, people might want me out of the way. It might even be a case of needing to give away someone to save their own skin. In short, I really feel I'm living on borrowed time, or rather that Oleg Nichakov is living on borrowed time."

David offered the obvious conclusion:

"So, you want to disappear . . ."

"Exactly."

"What about your assets in Russia?"

"I've got more than enough already outside with what you allowed me to bring in, plus some other stuff stashed away. Plus, who knows, my company may well have a future if Yushin disappears . . ."

"You haven't told us what your company does, have you?"

"No. I had actually preferred not to discuss that topic when I met with Mark in Tallinn. In a word, my company is the top firm involved in cyberwarfare in Russia: Visla Cybersecurity Group is its name."

Mark interjected:

"Cyberwarfare?"

"Yes. Both the defensive kind, protecting Russian installations against foreign attacks and the offensive sort: developing tools to attack others or sponsoring selected groups of hackers. I'm certain this will remain a useful business . . ."

"But won't they be missing you?"

Oleg surprised Mark and David arguing:

"Who says they must? One of the things I need from *Mossad* precisely is the ability to interact with my company and possibly even with some of its customers, without being in Russia."

"Is that realistic?"

"Remember, my wife has been a Swiss resident for quite a number of years and a Swiss citizen as well. People are used to see me on some videoconference or even just to hear my voice . . . on the phone."

With a wide smile he added:

"How quaint!"

■ ■ ■ ■ ■

The onset of the invasion of Ukraine by Russia quickly validated the choice which Oleg had made to create a second identity, and to establish his family outside of Russia, at least for some time.

Less than two months into the Ukrainian invasion, the news came out that two well-known oligarchs had "committed suicide" after having murdered their wives and children. That should have removed any doubt that remained that anyone who did not kowtow to the president should ensure he had substantial life insurance. The CEO of a major producer of natural gas had indeed been found hanging in the garden of a Spanish villa, while the bodies of his wife and daughter were lying in a pool a blood, not far away, having been knifed to death. Similarly, the ex-president of a large Russian bank was discovered in similar circumstances, with him, his wife and his daughter killed with multiple gunshots; a handgun was near the man. Finally, an American magazine noted that a total of twelve Russian oligarchs, including the two noted here, have been found dead in the partial year, since the onset of the Ukraine war.

In the end, was it despair or the desire by Russian authorities to eliminate possible dissenters? Maybe, it was just a warning to other oligarchs to toe the line . . . or else!

CHAPTER.03

TEL AVIV AND BEERSHEBA, ISRAEL

General Simon Rabinowitz, the head of *Mossad*, was having lunch with General (retired) Ariel Landau, his predecessor. Ever since Simon had taken over the position, he had made it a habit to have lunch about once a month with Ariel to catch up. Ariel was always still interested in what was going on in his old "haunt." Simon, for his part, felt he could only learn from his predecessor and mentor. Typically, though, one or the other would start on one particular train of thought and the other would plunge right alongside; Ariel's undoubted skill, besides being himself and deserving of his nick name "steel trap," was that he had a unique perspective on politics. He often called politics "the art of the possible" by which he did not mean that one should ever violate profoundly ingrained values, but rather that politics should be viewed as the skill of learning how far one could go without asking for too much or damaging a relationship. Simon enjoyed these exchanges even if he did not have anything special to ask, though he would still occasionally seek counsel from his former boss. That time, it was Ariel who surprised Simon:

"Have you heard of the latest breakthrough in cybersecurity?"

"If you're asking the question, the right answer is probably no. I'll simply say I don't think so. Now, seriously, what are you referring to?"

"Well, I was having lunch with the Prime Minister just the other day. He had just come back from the annual cybersecurity conference at Tel-Aviv University. He mentioned that the industry is growing at an exceptional pace, principally because it appears that there is no permanent solution."

"He means that someone always finds a way to break through, the moment a new barrier has been erected?"

"Exactly."

■ ■ ■ ■ ■

Simon knew very well that Israel is an unquestioned world leader in the field of cybersecurity, and in practice a de facto major exporter of cybersecurity products. Ben Gurion University of the Negev was the major driver behind the creation of the Advanced Technology Park. It is situated right next to the university's Marcus Family Campus, at Beersheba, about 70 miles almost due south of Tel Aviv. The Park is a public-private partnership which has been successful attracting virtually all leading players in the world. It is of more than passing interest to note that the Park is slated to become the base of the Israel Defense Forces' elite technology units. This underscores the essential truth that maintaining technology leadership is a matter of survival for the country. Though cybersecurity should never be a luxury for anyone, its crucial importance for Israel explains why it is using the military to incubate start-ups. As a matter of fact, there is another reason why things work out that way. Israel has a couple of programs subsidizing the most gifted among its engineering students. Since the scholarships come with an obligation to serve in the army longer than all other Israeli citizens, it becomes natural for these gifted computer engineers to keep working on their favorite subjects in the army. Interestingly, one of the countries, besides the U.S., with which Israel

works the most closely on cybersecurity is none other than Singapore, the small city-state at the tip of the Straits of Malacca, where despite institutional differences with Israel, education is highly prized and cybersecurity is of prime importance as well.

■ ■ ■ ■ ■

Simon asked Ariel whether there was anything special which had caught the Prime Minister's attention. After all, Ariel had asked about "the latest breakthrough" and his short explanation to Simon had not revealed much if anything of what that was. Ariel had two short coughs and replied that he really did not have anything concrete on which to go, other than the fact that the Prime Minister seemed quite excited. Simon did not show any reaction, but was somewhat disappointed until Ariel offered a last comment, which Simon actually took as a suggestion:

"Well, maybe there is something new. I have heard that Nathan Sharon, one of the senior researchers at The Advanced Technology Park may have come up with something quite unique. I'm told he has been working quite closely with the IDF (Israeli Defense Forces) though he remains on the academic side."

"Anything else?"

"Nope but thinking back of my meeting with the PM, I seem to recall that this was the main source of his enthusiasm."

"Say no more. I clearly had not heard that, but we're going to pay him a visit as soon as feasible. We never want to be far from the leading edge in that area."

"That's what I thought too, my friend. Thanks for lunch, it was great. Give my best to Jennifer and the family."

Simon immediately called David Heller to discuss the news. They quickly agreed that David should pay a visit to Nathan, with Simon adding:

"I'm only thinking out loud here, but I wonder whether we should not offer an assignment to The Shadow Experts of Countess Renate to see how their Singapore expert, Wong Hai Chock, reacts to the discovery . . ."

"I'm on it."

■ ■ ■ ■ ■

David had invited Mark Levi to join him for the trip to the technology park. They both had seen a number of reports of the park ever since it had been started. However, the vision of the spectacular Beersheba Station double arch footbridge was something they had not managed to get used to. Crossing as it does both rail tracks and the highway, it is designed to look like the double helix of a DNA structure; it is breathtaking and quite original. Visitors to the area also often comment on the number of relatively small buildings, almost like individual three or four-story glass covered cubes, each bearing the name of some major corporate player in the global technology world. Not widely publicized is the fact that a special defense system, a subset of the Iron Dome, was installed to protect the center from any missile attack. Nobody even bothered to hide the components of this defense: one can see here or there missile launchers, equipped with sixteen missile tubes ostensibly ready to fire to destroy any incoming projectile. That alone should serve to demonstrate the importance of that area for Israel.

David and Mark drove to the park from Tel Aviv on Yitzhak Rabin Highway and arrived barely an hour after having left their office. They parked the car and walked into the building where Nathan Sharon worked. There, in the lobby, they were met by an assistant who took them to the conference room where Nathan stood up to greet them.

He pointed out two seats on the other side of the large table in light-colored wood and brushed aluminum. He smiled and seemed to wait for them to start the conversation. David introduced the roles which both he and Mark played, focusing principally on the fact that his group's mission was to help neutralize threats against Israel. Nathan smiled again and thanked them for their service. David smiled back and replied:

"Well, it seems to me that we are both on the same side, right?"

"We absolutely are, though I would think of myself as the designer of the arms which are then used by people like you. Am I making sense?"

"Absolutely. In reality, I like your analogy."

Cutting to the chase, David moved the conversation to the main issue: cyber warfare and its cousin cybersecurity. Nathan welcomed the question and started with a general observation, as he put it:

"In order to make certain we're all on the same wavelength . . . Let me go back a bit to set a common base from which to jump forward."

He started by focusing on cybersecurity which, to him, involved the protection of electronic data and information. This extended naturally to defending electronic systems or devices which, in practice, are potential entry points into the storage systems where the data and information reside. He joked for an instant that everyone has been the victim of malicious attacks, noting however that most of them were benign. Yet, as he added:

"Though benign, they can be terribly tedious to fight, fix and eventually prevent."

His next point focused on the question most people who do not know much about cybersecurity might ask: why is it so important to prevent access to data and systems? Answering his own question, he plainly argued that the power that could accrue from gaining access to data or systems is enormous. With a wink in his eye, he noted:

"I surely don't need to talk to you of Stuxnet . . ."

■ ■ ■ ■ ■

Though not having taken place under his leadership but under that of Simon Rabinowitz his predecessor, David knew that Stuxnet had been quite a significant *Mossad* success in its attempt to prevent the development of nuclear bomb capabilities in Iran.[3] The Stuxnet worm had been created, allegedly, by Israel and the U.S. and introduced into computers, primarily in Iran. Analysts speculated that it was transmitted through thumb drives and infected tens of thousands of computers. In plain terms, the worm was able to burrow into operating systems and, unlike a virus, which is created to attack computer code, it was designed to take over systems. Once in place, the worm had taken over key instructions and caused several systems to malfunction. Rumors that were never confirmed by Iran were that the Stuxnet worm had targeted its uranium enrichment activities and caused damage to centrifuges by getting them to operate in the wrong condition, such as spinning too fast or not fast enough or operating at too high or too low temperatures. This was said to have caused minor explosions and mechanical breakdowns.

■ ■ ■ ■ ■

David smiled, though, as always, he would neither deny nor confirm officially anything that had not been publicly acknowledged. Nathan continued on his main topic, arguing that cyber-attacks typically use digital means to access, change or destroy information. He became visibly more serious and added:

"Now, most often, these intrusions, as we shall call them, have been meant to extort money from users. More or less money I should add, everything depending upon the target. Obviously, at one point, the extortion is too serious to ignore. But the ultimate form of

---

[3] By the same author, see "Operation Kovesh," Barringer Publishing 2020.

extortion had gradually shifted from money to more direct power. I say "power" because though I know that money provides power, there is currently more to the whole thing. Power is gained through spying, through damaging someone else's equipment, or literally taking a country hostage."

He paused to take his breath, which allowed Mark to barge into the conversation:

"I don't want to seem philosophical, but isn't this simply a new weapon in a well-established continuation across centuries?"

"Excellent point. The truth is that there have been very few instances, if any, of a new technology which would instantaneously replace an old one in war. New ideas come in, they help modify the way in which old technologies are conceived or employed. At times, new tactics must be developed to accommodate for them."

Nathan paused for a second. Fascinated by his topic, he kept going:

"When you think of it, the evolutionary force is indeed at the level of tactics. The best tactics make use of both the new and the old; eventually and gradually, they evolve and work together. Think of the long-term continuum which you mentioned, Mark. Artillery did not replace traditional warfare, it made it different. Similarly, aircraft, missiles or even satellites forced traditional warfare to adapt to new approaches. The one thing that would change everything is the application of nuclear weaponry to everything. But, as you know, that would lead to a super short war and the end of times."

He paused again and completed his logic.

"Let me take an example. You know that we, Israel, have been at the forefront of the development of drones; that too did not change everything, it just added dimensions which you must master. In short, I like to say that nothing gets replaced by something new. Something new becomes part of the dynamic nature of battle and it stays there forever, leading to an ever more chaotic state for those who don't

understand. And here I don't mean just don't understand the newest and shiniest technologies. What I really mean is that the key is to figure out how they integrate with everything else."

David needed to bring the discussion down to a more practical level and asked:

"Nathan, what do you mean when you say: "cyber warfare?""

"Wow! Do you have a few hours? No, seriously. Let's see. At a minimum, I refer to anything related to espionage or sabotage, which I know, you both know very well. At the other end of the spectrum, you have the classic propaganda. It's old hat, but it is a lot simpler and effective with modern tools than with having to drop pamphlets from the air. I should add that a variant on the theme could be censorship or even plain disinformation if you get surreptitious control over certain platforms, like social media."

He paused and seeing that David and Mark were totally on board, he switched to three of the activities which he felt were the most serious:

"To me, where things get really serious is when we talk of attacks on the electrical power grid or of denial-of-service attacks. In both of these, you work to deprive the adversary of services which are crucial. Imagine having to work without electricity . . . Now, and this is where I would argue the leading edge is:"

He picked up his glass of water to have a quick drink and was impressed by the fact that David and Mark seemed particularly attentive then. He continued:

"A form of denial-of-service involves affecting the way the enemy uses its own weaponry. You must have heard of Russia's hypersonic aero ballistic missiles. They're launched from the air and follow ballistic flight paths with a degree of maneuverability. Imagine that we gain some ability to tinker with their maneuverability . . . You turn what is supposed to be their greatest strength, their capability

to evade detection and retaliatory moves, into a potentially great shortcoming."

"Wait. Are we there yet?"

"Not quite. Not quite. But this is our current research direction. I would venture to say that we may not be as far from our goal as people think."

Nathan paused again and then resumed his narrative:

"You see, there are two ways of affecting the missile's maneuverability. The first, the Holy Grail if I can say it that way, would be to order it to do certain things. That's still in the future. But what about preventing it from responding to commands? What becomes of the maneuverability in that scenario?"

David and Mark were clearly captivated by the conversation and its potential. David felt he had to ask the one specific question that Simon had entrusted to him:

"Nathan, what about this newest capability which people were recently discussing at Tel Aviv university?"

"Oh. Still not totally perfected, but I think we have found a way of inserting into any program a few lines of codes which will effectively block any possible intrusion."

Mark was visibly excited and asked:

"That would be a defensive mode, right? In effect you'd be preventing enemies from accessing our systems. Correct?"

"Yes and yes. However, what about using classical cyber attacking modes, call them viruses, worms or whatever, and make it impossible for the enemy to access them unless they have the password? That'd become offensive, Yes?"

"I see. This is brilliant. And you are operational?"

"Not quite, but very close to it, Mark. A few more tests to prove that we have the accuracy we think we have, and it can be deployed. At present, please note, gentlemen, that any deployment would by definition be totally secret. This has got to be the one thing you don't

want to advertise. You want the enemy to question why things aren't working the way they should and to go down a few blind alleys. That is what we need in order to have the time to reinforce our own capability."

"The classic approach: stay one step ahead . . ."

"Exactly, Mark."

CHAPTER.04

TEL AVIV, ISRAEL AND SOMEWHERE IN THE AUSTRIAN ALPS

When Oleg had arrived in Tel Aviv, *Mossad*'s first order of business, after having taken him to his penthouse, was to make certain that he could not be traced. Mark asked:

"How many cell phones do you have?"

"Why, two. Why do you ask?"

"You'll see. Am I correct assuming that one is in Dimitri's name and the other in Oleg's?"

"Correct. I have been very careful to maneuver so that the two identities were completely separate."

Oleg did not feel the need to mention his third phone, the one he used to communicate with his Swiss banker, Adolf Edelblume.

"Can we take a look at Oleg's phone, please?"

Oleg looked somewhat surprised. However, he did not argue, other than asking:

"What do you expect to find?"

"We need to see if there is any geolocation feature."

"You should have asked directly . . . There is none, I've already made sure of that. But be my guest if you want to look for one. I

surely don't want people to see where Oleg is when I happen to be Dimitri."

Mark smiled and simply replied:

"I should have guessed. Anyway, would you allow us to run a few diagnostic checks on it while you're here. Better safe than sorry."

"As I just said, be my guest."

"Oh, while I think of it, does your wife have more than one cell phone?"

"No, the only one is registered to Irina Godunova and is based in Zurich. Naturally, she has a worldwide service . . ."

"Anybody in your entourage here has a phone?"

"We have no one here with us. My wife left the children's tutor in France, at least as an interim measure. Eventually, we'd like to have her with us. But that is not the highest priority item."

"Good. Do you want us to run a complete background check on her?

"Actually, that's not a bad idea. We've done what we could, and, to our knowledge, she has no connection to Russia. She is Swiss, from the Zurich area, though she speaks six languages: Swiss German, English, French, Italian, Spanish and some Russian she's been learning with us."

"Impressive. Good to know. Let's simply make certain that we remain on top of this issue."

▪ ▪ ■ ▪ ▪

Less than a week later, back in David's office with Mark assisting him, Oleg was asked to discuss his business in Russia. He had hitherto elected to play it quite cool and close to the vest. Clearly, he was intimately convinced that it was by far his best card. So, he only opened up when the process had made significant progress; he was by now, at least in his own mind, safely ensconced in Israel. David and Mark already knew from Oleg's own earlier comments that his

company was the Russian leader in cybersecurity and by implication in cyber warfare. They felt they needed to know more so that they could better understand how they could use it to penetrate the Russian cybersecurity apparatus.

David and Mark clearly remembered the smile of contentment which had appeared on Oleg's face, particularly when he gave his company the status of "unquestioned leader in Russian cyber warfare." They worried at that time that Oleg had not missed their reaction of surprise. Their suddenly massively heightened interest had demonstrated to him that his initial appreciation had been right on. They clearly had many of the trump cards in their hands, but he also held a major one. So, at present, the cat and mouse came would start with him working to verify that he could get the most without having to let go of everything. Interestingly, his state of mind betrayed a Russian oligarch trait: they worked with the "system" in that they could acquire wealth, and for self-protection rather than genuine loyalty. If truth be known, many observers of the Russian scene believed that the support which these individuals provided to the regime was due to the fear of what would happen to them if they were disloyal, rather than by some commitment to Russia as embodied by the current strong man. Oleg was therefore surprised when David asked point blank:

"Would you be willing to work with us to undermine Russian cybersecurity capabilities?"

"Do you mean spy for Israel?"

"Not quite, though in due course this might be welcome."

"So, what then?"

David followed on his original train of thought and explained that Israel did not want to take side in any of the conflicts in which Russia was involved, except for as long as they affected its own security. Oleg clearly was not following his logic. David had to clarify his point:

"Essentially, we're not going to try anything against Russia, except in cases involving Syria or Iran, and by extension any country which sides with the Palestinians. We are more than willing to live in peace alongside the Palestinians, even to the point of conceding territory as I am told, though this is obviously not within my purview. The only thing which we would require of them has to be a commitment to friendly neighborly relations. In other words, they would have to renounce terrorism and to prove it by both words and actions."

Oleg appeared to ponder David's "profession of faith" for a few seconds and still remained somewhat confused. He said:

"Honestly, I don't see where this is leading us . . . Can you be more specific?"

David replied:

"Oleg, we can't have a foreign policy discussion here. That's not my responsibility. Actually, I would argue it is not *Mossad*'s responsibility though General Rabinowitz might see it differently."

Oleg's body language signaled that he understood. David nodded and continued:

"Any ability we might gain, with your help, to interfere in the cyber capability of Russia and of its "client states" in the region would be a major plus for us. As I said earlier, we are really in a defensive mode vis-à-vis the Palestinians and not in an offensive mode against Russia. I'm sure that we would be very inclined to reward handsomely whoever helped us."

Oleg's face sketched a smile, though it immediately died as he replied:

"I see this and am very grateful, but the current environment in Russia is such that I am unsure that you can set the strict limits you mention."

Mark intervened:

"What do you mean?"

"Well, you must be aware of all the noise on the invasion by Russia of Ukraine. By the way, I have no idea how far that could go, but the risks of a third world war would increase exponentially if Russia elected to act."

Mark replied:

"David and I are well aware of the current geopolitical risk."

He paused briefly and then simply asked:

"How does this affect our conversation here?'

"Well, Mark, it does in many ways. For one, I would not have fled Russia as I did if that menace had not become increasingly credible. Second, you must have heard of the six entrepreneurs who were supposed to be close to Yushin and who were coincidentally found dead; suicide was alleged, but I would bet quite a bit that it was "assisted suicide" if you catch my drift."

Oleg allowed himself a wry smile at his gallows humor and continued:

"Third, my company really cannot differentiate between the cyber capabilities which are shared with the Middle East and the others."

David interrupted:

"In short, you feel that your life and that of your family is in danger. I get that. After all, you orchestrated an ingenious departure from Russia, not mentioning the way you had been organizing your family life for a number of years."

David could see a definite smile on Oleg's face. He added:

"The question for us is this: does this make it harder for you do help us?"

Oleg thought for a few seconds and calmly replied:

"Well, David, the obvious reply must be a resounding yes. Let me explain. I don't see myself ever travelling to Russia until the Ukrainian situation is cleared up, which, by the way, to me at least, means a regime change in Russia in one way or another."

"Ouch. You're really a pessimist on this one."

"No, David. I'm a realist. I've seen Yushin operate for many years, even before he became the top man. He has always been power hungry and has never shown any scruples. He had always been prepared to do whatever it took. Believe me, most people in the know in Russia understand he would not let anything stop him. By the way, that's why I'm worried, both for my family and more broadly for the world."

Mark could not help asking:

"Why?"

"Surely you get my drift when it comes to the safety of my family. But more broadly, I'm not sure I want an unstable character like him have his finger on the nuclear trigger. A cornered bear is much more dangerous . . ."

David could see the scope for the conversation going down a rabbit hole. He tried to retrieve it asking:

"OK. You can't go back to Russia. But can't you influence your company from abroad? After all, when your wife was living in Zurich or France, didn't you ever hold telephonic or video conference meetings with your executives?"

"Fair point. But, I have something stronger than that . . ."

"What?"

"Well, David, I still have direct computer access and know where most of the files are."

This time it was David's turn to smile. He could see a light at the end of the tunnel and was sure it was not an incoming train. He asked:

"So, what's the problem?"

"Truth is, most of our meetings when I am abroad have been by video conference. So, we need to be very careful that nothing in the background, whether a sight or a sound, gives any indication of where I am. Further, my guys know how I live. So, the solution of a completely bare room with no window won't cut it. They'd guess that

I'm either a prisoner or in hiding and probably would refuse to talk to me any further."

David's smile was quite a bit broader as he said:

"I would not worry about any of this, Oleg. We may need you to give some of our people access to your stateroom or wherever you work from on your yacht, or to one or several of your foreign residences. With that, we may have a great deal of fun, having you travel from one place to the next without ever having to leave Tel Aviv."

David saw Oleg smile. He paused for a brief second and asked:

"Do we have a deal?"

■ ■ ■ ■ ■

After Oleg had stepped out of David's office, David asked Mark to stay for a while so that they could discuss what they had learned from the conversation with Oleg. They wanted to evaluate it in the light of their visit to Nathan Sharon in Beersheba. Mark asked:

"How can we get this to work without disclosing anything secret to Oleg?"

He paused, but felt he had to add:

"I know that I may be too cynical or even paranoid, but what if Oleg was a plant? What if the Russians had always wanted to find out more about what their potential opponents knew and did in the space? The simplest way would have been to ensure that whoever was in charge of cybersecurity in Russia was also employed as a spy. They could have helped Oleg set up or more likely develop his company with that in mind. Now, fast forward, what if the Russians had found out something on our cyber progress? What if they were using him as a cover?"

"You know, I'm not sure you're too cynical. The fact is that this guy came to us out of the blue. Coincidentally, his specialty is cybersecurity. Could easily have gone to Singapore, just as "secluded"

and probably less likely to have "interferences" with Russia: no Palestinian issue in Singapore. It's also true that he's an oligarch and that he has a reasonable case for wanting to hide . . ."

"The one thing that makes me ask myself questions is the bit about the two identities. I don't know of any oligarch who has done that. In reality, they're all deeply indebted to the regime. Why would they even think of the need to hide?"

"True enough, Mark. Having said that, we know that at least six and maybe as many as twelve of these oligarchs have already been found dead. So, as I see it, the problem is that both scenarios are credible. He may be a Russian spy masquerading as an oligarch . . ."

"Which would explain the need to show off wealth even before he arrives . . ."

"Right on. On the other hand, how should he have behaved if he was truly worried by the regime and had been worried for a while?"

David concluded that they had no way of being sure at that point in time. He added:

"I know. That's why I think we must be careful, no, extra-careful but we cannot afford to miss the opportunity."

"You're right."

David paused for a few seconds and then smiled asking:

"How would the situation change if we asked Countess Renate and her Shadow Experts to help us?"

■ ■ ■ ■ ■

The Shadow Experts were a secret network consisting of specialists across a wide variety of disciplines who cooperated with and were directed by Countess Renate to defend "good causes." They ranged from micro-biologists to advanced material engineers, to art experts, to cyber engineers, to electronics experts and to many other specialties, each as esoteric as the others. All members knew they were members of the network, but most did not know who the others

were. They all knew Renate; most, if not all, had seen her in person or on some video conference call. However, no one could claim that he or she had met with her regularly. First, the specialists were all "part time associates" who came into a team to solve a problem and returned to the shadows when they were not needed.

■ ■ ■ ■ ■

Mark jumped on David's question and replied:

"Brilliant! They could serve as a front for our secret activities and yet get us where we want."

"Got it in one. Let me run this by Simon to see how he reacts and then let's proceed if he gives us the green light. Do you want to be with me on that call?"

"Why?"

"Well, after all, I have to talk about the risk Oleg is not legit and this was your idea, right?"

■ ■ ■ ■ ■

Simon listened very carefully to David's thoughts. He was openly complimentary of Mark's intuitions and admitted that the scenario he was painting was not only totally plausible, but practically at least as believable as the alternative. He asked:

"David, is there any way that you can dig a bit deeper into the Oleg character?"

"Sure can. Actually, we have already started as Mark really gave us a great idea. We need to find people who might know of him, or at least of his company."

Mark had another suggestion:

"Earlier, we had thought of Countess Renate to implement a plan. Couldn't we use her and Wong Hai Chock to find out what is known in the cyber world of Oleg Nichakov?"

David asked:

"Did we ask Oleg what the name of his company was?"

Mark replied:

"We sure did. Remember, the English translation was: Visla Cybersecurity Group."

David jumped up:

"The name tells it all; very interesting. You could argue that "Visla" is a combination of the names of the Vistula river, expressed in both Polish and Ukrainian. Oleg wanted to remember his Ukrainian heritage, but could not be too obvious, ergo the Polish connection. Just there to mess with us, using the obvious!"

▪ ▪ ▪ ▪ ▪

Though the Vistula river is the largest river in Poland and as such runs solely in Poland, it plays a symbolic role for Ukrainians as well. The Vistula flows from its source at Barania Gora, the mountains in the south of Poland that delineate its border with the Czech Republic and Slovakia, to the north and eventually empties into the Baltic Sea. Though the basin it drains primarily comprises Poland, it also extends into neighboring Ukraine directly and indirectly. Indirectly, it flows through the part of Poland where the 10% of Poles of Ukrainian ethnicity live; they are totally loyal to Poland, though they are surely quite sensitive to developments in "the motherland." Directly, it boasts two tributaries which originate in Ukraine, the Sian River, and the Buh River, and even has a direct connection to Ukraine's inland water system: the Dnipro-Buh Canal.

The connection between the Vistula and Oleg Nichakov's company becomes crystal clear when one learns that the name of the river is Vysla in Ukrainian and Wisla in Polish.

▪ ▪ ▪ ▪ ▪

Mark exclaimed:

"By God. You're damn right. Practically, he's just taking advantage of the fact that the letter "w" does not exist in Russian. So, the name he uses is the same as the way the river's name is spelled in Russian: Visla in the Roman alphabet and Висла in Russian."

Nonetheless, he almost immediately paused:

"Wait a second. Back to your explanation, David. Does it really help us with respect to our current quandary?"

He saw that David and Simon needed an explanation:

"Got you confused. Sorry. You know, the issue of whether he is for real or a plant."

Mark paused and seeing that David and Simon seemed back on board, he added:

"Let's see. Oleg told us of his Ukrainian or rather Cossack past. He told us he wanted, no that he felt he had to hide it. We worry whether he is a real fugitive or a plant. Does the name of the company help or hurt? You're with me now?"

David seemed albeit reluctantly to follow, but still said:

"To me, the name does not tell us anything more than what you and I have summarized in different ways. A bit like the fish which Christians at times affix to their cars: a way for the cognoscenti to recognize one another, but nothing sufficiently obvious."

He paused and added:

"So, the bottom line is simple: the name of his company does not hurt the scenario he proposed. Doesn't help it either. One question we might ask is this: did he really think of that himself, however far back he created the company or was it something which Russian security services suggested to him if he was then already a spy? The point is I'm not sure we gain anything by answering it!"

Simon agreed. He was starting to feel he needed to redirect the conversation in a more potentially useful direction. Thus, shifting gears, he asked:

"Back to your earlier point, Mark, what do you want to ask Countess Renate?"

Mark thought for a few seconds and replied:

"Well, my starting point is that his company would have had to have at least some passing contact with the broader, global cyber world if it is well-known and the Russian industry leader. Right?"

Simon and David nodded. Mark continued:

"So, based on that assumption, wouldn't it be highly likely that Wong Hai Chock would have heard of it?"

He paused again and noted that his two bosses were definitely following. So, he concluded:

"So, in my mind, we have two possible outcomes. If Hai Chock has not heard of him, a massive red flag just came up. If he has, even in a distant manner, he might be able to find out much more quickly than we . . ."

Simon interrupted:

"I like it. In fact, I like it a lot. Take this one step further. Though it's possible that Hai Chock has never heard of the company for whatever reason, there is no chance he would not have heard of Oleg Nichakov, particularly when the industry was in its infancy. So, whichever way it turns out, either we have just been given a great reason to demur or the guy might be for real and that opens super wide doors for us. You follow, Mark?"

"Absolutely right."

■ ■ ■ ■ ■

With Simon's concurrence, which he received like an approval, David sat down with Mark to call Countess Renate:

"David, what an unexpected pleasure. Please pass my best wishes onto General Rabinowitz."

David had to reply:

"Countess, knowing Simon as well as you do, I think you know that he is probably the last one to want to use his military title . . . Anyway, I sure will transmit your best wishes. By the way, my colleague Mark Levi is here with me. We may very well need your help."

"That would be wonderful. Hi Mark! I'm all ears. What's the problem?

David took the leading role in the conversation. He discussed what he called the "Oleg Nichakov situation" from two different angles:

"First, I'd like to check that we know as much as we can about Oleg. *Mossad* has a file on him and his company, but it's all from published sources. On the surface he looks clean, but the file is only five years old, though it did contain the information and placed it in the context of the broader advances which Israel had been making in the cybersecurity and cyber warfare areas."

Countess Renate replied:

"Has the company been around for longer?"

"That's the point. It has, but we couldn't find anything of substance about it prior to the inception we have in our files."

"Something created after the fact?"

"Could well be. But the fact is that whatever we have is not much. It confirms the business of the company, confirms that Oleg is the founder, confirms that they are a major supplier to the Russian military as well as to the non-military side of the economy . . . But that's about it."

"Do you mean that a doctored, or reconstituted file would have more juicy details, to attract the reader? In short, are you saying that it would be better if this was in the "too good to be true category" because then you'd know that it is fake?"

"Exactly. As it is, nothing is obvious. So, the question is this: is there a way that Wong Hai Chock might tell us or find out and tell us more about him?"

"Does not sound impossible. The second angle?"

David first stressed how totally secret this "second angle" was. He introduced the topic by musing on the possibility of having The Shadow Experts serve as a screen between the Russians and the Israelis. Countess thought for a few seconds and asked:

"That sounds fine. How much are you prepared to let me, or my team know? By the way, before you reply, you probably already know that the point man between us would be Wong Hai Chock. So, what do I tell Hai Chock?"

"I think you tell him the truth, i.e. what you know to be the truth—we've made significant progress in the domain, and here, by 'we,' I mean Israel. You don't know what the actual development is. We also have an opportunity to work behind the scenes with the owner and head of the largest cyber company in Russia. Israel's goal is focused on the Middle East, and we would only allow ourselves to be dragged into what looks like a probable conflict between Russia and Ukraine if that was inevitable, though there could be no visible link to Israel."

David then touched on the fact that Israel had made a couple of significant breakthroughs in the field and wondered whether Hai Chock and Shadow Experts could help serving as a screen, effectively hiding the key people in Israel."

"I'm not sure I understand what you're trying to do?"

"Well, if Oleg is legit and if his company is indeed quite up to speed, there may be a way to use him and his company to get into the Russian systems."

Countess Renate interrupted:

"I see, you would rather your scientist not be brought into the limelight. So, Hai Chock could serve as the counterparty to your friend, Mr. Nichakov, and work behind the scenes with your scientists . . ."

"That's exactly it. The first step would be to verify that Oleg is for real. Then we can move forward with the disinformation or sabotage. Note, however, that our principal beef here is with what the Russians do in the Middle East. We are certainly not trying to insert ourselves in any other conflict which the Russians may have."

Countess Renate replied that she would, as always like to think about it, and to talk with the associates, as she called the members of her network, who might be called to play a role. She concluded:

"Knowing you from our earlier adventures together, I am pretty sure that we can find a way to cooperate, but I need to ensure I know what we can and cannot do. I suspect you've got some similar work to do on your end."

CHAPTER.05

SINGAPORE, TEL AVIV, ISRAEL AND SOMEWHERE IN THE AUSTRIAN ALPS

Countess Renate had waited for a reasonable time of day before she called Wong Hai Chock, her top cybersecurity expert; he resided in Singapore. She knew that he was available 24/7; after all, so was she and it was a well-known and accepted condition for membership in The Shadow Experts. However, there being no inordinate urgency, Countess Renate felt no need to disturb Hai Chock for selfish reasons. He was normally employed as a professor/researcher at the National University of Singapore. Though he was as honest and straightforward as they come, he had a passion for puzzles. To him, dealing with hackers and all that was broadly known as the "dark web" and "cyber bandits" was of utmost interest—just like solving a puzzle. He picked up the phone on the second ring:

"Countess Renate, I haven't talked to you in a while. What's up?"

"Well, my friend, I may well need your help."

"Excellent! Always willing and sometimes able to help . . ."

"You're too modest. Anyway, the client would be the same as a couple of times in the last two years, our friends in the Middle East. They have just come across a Russian gentleman and his company.

They understand that they're involved in cybersecurity and by implication cyber warfare. Have you heard of them? The name of the company is Visla Cybersecurity and the fellow's name is . . ."

"Oleg Nichakov?"

"So, you know them . . ."

"Well, I know of him. He is known to be an oligarch, though he seems to maintain a lower profile than many others. However, let's not go too far; his profile is certainly not low by most standards. Yet, who knows by Singapore's? I believe that his company is very close to the regime, and Nichakov himself is understood to be quite a bit closer to the regime than others. Could simply be because of what his company does . . ."

"Could he be a part of what we used to call the KGB and we now call FIS, you know the Foreign Intelligence Service?"

"Nobody knows, but you could easily make up a case that this is why he maintains such a low profile despite having amassed what is said to be very substantial wealth."

He paused for a second and added:

"Having said that, let me add a couple of modifiers. First, what I just said about him could be said about just any oligarch you care to name. In his case, the only bit of extra suspicion would seem to be his field of activity. Cybersecurity IS a major priority in Moscow. Second, I have heard rumors, although I stress they were only rumors, that his company really was incubated within the successor to the KGB, probably just for the reason I just mentioned."

Countess Renate replied:

"*Mossad* would very much like to know if they could work with him or if he is more likely than not to be a spy . . ."

Hai Chock changed the topic for a short while, openly wondering why *Mossad* would work with a person such as Oleg Nichakov. He had to ask:

"What in the world would they want to do with him?"

"Well, I feel totally free to discuss anything with you since David Heller told me next to nothing . . . You know, his "need to know only" principle."

"I see."

"So, this is all I know. Here we go. I guess that they wonder whether they might be able to use him or his company to penetrate the Russian security apparatus, particularly as it deals with the help Russia provides to Israel's enemies in the Middle East . . ."

"I can understand the question. But why would he even consider talking to them? And how would they even get access to him?"

Countess Renate explained that this is where things became interesting. She told Hai Chock that it appeared that Oleg Nichakov had said he wanted to defect and reached out to Israel to do it. Hai Chock came right back:

"Now at least something makes sense. Let me think."

He paused for a second to give himself the time to check his logic and continued:

"However, to me at least, it makes more sense for him to be a spy trying to figure out what Israel knows than for him to offer them entry points into Russian cybersecurity. Don't you agree?"

Countess Renate could only concede that there was no obvious flaw in Hai Chock's thinking. However, she added that she really did not have enough actionable information to make an intelligent assertion. However, if only because she had precious few hard facts, she offered the thought that it surely made sense for him to have grown scared by all the noise which is made about maneuvers near Ukraine. She paused and added a clincher in her view:

"Let me add one point. We know that quite a number of oligarchs have seemingly committed suicide, and I should put this in the obvious quotation marks, in the recent past. All after the onset of these so-called maneuvers around Ukraine. So, the thesis of him being really scared and trying to escape the bear's hug cannot be dismissed."

Hai Chock had to reply:

"I see. That might make some sense, but I think "they," our *Mossad* friends, should proceed quite cautiously."

"That's the point, my friend. That's the point. That's where we, The Shadow Experts in general and you in particular come in. Is there any way you can dig a bit? Would your friends in the Military Security Department in Singapore know something they might be willing to share?"

"You mean Yeo Yap Min, the deputy director of the Agency[4]?"

"Exactly."

"Well, let me call him and ask. There is no harm in asking and, as it did before, asking a question might even give him a clue as to something he might want to investigate himself."

"I'm leaving this in your hands. Let me know as soon as you can."

■ ■ ■ ■ ■

It did not take Hai Chock very long to call Countess Renate back. Unfortunately, the message that he had to convey was if not useless at best not terribly helpful. Oleg Nichakov was indeed known to the Singaporean authorities, as was his company. There did not seem to be any firm indication that there was anything wrong with him or Visla Cybersecurity Group. Still, at the same time, there was no way of being 100% sure that everything was "in the clean" as Yap Min had said. In reality, he had essentially repeated, in his own words, everything which Countess Renate or Hai Chock had said or heard, or for that matter what David and Mark had told Renate. However, Hai Chock surprised Countess Renate when he added:

"The only thing he said which was new news was when Yap Min said, "In fact, we were even considering buying one of their services a few years back." That truly surprised me."

---

[4] By the same author, see "Below the Surface," Barringer Publishing, 2022

"You and me both . . ."

"Indeed. I asked him to expand. He said he felt he could not provide much more information, other than saying that in the end they did not buy the system and that their decision was based on precisely the same logic as stood behind Hai Chock's question. The government had decided that the field in which Visla operated was so crucial and the general profile of the owner, Oleg Nichakov, so apparently clean that we wondered whether there was more than met the eyes."

Hai Chock further reported that Yap Min had paused for an instant and offered the damning conclusion:

"After all, the people we most want to guard against when it comes to cybersecurity would have to be Russia and China. Why would we run the risk of letting the wolf into the sheep house?"

Hai Chock could only conclude for Yap Min's benefit:

"Exactly where we are in our own thought process. Let me pass on the information to Countess Renate and commit that I'll let you know if anything odd surfaces."

Countess Renate called David to let him know that they felt like they had reached a dead end. She couched her conclusion in a careful manner though:

"We didn't find anything that we believe would be in any way actionable. However, it looks to me as if everyone who has heard of Oleg Nichakov feels that there is something that might be too good to be true. So, I think it has to mean that we should be really cautious . . ."

David thanked her and indicated that he would be back to her soon with the second step in the assignment.

David decided to place a quick call to Simon to check his own logic. Simon invited him into his office which was only a few doors down the corridor. They sat in the corner with the sofa and the two wing chairs and focused on the one question which David felt he could not or rather should not decide on his own: do we trust Oleg Nichakov? He gave Simon a summary of what he knew so far and was maybe a bit surprised when he saw a smile light up Simon's face as he said:

"David, my friend, we may have received a great gift, but it could also be a poisoned gift."

David decided to stay quiet and wait for more from Simon, as he thought he understood, but was not sure. After all, Simon was known to give himself some time in these kinds of conversations: he would make a general comment to delay having to come up with the real answer. At times, people would jump to a conclusion and not ask more, at which point Simon would simply say no more and let the topic die. In other circumstances, particularly with people who knew Simon and really valued his opinion, they would let him take the time he needed and wait for the pearl to come out of his mouth. Today, Simon asked:

"Assume for a minute you knew Oleg is a plant. What would you do?"

"I would turn down his offer to help us, I think."

"I don't disagree, but I might not have been as forceful as you in my reply."

David looked definitely quizzical. Simon noticed and added:

"A known spy is totally ineffective. Well, maybe not totally, but certainly somewhat ineffective. We would know what to show and what to hide. After all, I trust you and your colleagues to manage that line, though I'll concede that it may not be obvious,"

David was smiling. Simon continued:

"Yet, we could use him to find out about his side. Now, at some level, he probably would know how not to divulge anything secret, but he has to keep us interested in what he has to offer. Right?"

"Right. I see. You're saying we can try to outsmart him, given the fact that he has to deliver something while we are merely waiting for whatever he is delivering."

"Precisely. So, I might not totally reject the idea of working with him, though I would be extremely vigilant. On the other hand, take the other side. What would we do if we knew that he was legit?"

"We'd jump on the opportunity, wouldn't we?"

"Agreed, though, again, we still have to be cautious. Anyone who is prepared to be a traitor to one master, could easily decide to double cross the other "master" as well, immediately or down the line: a mercenary is always for sale to the highest bidder. Let someone come up with a better deal and you've got a liability on your hands."

"Makes all the sense in the world. So, if I understand your point, we should be careful in either case, but still might try to move forward with our eyes wide open . . ."

"Exactly my friend. Initially, you talked, or rather was it Mark's idea, of bringing Countess Renate into the process, sort of to create a screen between Nathan Sharon and Oleg. Well, it seems to me that the idea remains, with one caveat. We should warn Hai Chock and Nathan that we may spread a bit of disinformation in the middle of everything, just to see how Oleg deals with it. Makes sense?"

"Totally."

■ ■ ■ ■ ■

David asked Mark to join him for the next phone call to Countess Renate. He had briefed him on the idea that some disinformation might appear here and there but made the point that he was going to play it straight with Countess Renate. Again, she picked up the phone quickly:

"David, you're back even faster than I expected. Must be a real important thing . . ."

She had a short laugh.

"Simon sends his best."

"Well, thank you. Tell him that the same goes for me when you get to talk to him. So, what's the next step?"

David explained that though he was quite grateful for the additional information provided by Hai Chock, *Mossad* had concluded that they could not determine whether Oleg was legit or a plant. He briefly outlined the pros and cons and said that, in his own view, he was firmly on the fence. He could hear a short chuckle at the other end of the line. However, in his words, he matter-of-factly declared:

"This is an opportunity which we cannot miss."

Renate interrupted:

"I understand and would agree."

"Thanks. So, I think that what we must do is establish a couple of distinct channels. One will have us introduce your team, Hai Chock I presume, to Oleg, arguing that he is a cyber consultant whom we have been using in his capacity as researcher/professor at the National University of Singapore. It is public knowledge that Israel has been working with Singapore on these issues, so that should not raise any flag in Oleg's mind. Agreed?"

"So far so good. I'm waiting for the second channel as you call it."

"Yes. The second channel is to have Hai Chock introduced to Nathan Sharon, the top scientist in the area at Beersheba, By the way, his sharp focus is known as he, Nathan, has spoken at various conferences. Should add that the fact that he has gone beyond the civilian world is not widely known. After all, a cynic might assume that Oleg, if he is a plant, is precisely here either to get to know what he knows or to eliminate him."

"Eliminate him?"

"Well, you know how Russians deal with their enemies, don't you?"

"I do. I do. I'll confirm Hai Chock knows this. But what do we want Hai Chock to find out?"

David explained that the goal would be to find out where the Russians are, particularly their newest applications, adding:

"Ultimately, our real goal is to see if we can sneak stuff into their systems so that any cyber-attacks on Israel coordinated with or thought Syria or Iran, not only fails, but allows us to burrow even deeper into their and their clients' systems."

"Now, correct me if I am wrong, but Hai Chock would be allowed to claim a business relationship with *Mossad*?"

"Well, technically, I don't think it would be with *Mossad*. It would be with the Israeli Defense Forces."

"Point taken. Sorry. So, he would be asking Oleg if he knows of something that might help Israel fight cyber-attacks from Russian client states, but not attack Russia. Correct?"

"Absolutely. It would in truth be quite interesting to see Oleg's reaction to this. Mind you, that won't necessarily tell us anything about his ultimate motives. Imagine he is a traitor against Yushin, but not against the greater Russia. He might want to avoid weakening the mother country."

Mark interrupted:

"Right, David, but let's not forget that one of his first few statements to us was that he had never forgotten his Ukrainian roots . . ."

"Good point. But that could be something to lead us down the wrong alley . . ."

Renate concluded:

"Gentlemen, I think I have enough to brief Hai Chock. I believe that we should be planning on getting him on a video conference call with you two. That's where we will be able to put a bit more flesh on the bones of the outline we have so far."

CHAPTER.06

TEL AVIV, ISRAEL, SINGAPORE AND SOMEWHERE IN THE AUSTRIAN ALPS

A short six weeks earlier, Hai Chock had found himself in Tel Aviv. The trip being strictly of an academic nature, neither Countess Renate nor anybody else outside of Singapore knew about it. Tel Aviv University was holding a two-day conference on cybersecurity, actually, the one that had impressed the Israeli prime minister. Speeches were expected from a number of the thought leaders in the field. Hai Chock for his part was going to speak about the need to maintain a high degree of vigilance and on one of his pet topics: *Offence is often better than defense.* The program indicated that Nathan Sharon was also expected to give a speech on the topic of a new and virtually undetectable way of taking control of "foreign" networks. All the participants, speakers, or only delegates understood that true secrets of breakthroughs were unlikely to be brought up in enough detail to be "actionable." Any real "transfer of knowledge," if there was going to be any, would occur behind closed doors, among people who already knew one another and who were often already working together. It was indeed a wide-open secret that at least a quarter of all the delegates in these conferences, despite posting

apparently authentic credentials and aside from the press, only attended to find better ways of penetrating cybersecurity. In other words, they were hackers or, worse yet, spies who were hoping to get better at their craft, but surely not for the benefit of science or of the whole community.

■ ■ ■ ■ ■

Cyber warfare, or the use of digital attacks against an enemy state, though relatively new has still been around for quite some time. However, there is considerable debate within the community whether the term is actually even acceptable. Indeed, it has been argued that no offensive cyber action could be viewed as war, though many people might disagree with the statement, on the grounds that it confuses the concept of "war" with the reality of an "act of war." Cyberattacks are liable to inflict physical damage to people or even objects in the real world. Israel, for instance, targeted and destroyed a building which it had identified as the source of an ongoing cyberattack, in May 2019. One could describe the process that unfolded as an act of war, the cyberattack, followed by a military response. The act was not a war; at most, some action within a war.

One way of getting the protagonists closer together on this question is to distinguish between cyber warfare and cyber war. While the latter implies scale, duration and violence, the former only conjures up the use of techniques, procedures or tactics which make use of cyberspace. For example, still in 2019, the United States launched a cyberattack against Iranian weapon systems in response to the shooting down of a drone over the Straits of Hormuz. Their response can be viewed as an instance where cyber warfare is used to support traditional warfare, all the while with some degree of distance to avoid what might otherwise be seen as an unequivocal direct confrontation.

Each of the dimensions of cyber warfare indeed straddles the line between direct confrontation on the one hand and disguised and plausibly deniable intervention on the other. Sophisticated computer-based systems have long been crucial in the toolbox of the espionage community. Sabotage, which one could argue is one step-up from espionage in terms of confrontational attitude, is definitely a beneficiary of the use of cyber tools. Consider an effort to prevent air defense systems from identifying or shooting at an intruder, directly, or as a means to conduct an air attack. A similar kind of activity can bring about disruptions to the provision of power, water, fuel or communications, and quickly cross into the category of denial-of-service; denial-of-service is a broad category which simply covers any action which incapacitates an organization and makes it unable to provide the service it normally does. The well-known vulnerability of the electrical power grid, both within individual countries and even globally, is often considered only from the point of view of a nuclear explosion in space. Systems intrusion, of the same nature as the Stuxnet virus allegedly introduced by Israel into the Iranian uranium enriching environment, could achieve the same end without crossing the line into nuclear warfare.

■ ■ ■ ■ ■

The one element of the cyber world which was of particular concern to Hai Chock was what he deemed "special, surprise attacks." It is not a new idea for anyone to try to capitalize on a surprise element to achieve some initial, potentially vital, advantage. Al-Qaeda terrorists probably knew that, as they planned and executed their coordinated attacks on the U.S. on 9/11. Still, the much broader reach which cyber warfare potentially enjoys could transform what might initially seem as a minor advantage into an overwhelming benefit.

Given the relatively small size of Singapore in geographical terms and its advanced use of computerized systems, ensuring that the

Republic remained at the leading edge of capabilities on that front was a top priority. Though their potential enemies were totally different, it was the simple recognition that both countries needed to use every possible means to succeed and survive that had led Singapore and Israel to their close cooperation in the cyber world.

One of the speeches in which Hai Chock was really quite interested was scheduled to be delivered by an Israeli scholar, Nathan Sharon. As advertised, Sharon discussed the use of computer code to disrupt the normal functioning of routine systems. Hai Chock had already met Nathan a few times, including a couple of visits to his Beersheba laboratory, and felt like they were kindred spirits. Both were more interested in the science than in the military implications of their work. Both viewed tinkering with computer programs or systems as fascinating intellectual exercises, somewhat akin to solving puzzles whether these were based on images or algorithms.

This time, both certainly enjoyed each other's presentations. They were delighted to catch up and used a dinner away from the conference site, but still walking distance from the campus of Tel Aviv University, to discuss their work in more depth. Neither could tell the other any of the elements of their results which both would consider state secrets or at least business secrets, but they were sufficiently open with each other that they could share pointers or "research avenues." Further, they reiterated their commitment to stay in contact and see whether there was room for further cooperation. Hai Chock as it turned out had a further goal in mind; he wanted to suggest to Countess Renate that Nathan Sharon could be a wonderful addition to The Shadow Experts. He knew that he could not raise the issue directly with Nathan; that was Countess Renate's preserve. However, he danced a bit around it for a couple of minutes, talking of the ability to serve a greater cause. In practice, that might in truth be somewhat more difficult a move. Indeed, the one thing which Nathan had not disclosed to Hai Chock was the fact that his job description

was not limited to the academic world; he had a direct line to the Israeli Defense Forces, which would make the idea of working for The Shadow Experts a potentially difficult challenge at best.

■ ■ ■ ■ ■

Hai Chock almost broke out laughing when Countess Renate talked to him of the second element of the mission.

"You mean that I need to get to know Nathan Sharon?"

"Yes, that's the name which David gave me."

Keeping as serious an expression as he could, in order to prolong the joke for a few extra seconds, Hai Chock simply replied:

"And what if I already know him and of his work?"

"You do?"

"Yes. As a matter of fact, we've met a number of times and admire each other's work. Come to think of it, we attended the same conference in Tel Aviv as recently as six odd weeks ago."

"Tel Aviv? Six weeks ago? Wasn't aware of that."

"I know Countess. This was really work that I was doing on behalf of the National University of Singapore. I surely could not guess that this was going to morph into a project . . ."

"No harm done. So, what do you think of this fellow?"

"Super smart and at the same time immensely practical. He has what seems to me to be an excellent grasp of theory, but he strikes me as being driven by results. By the way, this is not a huge surprise. In the world of software, people often deal with bugs one at a time rather than revisit the whole program. That's why discussions with technicians can be mesmerizing for non-specialists; the focus is on fixing the problem rather than understanding how it arose. Traditional engineers suggest that any such solution will be at best sub-optimal; software engineers know that such is the only practical way to get to a solution within a reasonable time frame."

Countess smiled and added:

"Well, this is going to make our job a lot easier. At this point, I don't have all the details, but I suspect that we should plan on a three-way video conference with you, David and me in the very near future."

"Just let me know when."

He paused and with a smile on his face added:

". . . and let's try to have it at a time where no one is having to wake up in the middle of the night."

■ ■ ■ ■ ■

Though she had left the prior conference call with the idea that the next step was the video conference she had just discussed with Hai Chock, Countess Renate felt that the new information she had just learned made it imperative for her to have another conversation with David. She surprised him with her introduction:

"Hai Chock knows Nathan Sharon. They have met several times and Hai Chock has even visited Nathan in Beersheba."

"How interesting. That changes things a bit, Countess. You're right."

David paused for a few seconds and added:

"I must talk with Nathan and bring him a bit further into the loop. Wouldn't be fair to him to keep him in the dark. In the end, I don't see this as a major issue, but he needs to know the full picture. After all, that can only make our work together more fruitful."

"Can't disagree. I have to tell you that I was surprised when I found out that Hai Chock had met Nathan and actually already cooperated with him. In a sense, I shouldn't have been surprised; after all, they're in the same world. However, it made me realize anew how my associates have their own professional lives and how, at times, their professional lives and mine actually overlap. Not a discovery, but a good reminder . . ."

"You know, Countess, that's probably what makes their strength."

"Can't disagree. I guess you can't have it all, excellence and total control!"

"Turning philosophical on me Countess?"

CHAPTER.07

TEL AVIV AND BEERSHEBA, ISRAEL, SINGAPORE AND SOMEWHERE IN THE AUSTRIAN ALPS

Mark and David had invited Oleg back to their offices for a further conversation; David was determined to start "using" Oleg and, if not possible, to close the chapter. He did not want to waste any time. All security precautions had been taken care of, as Oleg was accompanied by a bodyguard and driven in an unmarked *Mossad* car. Surveillance of the penthouse was reinforced while he was away. Irina and the children were staying "home alone" in what looked a lot like a golden prison, though one they had chosen for safety reasons. Given the weather on that day, it was a good bet that some splashing in the pool had to be on the menu. Mark and David used a conference room with all the appropriate hidden recording apparatus for the meeting with Oleg. Oleg was not surprised, as his prior visits to *Mossad* headquarters had involved the same room, and, he assumed, the same security precautions.

Mossad headquarters were located in the north of Tel Aviv; specifically, three miles north of Hayarkon Park. The park is often referred to as "the lungs of Tel Aviv," as it is if not the largest, one of the largest parks in the city, covering nearly 1.5 square miles. It

is named after the Yarkon River which flows through it, The park comprises extensive lawns, botanical gardens, sports facilities, a water park, an aviary, and a lake in addition to a couple of concert venues. *Mossad* headquarters occupy a modern structure angled to face to the northwest; the complex is made up of seven connected individual structures, five of which are arranged as the two sides of a right angle. Each of these five looks somewhere between square and hexagonal and have a large internal light well which provides natural light to most rooms within. Most of the offices facing the outside and to the northwest have a nice, virtually unobstructed view, across the Glilot Ma'arav Interchange, of the Mediterranean, and of the Herzliya marina. The latter stands barely more than a mile in the distance with undeveloped but cultured agricultural land between *Mossad* headquarters and the seaside. Barely a half of a mile straight to the west was the scenic and much visited North Cliff beach.

David opened the conversation asking:

"How have you been doing, Oleg?"

"Well, as you know, it truly is a golden prison, but it remains a prison . . ."

"Anything we can do about it?"

"Not at this point I am afraid."

"And the family?"

"Again, as well as could be expected. You wanted to discuss something, David?"

David was thankful that Oleg had cut short the chitchat as rapidly as he had. He knew that he was going to ask hard questions and had somehow "played for time" at the outset. Mark, on his side, viewed the move as suspect, wondering *"is this a sign of a spy who wants to get into the thick of things?"* He still preferred to let that thought pass for then, though he did file it in a corner of his memory for later use if needed.

David confirmed that they were now in a position where they could begin to work together. Matter-of-factly, he stated:

"We would like to introduce you to a consultant whom we use. He is as good as they get in the cybersecurity front. He is not based in Israel, but he has our total confidence."

"Where is he or she?"

"It's a he and he is in Singapore."

"Why wouldn't you use someone local? After all, I believe you all are at the forefront of the industry. Or at least, this is what I read in the academic literature and hear from everyone with whom I talk."

He paused for a second and conceded:

"Though I hear that Singapore is also quite skilled in the matter."

Mark could not resist asking:

"Oleg, have you been able to achieve all that you and your company have achieved without direct contacts with anyone outside of Russia?"

Oleg looked a bit embarrassed and did not reply right away, other than saying:

"No, absolutely not. I surely attend many conferences, and so do my top technical people."

He stopped, and Mark assumed that his apparent embarrassment was caused by the fact that Russia—as did China—had been relying on spying for a good part of their technical developments. Oleg regained his composure and added:

"Well, gentlemen, as you know, we take full advantage of all published materials, as I just said we try to attend as many conferences as possible . . ."

Mark looked like he was going to cut him off, but David motioned to Oleg to continue.

"So, that information plus the work of our own technical experts has taken us to where we are. I should add that the technology behind what we do is not terribly complex. Tedious would be a better word

than complex to describe it. We keep looking for opportunities to penetrate systems and insert our viruses, worms or related mini programs."

David nodded. Mark smiled and asked:

"What about the defensive work which you must be doing?"

"Great question. The principle is the same, but somehow in reverse. We have within our company a group of people whose only job, based on the same information, is to look for ways and try to penetrate our own systems. Think of them as our in-house spies. Once they find a weakness in any of our tools, they immediately alert the rest of the firm which then works to close that loophole."

"I suspect you're making it sound simpler than it really is, but I understand."

Oleg smiled and seemed to relax a bit:

"You know, Mark, it is really not that much more complicated. The key skill is found in people who have experience debugging software programs. It's all a case of looking for a weakness. As you know, software developers rarely go back fully into a program. When told of a bug, they fix it. Well, our role, and I suspect the role of the people you have here or your consultant in Singapore, is to find bugs before others find them."

Oleg paused, drinking from the chilled water glass that has been set before him. He then asked David and Mark:

"So, what would you need me to do?"

David replied:

"Well, we would like to have you meet, by video conference or in person here, our consultant and bring him up to speed on what you have, where you see your strengths and where you believe there may still be weaknesses. This should be quite an interesting conversation."

Oleg nodded, but corrected David's understanding:

"I'm happy to go through that, but you must understand that my role in the company never was to work "on the line" so to speak.

I run the company, determine strategic directions, secure contracts, primarily government contracts, and manage the income statement so that we have the resources we need while still turning in a profit. If you just listened to developers, you'd keep adding resources and pretty soon you'd be losing money hand over fist."

Mark had to ask:

"Can you have a technical conversation?"

"Up to a point yes, but I cannot guarantee that I am able to take it deep enough for your consultant."

David looked somewhat crossed, and truthfully was again beginning to ask himself whether Oleg was for real. Without allowing his displeasure to show and forcing a smile he asked:

"Oleg, how can you offer to help us if you cannot have a full conversation with our techies? More to the point, how could you run the business if you could not stay on top of what your top engineers were telling you?"

"Dealing with your second question first, I have a Chief Technology Officer who serves as a go-between between those focused on day-to-day software issues and me. He and I have been together for quite a long time, in reality pretty much from the very beginning. I would not describe him as an intimate friend, simply because when I married Irina, I decided not to have any close friends in Russia. Preferred the reputation of a workaholic who needed rest when in St. Petersburg."

David decided to allow Oleg to respond to his first question before asking the obvious follow-up question. Oleg continued:

"With respect to the first question, I am sure that I can have a discussion with Yuri . . ."

"Yuri?"

"Yes, Mark, Yuri Vassiliev, our Chief Technology Officer."

"I see. Sorry to have interrupted. Please continue."

"Not to worry. We have a good enough relationship that he knows my strengths and my limitations. And I know his."

David had to ask:

"How can you do that without returning to Russia?"

"We're used to it . . ."

Mark interrupted:

"We know that. However, imagine that your fears of your being on a blacklist are warranted. Wouldn't you expect Mr. Vassiliev to try to lure you back to Russia?"

Oleg seemed to think for a short while. Then he replied without his face displaying any more emotion:

"He certainly might if you assume he is not loyal to me and to our company, but to the regime. But frankly that's not how I read him. I think he's clean, by which I mean that he is not working for the Kremlin, at least not directly. So, as I said, he might, but he won't be successful anyway. I know how far I'm prepared to go and that bit, going back to Russia is off limits, period, paragraph."

Mark did not let go:

"What if he refuses to answer when you try to communicate other than in person?"

"First, as I just said that would be a change, because so far we have spent a lot of time on the phone or in videoconferences. So, that change would have to mean that he knows that I have fled, and that pressure is applied to him to get me back. We'll cross that bridge when we get there. But I think I have a few trump cards still in my hand. Everybody in Russia has a price!"

Mark smiled and concluded:

"Understood."

Mark looked as he was about to get up and leave the meeting, when he suddenly seemed to reconsider and asked:

"How well does Yuri know the inside of your homes or even of your yacht?"

"He's been on the yacht and has seen the inside of the house in St. Petersburg. But, he's never set foot in the houses in Switzerland or in France. In fact, I'm sure he doesn't know about them."

■ ■ ■ ■ ■

After Hai Chock and Nathan Sharon had had the opportunity to discuss their joint mission and be candid as to the limits that had to be imposed on their cooperation, they agreed with Mark that a video conference call including David and Countess Renate would make sense. It would allow everyone to know that they were all singing from the same hymn book. They had made an important decision: they would share with Nathan the existence of The Shadow Experts. Initially, Countess Renate had been lukewarm on the issue. She agreed when Hai Chock made the point that Nathan could actually be a great potential new associate. The issue of his work with the Israeli Defense Forces obviously was raised, but she herself simply added:

"In truth, he would not be the only associate who must limit his activities because of a conflict. You know my key principle: a disclosed conflict is no longer a real conflict; we simply work around it."

David opened the video conference call with thanks to Countess Renate and her Shadow Experts for, once again, joining in *Mossad*'s efforts to fight back against their regional enemies. He made it very clear that they were not aiming at the Soviet Union, a particularly important side note to the extent that the recent start to the invasion by Russia of Ukraine was raising the specter of a third world war. He argued:

"Though it's painfully obvious to all that I'm not in the foreign affairs ministry, let me verify that everyone understands what we are trying to achieve here. First, we do not want to be seen to be targeting Russia. Our principal goal, as you all know, is and has always been to ensure first the survival and second the prosperity of the State of Israel. In this particular case, second, we believe that we may have an

ace up our sleeves in the person of a Russian oligarch whose business we're told is the largest cybersecurity company in Russia. We know that the large bulk of their work is done for the Russian government, though we are aware of other contracts. Before you say anything, know that these other contracts are mostly with government-owned or controlled enterprises. So, it would not be dumb to say that they are as close to a branch of the government as can be . . ."

He let that sit for a short while . . . Countess Renate interrupted:

"David, this closeness to the Russian government? Isn't it strange? Could it be a trap?"

"Well, Countess, I have to say that you could well be right on all counts. We are fully aware of the strangeness of the situation. Let me simply assure you that we have a plan to deal with that contingency. There will be an exchange of information, for sure. But there will also be a fair dose of disinformation. Whatever disinformation comes from us will be deliberate. Whatever comes from him would be seen as a serious deal breaker if we ever found out."

"I suspect you can't discuss that . . ."

"I can't indeed, not because of any distrust of anyone. We're among friends and kindred spirits here. It's more a question of making sure that everyone reacts as naturally as possible in the moment. I should also say that the plan should not affect the interactions between Hai Chock and Nathan. Everything between the two of them ought to be above board, though I do not want to prejudge anything."

He paused to take a short sip of iced coffee and went on:

"I suspect that some part of Nathan's work is covered by national security secrecy. In a bind, do not hesitate, Nathan, to contact me, or to have your controlling authority go directly to Simon for guidance. On Hai Chock's side, same thing; I don't know what I don't know, but I leave it up to you Hai Chock, with or without Countess's help, to decide what you can and cannot share."

Hai Chock opened the meatiest part of the conversation:

"Now, you said your goal is limited to the Middle East, David?"

David nodded.

"I understand that this might sound narrow, but that's where we are. Yet, at the same time, the truth is that cybersecurity is very much a global issue. I will let Nathan comment on his end on that if appropriate. Our intention is to use certain tweaks which the team will suggest to us. These tweaks could have global implications, but we would only be applying them against a Middle Eastern foe, rather than in Moscow or in Beijing."

Nathan took this further, with an important twist:

"I agree. However, David, do I understand you correctly to mean that anything which we do, in an offensive mode, should be directed to communications or installations that are liable to have a bearing on the Middle East?"

"Exactly."

"This is very important. Hai Chock and I haven't discussed this yet, but we, here in Israel, have come up with a very discreet manner of sending foreign systems around the bend. Let me simply say that, once in, we effectively make them run in circles and therefore prevent them from doing their jobs."

Hai Chock cut in:

"I'd love to see what you mean in practice, Nathan. We have a routine which we used in another operation, actually a joint mission with *Mossad*, where we got computers to run such endless loops to the point they overheated and melted down . . ."

"Well, as they say, I'll show you mine if you show me yours. I just hope we did not independently come up with the same thing. It would be a waste of talent. But, back to the point of the direction of our interference, remember that a lot of what Russia has sent to Syria and Iran is still in one way or another controlled through Russia. I'm sure they would not spill the beans to people whom they know to be anything but reliable . . ."

He paused for a second, seemingly uncomfortable with his last statement, though in the end only added:

"We know they have plenty of technical advisers who might mitigate the problem for them to some extent."

"Fair point. I would suggest that you both think in terms of focus and then let the chips fall where they may. Makes sense Countess?"

"Absolutely David. The last thing we want to do is to provoke the Russians. However, if they offer us an opportunity on a platter and if we can take advantage of it without showing our faces, I suspect that we should not be shy about going ahead."

Mark simply nodded and smiled his total agreement; he then asked:

"Is there anything else which either of our cyber wizards need from us?"

CHAPTER.08

TEL AVIV, ISRAEL, CAGLIARI, SARDINIA AND SOMEWHERE IN THE WESTERN MEDITERRANEAN

Ever since his "move" to Tel Aviv, Oleg had made it a habit to correspond at least weekly with Yuri Vassiliev. Though technically not his "second" as Yuri headed up the technology hierarchy but did not run the business, it was widely accepted that the pair made up the top duo, with the Chief Financial Officer, Igor Zatopek, a somewhat distant third. Interestingly, Yuri was not personally viewed as an oligarch, though rumors occasionally circulated that he had been seen here or there driving a fancy car or enjoying the life of the jet set outside of Russia. An easy internet search would have shown that Yuri's home definitely was in a highly desirable part of town, in the Palace District, and one in which the really wealthy or well-connected live. The Palace district also called the Golden Triangle has a timeless, opulent feel, with its picturesque and serene waterways and treasure trove of European-style architecture and highly ornate palaces and museums. The world-famous Hermitage Museum is located on Palace Square, in the Tsentralny district, the center of Saint Petersburg. This square, along with the section of Nevsky Avenue that runs down to the Fontanka River, is one of the most scenic and frequently depicted

parts of the city. Hence, it ought to be crystal clear that Yuri was not lacking for money.

Early after his departure from St. Petersburg, Oleg had called Anton, the captain of his yacht, the *Volga*. At the time, she was moored in Odessa, in Ukraine, on the Black Sea. He had instructed him to sail south through the Straits of Istanbul and into the Aegean Sea. He had indicated that, as he had been known to doing in many previous instances, he might use a helicopter to get to the boat near one of the Dodecanese Islands. This allowed him a quick roundtrip to and from the yacht to enjoy some time in the environment he found the most peaceful or take care of the business of the ship.

Anton had more recently heard from Oleg. After Oleg had "settled in Tel Aviv," Oleg had asked him not to stop in the Aegean Sea, but rather to sail the *Volga* to southern Spain. Anton knew that Oleg liked to play golf, in Marbella, less than 40 miles from Malaga. Though he did not have a house on the Costa del Sol, as the area is known, Oleg would indeed occasionally fly to this golfer's paradise. He would routinely use the *Volga* that he would have sent there ahead of time as his floating home. He would then typically use either the yacht's tender or a helicopter to get from the yacht to the golf course. He occasionally did something similar if he wanted to play in a place where he could access several first-class golf courses.

■ ■ ■ ■ ■

The Marbella area certainly qualified as a place with somewhat unique access to high quality golf, with many championship golf courses dotting the landscape from Sotogrande and Valderrama, near Gibraltar to Torrequebrada near Malaga. In point of fact, the Malaga tourist board, as Malaga is the capital of the province, claims that there are more than fifty championship golf courses along the Costa del Sol; they have no difficulty touting plenty of sunshine, wonderful beaches and the Sierra Blanca with the Pico del Lastonar culminating

above 3,500 feet as a distant background. Indeed, golfers love to mention that there is one spot in Marbella where one stands less than 100 yards from three championship courses, all three designed by famed architect Robert Trent-Jones: Las Brisas, Aloha, and Los Naranjos. Residents of Naples in Florida might take issue as to where the largest number of golf course per capita can really be found, but, fortunately, they operate in different circles.

■ ■ ■ ■ ■

For the first couple of weeks of his "exile," Oleg needed to rely on a simple phone connection when dealing with Yuri or other business associates or even clients. He knew very well that a zoom conference call would show background images that should surprise Yuri, probably more than others, as he was more used to seeing Oleg in these different environments. Yet, quickly, Yuri started asking perfectly reasonable questions as to why they could not use a so much more practical videoconferencing system. His logic was impeccable: he needed access to a screen at times if only to demonstrate or show something to Oleg. Something needed to be done, but that was well within the skillset of *Mossad*.

■ ■ ■ ■ ■

Mark had agreed to visit Yuri at his penthouse apartment, when it had become clear that they had something important to discuss. Mark smiled when he noted that there was someone to open the door to the penthouse after he had rung the bell, from the lobby of the building, as the apartment had its own private elevator. The person who answered the call had been warned by headquarters that Mark would be coming; she was a *Mossad* agent, one of three people assigned to keep Oleg, aka Dimitri and his family safe. She was a black belt in Krav Magra, as were the two other people assigned to keep a protective watch over Oleg and his family.

Mark was shown into a nice library that also served as the host's office. Oleg was there waiting for Mark. He said with a smile:

"Please, do come in. Make yourself comfortable on the sofa. Anything to drink?"

"A glass of cold sparkling water would be nice, thanks."

For his part, Oleg chose to sit in one of the two matching armchairs at each end of the sofa. Once the glass of sparkling water, Neviot bottled water carbonated with a SodaStream machine, was delivered to him, Mark asked:

"I understand you need to talk to me. What can I do for you?"

"I'm beginning to feel that the weekly conference calls with Yuri may have become an issue."

"Why? In what way? I thought you were used to communicating in this way."

"Well. Yes, we are used to not being in the same room. But we typically used some form of video conferencing. The last two calls have been by telephone, and I sense that Yuri is not comfortable."

"Not comfortable or asking questions?"

"Fair enough. Both. He's asking why we can't use the video system."

He paused and added:

"He's asked me if I was sick or something."

"Well, let's be glad he hasn't asked whether you're hiding."

Mark did not let Oleg reply and immediately suggested that *Mossad* would need to find a way to create enough "background material" as he called it to allow Oleg to get back onto Zoom. Oleg agreed that it was a good idea. Mark suggested that *Mossad* should go take pictures of the inside of the yacht and a couple of homes. Oleg replied that he was not sure there was a need for any of the houses. He explained that the house in the Domaine des Terres D'Azur and the family home in Zurich, though they may have appeared in conference calls Oleg had placed or received while there, were not officially owned by

Oleg but rather by his alter ego, Dimitri Godunov. He had certainly never welcomed anyone official, even Yuri whom he considered as his right-hand man, there; no one in Russia should know that Oleg and Dimitri were the same persons. With a smile, he added:

"And we don't need to worry about St. Petersburg . . . If I was there, Yuri and I could meet face-to-face."

Still, to the extent that they had certainly appeared as backgrounds, Mark argued that *Mossad* should arrange to have pictures taken in both places, focusing on the room which was used as Dimitri's office. A "white lie" concocted by *Mossad* had the domestic help in these two homes told that the pictures were meant for some decorating magazine, something which Oleg, aka Dimitri, was happy to confirm. These pictures were taken at various times during the day and night to deal with all contingencies, together with a recording of the sounds that one would expect to hear at the appropriate time.

At the same time, the more probable location, the yacht, could not be dealt with in the same manner. Mark did formulate a plan which had every chance to succeed. Unfortunately, it would take a few more days to organize its execution. He suggested that Oleg should take the next conference call with Yuri physically from the yacht:

"But what if they try to get me there?"

"Perfectly reasonable concern, Oleg. We will however organize ourselves so that the visit surprises them in a way such that they do not have the time to plan anything, unless your Captain or the crew are loyal to Yushin, and Yushin has already ordered your assassination."

Oleg mumbled:

"That's a risk, isn't? After all, we don't know. Though I'm sure Anton is loyal to me."

Mark smiled and first tried to calm Oleg who appeared truly frightened. Mark at that time was thinking *either he is a great actor, or he is really afraid. That would tend to tell us that he is not a plant, but a real fugitive.* For Oleg's benefit, he started with a calming assurance:

"You will not be alone. You'll have official bodyguards."

He proceeded to suggest that Oleg should send an email to Yuri to tell him that he'd like their usual weekly conversation to take place the next day or the day after that. Oleg dutifully walked away from the sitting area to his desk where Mark could see him compose an email message on his laptop. He took his computer tablet with him when he returned to the sitting area, so that he could quickly read Yuri's reply. He did not have to wait long, as the reply came within less than a minute. It suggested an early afternoon call the next day. Oleg looked to Mark as he read it; he had to translate it for Mark who did not read or speak Russian. Mark suggested that he should accept it and add that he would like to have the call using Zoom. Yuri agreed and waited no time to forward a Zoom meeting invitation. Mark asked Oleg to give him a couple of hours to set things up, though, just before leaving he asked:

"Where is your yacht at present?"

"Let me see . . . It looks as if she's just sailed between Tunis, in Tunisia, and Marsala, at the western tip of Sicily."

Mark wondered at the fact that an app on Oleg's smartphone would allow him to see where his boat was. Still, looking at the map, he immediately saw how his plan should unfold.

▮▮▮▮

Very early the next morning, Mark stopped in front of the building where Oleg's penthouse was. He stepped out of the car while his driver kept the motor running. He called Oleg on the interphone and waited for him in the lobby. Oleg quickly stepped out of the elevator and greeted Mark with what seemed like a mix of excitement and discomfort. The rear left door to Mark's car was held open by Mark's driver, for Oleg to take his seat. Mark walked around the rear of the car and sat on the rear right side and closed his door himself.

It took less than 20 minutes for the car to reach Palmachim Airbase, given both the early hour and the discreet police escort. The car was allowed to drive right onto the tarmac, all the way to a private jet which was waiting for Mark and his charge. They climbed up the stairs and were met in the cabin by the two-man crew and a couple of additional men who Mark introduced to Oleg as his bodyguards. As is so frequent both within *Mossad* and in Israel, the two men did not look like the traditional bodyguards, complete with dark suits, towering heights, bulging muscles and visible earbuds. They were clothed in khaki pants and blue blazers, with open neck shirts; they did have a communication device, but it looked more like a classic earbud than the typical secret service earpiece, complete with the beige cord disappearing into the shirt collar.

The plane took off as soon as the departure procedures were completed. Prevailing headwinds made the trip last almost four hours. The jet landed in Cagliari Elmas International Airport, near the southern tip of Sardinia, just after 10:00 a.m., local time, or 11:00 a.m., Tel Aviv time. About an hour before landing, Oleg had placed a phone call to Anton, the captain of his yacht to let him know that he would be arriving in the next two hours by helicopter. Anton did not appear surprised and indicated that everything would be ready for him. He did ask:

"How many nights will you be spending onboard, sir?"

Oleg hedged his reply saying that he had a business meeting he was conducting with three friends who would be with him and the office in St Peterburg. He added:

"Depending upon how long the meeting takes, I will stay one night and need three guest staterooms for my friends, or we will fly back ashore. Can you stay flexible?"

"Not a problem, sir."

Four men walked down the stairs of the plane and were met by a car which took them to a helicopter pad located less than 3,000

feet away. The helicopter flight was uneventful, and the men reached the *Volga*, just south of Marettimo, the westernmost among the five islands in the Aegadian archipelago, less than two hundred miles southeast of Cagliari. Oleg was able to take his videoconference call undisturbed, while Yuri could surely not doubt that Oleg was where he said he was.

■ ■ ■ ■ ■

Before leaving the boat, as it turned out that by mid-afternoon the conference call had not taken too much time, Oleg took Anton aside. He told him that one of his dear friends would visit the *Volga* in a few days and would like to spend a night aboard. Oleg had asked that his friend be given his stateroom, although there were plenty of other guest staterooms available. That surprised Anton as it surely was the first time that Oleg would let any company "invade" what he called the "yacht's family quarters:" a suite which comprised the master stateroom, an office, two smaller staterooms one each for the children and a playroom that included plenty of space for television and other video games. Matter of fact, just next to the entrance to that family complex, there was a private elevator which could be used by the crew or any other domestic help, to go quickly from the crew quarters to respond to any request made by the family.

He also warned Anton that his friend was a fan of photography and would probably shoot many pictures inside and out of the boat, adding:

"Don't worry. He just did me a big favor and is not used to this kind of luxury. Offer to take him on the bridge as well; I'm sure he'll love to show the picture to his friends. Just make certain that he knows of one restriction: I do not want the name of the boat to appear in any picture. Moreover, I don't want any pictures that would allow anyone to recognize the *Volga*."

Anton was surely not surprised and promised to show Oleg's friend a good time. It was not the first time Oleg had offered hospitality on his yacht without being there himself. He asked:

"Should I organize company for him?"

"Don't think that will be necessary; not his style."

"When should we expect your friend?"

"Excellent question. When would you expect to reach Marbella?"

"Less than two days . . ."

"Let's assume he will arrive in three days, is that OK?"

"Sure. I'll reserve a berth at Puerto Banus. They have plenty, but the number shrinks the moment we're dealing with yachts this size or even larger."

Oleg knew that Puerto Banus was Marbella's harbor, about 6 miles west of the center of town, with the famous landmark: the Don Pepe Gran Melia, a luxurious beachfront hotel. Though Oleg's yacht with a total length of about 200 feet was sizeable, it was more modest than the boats to which most oligarch had treated themselves. It did not dominate the harbor, where at least two or three bigger boats throned. It had four decks for the use of the owners and their guests, including a flybridge at the top, with a small open-air terrace at the back, which provided wonderful views. The promenade decks ran virtually the full-length of the boat, except for the bow, where the pool was located and the stern which had a small open terrace. The staterooms were on the main deck, occupying the front two thirds of the length of the vessel, with the rest serving as reception and living areas, which extended to the promenade deck one floor up. The bridge was one further floor up, just below the flybridge which only offered replicated operating commands. The yacht also had two other decks below the main deck but above the water line; they served for mechanicals and, most importantly the crew, including their living quarters, with separate staterooms for the four most important positions, the captain, the first mate, the chief engineer, and the chef.

All other crew members had to sleep in bunk beds, although Oleg had made sure that there were recreational areas, to provide some comfort to them; many who had seen the inside of these crew quarters would agree that the owner had surely demonstrated more care for his crew than many.

Anton had rented a car and organized for one of his crewmen to meet Oleg's friend at Malaga Airport and drive him back to Puerto Babus. As soon as Oleg's friend was onboard, they set sail for a short one-day cruise in the Mediterranean. The agent, who was normally based in Madrid, enjoyed the Captain's hospitality and as predicted by Oleg shot plenty of still pictures and movies. Anton surely did not notice that a mini sound recorder was activated as soon as the agent stepped on board; it would keep recording the sounds which could be heard both in the office, which was a part of the master stateroom suite and on the promenade deck. Another unit was activated when the agent was on the rear deck enjoying the sights.

Another of the agent's activity which Anton did not notice was the care with which he completed the dissimulation of the various recording and communication instruments which the two "bodyguards" had installed when Oleg and Mark had come on board near Marettimo. While they only had the absolute bare material needed to allow them to place their equipment and ensure they were not immediately noticeable, Fernando, the Spanish agent, took the time to complete their work: hiding, and at times relocating even the most minute detail of the installation. Even a very careful chambermaid would be unlikely to find anything amiss. Nothing should be uncovered short of a professional sweep. Though this prevented Fernando from enjoying the full hospitality of Oleg, he still managed to catch a long enough sleep that he appeared totally rested the next day. He was served a nice breakfast in the dining room of the owner's suite and eventually, after the *Volga* had docked anew in

Puerto Banus, packed up his belongings and went to the terrace at the aft of the deck waiting for his transfer back to Malaga airport.

Anton had maneuvered in a way such that the same deck hand who had fetched Fernando from the airport could help him get to Malaga on time to catch his return flight.

CHAPTER.09

TEL AVIV, ISRAEL, MARBELLA, SPAIN AND SOMEWHERE IN THE WESTERN MEDITERRANEAN

Mark and his two agents could not help but be impressed by the *Volga*. Sure, she wasn't the largest yacht they had ever seen, but she was certainly still in the running. Since they were early for the call Oleg was to place to Yuri, he offered his guest a tour of the boat. Everybody agreed with pleasure, though Mark, in the end, found the visit of all the staterooms somewhat tedious. The decoration was varied and, unusually for many Russian owners, somewhat classical and understated. The luxury was still somewhat overwhelming. The three *Mossad* people became much more interested when Anton showed them around the more technical parts of the boat, specially its communication center. Practically, Mark had found it necessary to distract Anton and ask numerous questions the answers to which were in reality not terribly relevant. He was playing for time so that the so-called bodyguards were able to sneak a few unobtrusive pieces of equipment that would henceforth ensure that no internal or external communication within the ship would go unnoticed. Marvin Goldstein, the technical guru of *Mossad*, had been able to give them

a prototype of a tool that could capture communications between cell phones, for as long as one of the phones was on board.

Oleg's call to Yuri did not take particularly long. On Oleg's side, with Mark and his two "bodyguards" outside of the field of vision, the principal goal was to quiet any discomfort which Yuri might have experienced at the conference call having only been by phone. The goal was achieved in spades, as Yuri surely recognized the appearance of Oleg's office on the yacht. Nonetheless, it was long enough that the two "bodyguards" had the time to install tiny relays which would strengthen the small network they were creating within the boat. They continued on that path when the group moved to the terrace on the main deck where drinks and tapas were served.

Returning to the call between Oleg and Yuri, as per usual, they focused on any particular technical issue which might at the moment be specially topical or pressing. Yuri rattled off a series of minor issues, bugs really, that his team had addressed. Oleg asked:

"Is there a pattern there?"

"No, not really. I think it's just a question of having pushed the developers a bit too much when we found what we thought was the "hole" in the General Manufacturing European systems. Remember, the U.S. company which had to pay us a nice ransom?"

"I do. I do. How are these recent problems related to General Manufacturing?"

"They're not. It's simply that we had diverted resources to milk General Manufacturing as much as we could. The key was that the whole thing had to remain secret. They had been told that the ransom request would triple if news of it made it into the papers or worse yet to the U.S. Government."

"Now I remember. Never been too comfortable with these activities, though I know as well as you are why we are asked to carry them out."

"Our way to pay our dues to Moscow . . ."

"Exactly. Anyway, you know that I am always concerned if we make too many waves. To be blunt, I really don't want to attract the attention of the U.S. They're sufficiently worked up with Ukraine . . . I'd rather we maintained as low a profile as our government will allow us to maintain. So, I'd rather if we did not participate in any similar ransom work in the near term, unless we have to. Let's remain as much under the radar as we can."

"Have you talked to "you know whom" about that?"

"No. Not yet. First, he's got a lot on his plate. Second, I'm told it's hard to get ahold of him and third I also want to keep as low a profile as possible."

"Is that why you've disappeared from the face of the earth for the past two weeks?"

Oleg winced, but he and Mark had specifically prepared for that question. Oleg replied matter-of-factly:

"No. Just a routine health checkup. You know, I've tended to believe that an annual checkup is a very cheap insurance against something nasty. Everything is fine, I should add."

"When are you back in St. Petersburg?"

"Probably not for another few weeks. You know . . . This is not the most attractive season there. The weather in southern Europe is much better . . . Give me late spring or summer in St. Petersburg anytime, but winter? Nah!"

"You and your golf!"

"Well, that and swimming and being in the sun. Anyway. How about having our next call about the same time next week. Does that work for you?"

"Let me see. Well, I don't see any conflict. So, no problem."

"I'll let you know where I am."

Though they did not speak much while on the helicopter taking them back to the plane in Cagliari, for the flight back to Israel, Mark had one burning question for Oleg ever since they had toured the *Volga*. He was sitting across the aisle from him on the plane and discreetly asked him:

"Oleg, something is concerning me here."

"What? Any problem with the call?"

"No."

"With the way the meeting went on the boat?"

"No. It has to do with the boat itself."

Now, it was Oleg who looked quite surprised:

"What was wrong?

"Well, you told us that Oleg was a ladies' man; didn't you?"

"I sure did, but remember I also said that this had been more for show in the last few years."

"Well, the owner's suite of the *Volga* . . ."

"Nice, isn't it?"

"Absolutely. Well, tell me, unmarried men do not need children quarters, do they?"

Oleg could still not see where Mark was going with the thought. So, he asked for further clarification. He finally got the whole idea as he was formulating the question. He stopped dead in his tracks and asked Mark:

"I understand. Looks odd. But the excuse is simple: the design of the boat called for it when I ordered her. I bet you're going to ask me whether Irina and the children have been on the yacht. Right?"

"Correct. So?"

"Well, they have, and they enjoy the family amenities as you might call them. I bet your next question has to be they wear the Godunov name, not the Nichakov's."

"Right again."

Oleg smiled and said:

"Well, there is one thing that I did not tell you."

Mark allowed himself to look mildly shocked but did not say anything. He was hoping this was going to be a breakthrough. Oleg continued:

"Anton is Ukrainian. In fact, we are second cousins. He is the only person who knows of my two identities. Though he is the captain of the yacht, I can assure you that he is quite wealthy by Ukrainian standards. I trust blood, but I trust money even more . . ."

"I see. So, in short, you are not worried that he could betray you?"

"It would be foolish to say that I am not worried, but let's face it. First, I trust him. Second, he has been doing this for a number of years now and could easily have betrayed me several times each year. So, again, worried, probably not, but concerned. I frankly don't have much of a choice."

"Other than dispensing with the yacht . . ."

"Status symbol within my peer group. I bet people would ask more questions if I did not have one. Also, can you imagine the cost and the hassle of having two yachts?"

Mark smiled interiorly noting that Oleg was more ready to consider having two yachts rather than having none at all. He thought: *luxury can surely become a bad habit* . . . He thanked Oleg and made a note to himself that this was another element which should be discussed with David. After all, this one overlap between the two identities could well be real and have been around for as long as Oleg said it was. However, it was at least equally reasonable to think that the distinction between Dimitri and Oleg may have been manufactured just for *Mossad*'s benefit.

■ ■ ■ ■ ■

Oleg's next call to Yuri occurred on schedule and from the *Volga* again, though this time the only part of the *Volga* in the image was the background picture which the *Mossad* agent had taken on his short

visit aboard the yacht. Oleg was in reality in a *Mossad* conference room, in Tel Aviv.

"Hello Yuri, how are you?"

"Just fine, thank you. Where are you?"

"In the Mediterranean on the *Volga*, offshore the Costa Del Sol."

"I did recognize your office. What do you need?"

Oleg calmly asked a number of questions which all would be a normal part of his routine conference calls. They were all principally focused on current developments on the technology front, as a firm such as his seems always to be busy fixing bugs or identifying new areas of opportunity. Out of the blue, toward the end of the call, Oleg surprised Yuri:

"One thing that I have been worried about, Yuri, has to do with weaknesses in the systems which we use, I mean Russia uses to correspond with Syria and Iran more specifically . . ."

"Weaknesses? Why would you ask that?"

Oleg replied that he had recently read a detailed analysis of the Stuxnet virus which Israel and the U.S. allegedly had used to interfere with Iran's uranium enrichment capacity. He conceded that he did not learn anything terribly new, as the issue had been analyzed in detail in a number of places, Moscow being no exception. Still, he pointed to a sentence which said that the damage could have been anticipated and therefore partially controlled if a particular weakness in the Iranian enrichment infrastructure had been better understood. He concluded:

"That gave me a thought. Are there any other similar weakness which an enemy might exploit?"

Yuri could not have known that the material to which Oleg was referring was a total fabrication by *Mossad*, though one element of the story was correct: everyone knew of the weakness which the Stuxnet virus exploited. It was therefore easy to point to it and play the role of the "Monday morning quarterback" who judges everything with the

benefit of hindsight and can appear to be much more knowledgeable that he or she really is.

Yuri appeared to be fooled by the story and asked for additional details, which Oleg was only too happy to provide, since they were actually the details which had opened for Israel the door to the Iranian uranium enrichment facilities. Yuri let go of a sigh and said:

"I'm afraid that this is totally correct. However, I must also admit that I don't see much in there that is new. More to the point, nothing seems new."

"I'm sure that's true for you my friend, but remember, I am a bit removed from all this technobabble."

"Understood."

"So, do you know of any weakness of a comparable nature in the way we deal, or rather Moscow deals with the Syrians or the Iranians, or with anyone in the region for that matter?"

Yuri rattled off a number of activities which had to be carried out for the help Russia provides to her friends in the region to work. They included all the usual, each of which had its own potential vulnerability: communications, control, instructions in cases where Russia would want to take over the running of an installation, satellite links and several others. He was starting to go down into a minute degree of detail when he suddenly exclaimed:

"Oh my God. You're right Oleg. This one is staring us in the face."

Yuri could see on his screen that the face of Oleg was lighting up. He could not see that, beyond the reach of the camera, there were other people in the room who were monitoring the conversation. One of them was Hai Chock. He discreetly passed a few handwritten notes to Oleg to help him dig more into what Yuri had just mentioned. Yuri was taken aback:

"You will always surprise me, Oleg. From time to time, you ask questions that seem so incredibly focused that I frankly did not realize that you understood that level of detail."

Oleg smiled a humble smile and simply replied:

"Remember, I did found the firm. So, I used to know a lot more. A lot of this has faded back into my memory bank, but once in a while something comes back . . ."

"I can see this. The question you just asked is in truth both an "old" topic and incredibly pertinent. Why don't we do this? I've got to go do some digging because I don't have all the information at my fingertips. Hopefully you're not playing golf at this time tomorrow, because if you can I'd like to regroup."

"Fine with me. You know any golf game can be moved. Around here, there are so many courses that I can always get a tee-off time on one of them. You should try golf someday."

"Maybe later. But right now, I hardly have the time for a simple game of tennis!"

■ ■ ■ ■

Having hung up with Yuri, Oleg turned to the people in the room with him. Mark and Hai Chock were both connected through a *Mossad* interpreter to the call and were therefore able to follow the full conversation, albeit with a small translation delay. Just as Oleg was hanging up on Yuri, Hai Chock passed a message to Mark:

"Let me deal with this. There is a trap in there."

Mark dutifully let Hai Chock captain the debrief which proved to be a more elaborate and complex exercise than anyone had anticipated. Indeed, while Oleg's knowledge of English was in truth quite good, there were still a number of voids when one started to dig deeper into technological matters. The trio therefore still needed the interpreter to join them in the room, as there was no longer any issue with Yuri being able to hear her voice. Hai Chock initially thanked Oleg, and then dove directly into the issue which Yuri had identified, and which, truth be told only he understood. Oleg was pretending to understand but was ostensibly beyond his depth and certainly so was

Mark. The conversation extended for several minutes, but Hai Chock soon enough indicated that he had nothing more to ask.

As Hai Chock and Mark exited the conference room and let Oleg be driven safely to the penthouse he occupied with his family, Mark was surprised to hear Hai Chock say:

"The hole they are discussing is relevant, but not terribly problematic. Thruthfully, my bet is that Yuri will tomorrow announce that he has plugged it."

"So, back to square one?"

"Well, not quite. I don't know whether Yuri figured it out or not, but there is something generic there. I want to spend time with Nathan as soon as I can, preferably before tomorrow, because I suspect they have opened a door for us . . ."

■ ■ ■ ■ ■

Though, with the benefit of hindsight, he should not have been, David was still surprised when Mark asked to see him.

"Didn't take long . . ."

"Mark, my friend, you're gonna have to explain. I'm not following."

"Sorry. The excitement. Well, there was a phone call from St. Petersburg to the *Volga* the day after Yuri last talked to Oleg."

"Well. Interesting I would note. What did they say?"

"That's the part that is more puzzling than interesting. The caller was Yuri."

Mark paused. David displayed a minor sign of impatience, though he knew that it was a part of his second-in-command's normal behavior to pause and take his time to choose his words as carefully as possible. Mark continued:

"It seems that the only questions that Yuri asked were first where the ship was and second when they were returning to port."

"Strange. At first I thought it was going to show that some people were spying on Oleg. But, if that was the case, I would have expected Yuri to ask what Oleg was doing at that time . . ."

"Thought about that sir and decided it would be difficult to explain, unless both Yuri and Anton are ex-KGB or current Foreign Intelligence Service. My thought went in a different direction."

He paused again, triggering David's comment:

"You're testing my patience my friend . . ."

"Sorry. Want to confirm I'm on the right track. I am wondering whether the question on returning to port is not meant to indicate a possible attempt at kidnapping Oleg."

"Which they can't do since he is not there . . ."

It was David's time to pause. Then he continued:

"That means that we may well be seeing the onset of some chase between Oleg and Yuri, assuming that Yuri represents the danger to Oleg's life . . ."

Mark nodded and agreed that he was going to have to play that one quite carefully. He quickly smiled and mentioned to David the plan he was going to implement to stay on top of events.

CHAPTER.10

TEL AVIV AND BEERSHEBA, ISRAEL, MARBELLA, SPAIN, ST. PETERSBURG, RUSSIA AND SOMEWHERE IN THE AUSTRIAN ALPS

Mark placed a quick call to David Heller, just to confirm he remained fully in the loop.

"Ready for a quick update on the Oleg Nichakov saga?"

"Sure. Shoot."

"Well, Marvin's toy delivered exactly as advertised . . ."

"Marvin's toy?"

"Yes, you know. The system that allows us to pick up cell phone conversations if at least one of them is onboard the *Volga*."

"Oh, yes. Now I remember. Sorry. So?"

"Well, less than hour after the *Volga* had anchored at Puerto Banus, someone called Anton Chernenko, the captain, on his cell phone. We were able to record and as such hear the whole conversation. They asked where Oleg was. He replied that he was not onboard."

Mark paused a short instant and continued explaining that there followed some clear sign that the voice on the phone was definitely not happy. He was asking how it could be that Mr. Nichakov was not onboard, since he had been told that Oleg had placed a call to Yuri

Vassiliev from the boat only a couple of days earlier. Mark mentioned that, after some further frustrated-sounding back-and-forth, Anton blurted out something like:

"Where did Mr. Vassiliev get that idea?"

Mark reminded David that Vassiliev was Yuri's last name to verify he did not lose him. He went on saying that the man on the phone said that he needed to find out more and had hung up all the while promising he would be back on the phone quite soon. Mark ventured the guess that the excuse that the man needed more information sounded weak at best, adding:

"If you ask me, the man was calling for instructions."

David nodded his concurrence. Mark indicated that Marvin's tool picked up a second call less than a half an hour later. The same voice was calling back, and started that time with a statement:

"Mr. Vassiliev doesn't understand. He tells me that you were the one that said that the vessel was off the coast of Marbella when he had spoken to Mr. Nichakov."

The lightbulb went on in Anton's mind and he simply replied:

"Indeed, Mr. Vassiliev asked me where the Volga was, and I told him. But he surely did not ask whether Mr. Nichakov was still onboard. I can guarantee you that I would have told him he wasn't if he had asked."

"Where was he then?"

Anton could only reply:

"That, I don't know. This time, just like the last time, Mr. Nichakov came onboard with a helicopter to take a videoconference call; standard practice for him, you know?"

He paused for effect and added:

"The first time he came onboard, about ten days ago, we were off Marettimo Island, about halfway between Sicily and Sardinia. He told me the helicopter had taken him from Cagliari, on Sardinia, and, when he left said he was going back to Cagliari. You follow?"

"Yes, so far."

Anton continued:

"He was scheduled to be back on the boat for the next call. Then a couple of days ago, he called to say that he had a conflict and could not come when he had said he would. That's when he asked me to go ashore and prepare the ship for a cruise. He asked me to sail to Marbella. He said that he would meet us there one way or another. Frankly, at that time, I understood that either he would meet us in Puerto Banus at the quay, or at sea with the helicopter. He asked me to wait in Puerto Banus until he knew for sure when he would like us to meet him next. That's what I did. In the end, he told me to sail away from Puerto Banus. Mr. Nichakov joined us for the call, still by helicopter. At the time, I presumed from Marbella, but come to think of it, he was probably not there, but rather somewhere on the Costa Del Sol; maybe simply Malaga, because that's where he would have flown if he was outside the country."

Anton clearly heard a grunt at the end of the line just before the caller hung up. David could only comment:

"They're after him. Wish I knew who "they" are. I assume there's no way we can figure out who is the character who was on the phone to Anton . . ."

Mark replied:

"Afraid not. Anton probably knows him or at least who he is; otherwise, he would not have answered. My bet is that the fellow works for Yuri. But, telling Anton we know of the phone call would blow up our surveillance apparatus. The one thing we know is that the person who called knows Yuri but is not Yuri; however, we don't even know if the man used Yuri's name simply to get to Anton."

"Let's keep on it, Mark. At one point we may be lucky or they, whoever they are, might get sloppy At this point, I can't think of anything more we can do."

■ ■ ■ ■ ■

Hai Chock and Nathan had decided to spend a couple of days together in Beersheba. In the end, to the extent that it made very little sense to have Hai Chock and Nathan fly to Singapore, the simplest step was for Hai Chock to travel back to Beersheba with Nathan. They could use his lab while Hai Chock carried a lot of his insights in his laptop—the rest was hopefully not too deep in his memory bank.

Hai Chock was definitely impressed by both the installation and the types of equipment that were available to Nathan. They were not necessarily better or more sophisticated than anything he had in Singapore, but Hai Chock surely noted that he was not ahead of him. He thought to himself: *need to keep abreast of everything if I don't want to fall behind.* They had a long conversation during which they exchanged what they would both readily admit was all but the top 10% of their knowledge. Neither was ready, unless ordered to, to disclose the most sensitive work they had done.

They quickly came to the conclusion that they had been working on somewhat parallel tracks, with an interesting difference. That difference meant that their working together might be quickly leveraged into something neither could achieve rapidly on his own. Nathan's focus had principally been on "penetration" or the ability to get into other systems, or of other systems to get into Israeli installations. This made all the sense in the world: after all, Israel is the target of many cyber warfare activities and defending against them meant being sure to catch and quickly fix any entry point that could be available to the enemy. Hai Chock had spent more time working on finding newer and meaner viruses or worms that would allow him to get other systems to do his bidding. Again, after all, this also made a lot of sense, as the Singapore Internal Security Department (ISD as it is known in the Republic) was all over the issue of making sure that they kept all entry points secure.

This "discovery" led them to the conclusion that they should both consult with their "superiors" to ensure that they could keep on with their collaboration. Nathan put it best:

"I think that we can both make a significant leap forward if we combine my insertion capability with the tricks you have taught your viruses."

Hai Chock readily agreed, though he still wanted to ask an important question:

"Nathan, what we learned on the call about the weaknesses which Yuri mentioned to Oleg. Is it really new to you?"

"Well, new to me, yes . . . Up to a point. More important is that it confirms something I have believed but had not been able to prove."

"Is there anything we can do about it as we speak?"

Though he could have been surprised by Nathan's reply, Hai Chock heard almost exactly was he was expecting:

"Personally, I wouldn't. Remember our conversation right after the debrief . . . The hole they put forward is quite generic. The instances they have found can be easily plugged."

Hai Chock immediately understood that Nathan and he were on exactly the same wavelength. He let Nathan continue:

"Assume we use these entry points, Yuri should have immediate suspicions. Clearly, he does not know about us, nor did he know we were listening in on the call. So, he would not suspect either of us. However, everything would point him in the direction of Oleg as the traitor. I've just read in the papers an article saying that Yushin is continuing his push to get at those oligarchs that he believes are not with him. We'd be signing a death warrant."

Hai Chock interrupted:

"Agreed. Not doing anything now but looking for the other entry points suggested by their generic error could be just as successful and quite a bit less incriminating."

"Couldn't have said it better."

■ ■ ■ ■ ■

Just after the individual had hung up, Anton called Oleg on the phone. He reported on the call he had just received, adding:

"I hope I did the right thing. I said that you were onboard when you made the last call, though I know very well that you weren't."

"How did you describe it?"

"I said that, just as the first time you had flown in by helicopter, I assumed you had flown in from Marbella but was less sure then; I said it could have been from anywhere on the Costa Del Sol, all the way up to Malaga."

"Great job, my friend. You did exactly as I would have hoped. The one error was mine. The next time I use the ship as a background on a call, I'll make sure to let you know."

■ ■ ■ ■ ■

As the *Volga* had returned to harbor and had moored at the Puerto Banus harbor, all but a couple of crew members had gone ashore. A few would come back to the yacht after having acquired the provisions they needed, while others were simply enjoying the usual R&R which sailors have known for centuries when coming to port for a short while.

Puerto Banus Marina has an elongated U-shaped quay. The southern part of the quay is really a seawall designed also to provide anchoring space for the truly larger vessels particularly at its western end, besides its normal role as a protection against the waves associated with at times rougher seas. Smaller vessels are moored parallel to the shore on individual peers that jut out from the northern wharf. Larger boats can either use the couple of spaces provided against the seawall or two piers reserved for them. In season, it is not unusual for several large yachts to be anchored just outside of the harbor, either waiting for a space to open up or simply choosing to use their tender

boats, which are needed on larger ships to perform the tasks which the bigger boat cannot, to shuttle back and forth to the harbor and beyond it to town.

Restaurants and bars were plentiful both along the northern quay and in the entire neighborhood. The establishments located right alongside the harbor tended to be higher-end and patronized by well-dressed tourists ready to spend significant amounts of money. One could also see the usual entertainers, providing more or less realistic portraits with a caricatural bent or not; shops looking to sell their inventory of more or less tasteful T-shirts most of which were typically made outside of Spain in a place where labor is cheap; and even the odd bar, which was willing to cater to well-behaved sailors, usually meaning the more senior members of the crews. In practice, however, most sailors preferred to retire a couple of blocks away from the water where the noisy bars were located and the odds of finding suitable professional or amateur female company considerably higher.

A group of five sailors from the *Volga* had chosen a bar a block away from the quay to start the evening. Though Anton's two closest aides were Russian, and he was Ukrainian, from the Kiev area, the rest of the crew came from Rumania and Georgia. While it made for an interesting cacophony when they were communicating, equilibrium was found with the new national groups having one leader who spoke both the national language and enough Russian to serve as a translator. It was therefore not unusual that when on shore leave, however short it might be, the men remained grouped along national lines. After all, it was the only way they could communicate among themselves, particularly after having ingested copious quantities of alcohol, often Chinchon, a Spanish variant on the Ouzo-type drinks available throughout the Mediterranean basin.

As they were enjoying their third round of drinks, another sailor who claimed to be a Rumanian native joined them. His entry ticket into the group had been his offer to buy the next round of drinks. Who

would refuse free alcohol on what was going to be a 12-hour shore leave? The group, then comprising six rather than five people, moved to another bar when the owner of the first bar started complaining of the excessive noise. Again, the sailors were not surprised by the turn of events. They were in reality quite used to it; they would stay at a bar until they were chased out, only to resume the same noisy conversation in another bar until it turned into a ruckus which would get them chased out again.

A couple of bars later, as the group had moved, almost instinctively, closer to the red-light district, one of the sailors passed out. The new member of the group, who had said his name was Cristian, immediately took over, called an ambulance on his smart phone and assisted the EMT staff when they arrived. The rest of the group, in some serious degree of inebriation, was impressed to note that their new comrade was also fluent in Spanish. Little did they know that he was in effect a *Mossad* agent. He had not been a simple bystander in the incident, as the individual who had passed out had received some help from Cristian in the form of a small prick from a needle hidden in Cristian's pinky ring.

The group dispersed for a short period of time to deal with their animal instincts and got back together, not much less inebriated, but calmer. Cristian explained to his new friends that the other sailor had been taken to Marbella Hospital where he would likely be kept for observation for at least a few days. The leader of the group, Alexandru, was concerned that returning onboard with one fewer sailor would create a challenge. Cristian volunteered to help and take the sick man's place for a few days as needed. Alexandru welcomed the offer although he said that he would have to clear it with Anton, the ship's captain.

Though Anton obviously was unhappy at the development, he reluctantly agreed to having Cristian on the crew as an interim member. What may have been key to his decision was the offer

Cristian made to help him talk to the hospital and inquire directly as to the situation of his sailor. Anton never found out that he had not been connected to the hospital, but to a private residence one room of which had been converted into a believable hospital room. The attending physician, after explaining that he was not at Marbella hospital but at a private clinic since the emergency room at Marbella Hospital was too full, said that he was himself an emergency room specialist; why should he even have considered telling Anton he was in reality a *Mossad* agent as well? He gave him sufficient details on the health of the sailor. He made it clear that the problem was not related to alcohol nor to some major cardiac or nervous system issue, simply saying:

"He must have swallowed something that did not agree with him. We pumped his stomach out and he looks OK. We will need to keep him probably three or four days until we can get the results of the various fluid tests we have performed. We want to confirm that whatever he has is not contagious."

Anton going through Cristian as an interpreter asked whether there should be any worry with respect to his comrades, those who had not fallen sick. The doctor replied that it was always possible, though there was no way of telling. He suggested that they should be monitored onboard. He asked:

"Do you have any medical facility on board?"

"We have a mini-clinic with a nurse on duty."

"That should be plenty. Would you like me to talk to her?"

"Actually, it's a "he." The nurse is a man. But yes, that would be helpful."

The rigmarole was replayed, through Cristian, with the nurse. Cristian was elated to see that his *Mossad* colleague knew enough by way of medical terms that he was able to fool the nurse as well.

At dawn, the *Volga* started to maneuver out of the harbor, with the help of a couple of tugboats until she had passed the mouth of

the harbor and could move on her own power. Anton had received a call from Oleg asking him to sail in the direction of Mallorca, the largest island in the Balearic Islands, in the Mediterranean Sea, about 150 miles off Barcelona

■ ■ ■ ■ ■

Hai Chock called Countess Renate from his room at the Hotel Leonardo Be'ersheva, which Nathan had recommended. Though certainly not the fanciest hotel in town, it was still among the top five and, quite important for Hai Chock, offered a pool. It would allow him to go and swim a few laps to provide for his usual exercise, which he missed in hotels where the pool was either too cold or too crowded.

"Countess? Hai Chock here."

"What's new?"

"Well, I would argue that the news is excellent, but we have come to an important decision point."

"And?"

"Well, the issue is simple. The good news is that Nathan and I have not been duplicating each other's work; we are therefore quite complementary. The bad news is that we need to go and discuss stuff that has been kept quite close to the vest, both in Singapore and as far as I can tell in Israel as well."

Countess Renate replied:

"Very interesting. I'd suggest that we bring David into the loop. He may even have to ask Simon's views. On your end, are you in any conflict with anyone in Singapore?"

"No. You know how I work. I do my research pretty much alone and bring colleagues at the National University of Singapore when I am sure that they are ready for it and would not create a weakness for The Shadow Experts."

"Can you hold the line for a minute? I'll try to conference David in if he is available."

Less than a minute later, Countess Renate was back on the line. She mentioned that David was with her and asked Hai Chock to summarize for David the current quandary. David listened attentively to Hai Chock's presentation and simply replied:

"Sorry, but that's above my pay grade. Nathan's work is classified for the bits that are the most sophisticated and it is not a part of my world at *Mossad*. I need Simon's permission. I think you gave me more than enough to talk to him. Further, if I can't answer all his questions, my suggestion will be to have him, and Nathan join us on a video conference to make the definite call. Having said all that, my own guess is that Simon will have no problem letting you all work more fully together."

CHAPTER.11

TEL AVIV AND BEERSHEBA, ISRAEL, ST. PETERSBURG, RUSSIA, SINGAPORE AND SOMEWHERE IN THE AUSTRIAN ALPS

Mark wanted to have another conversation with David. He was becoming less comfortable with several developments on the Oleg front. He described his worries:

"You remember that I had issues with the legitimacy of Oleg at the beginning. The story of the phone calls to Anton and between Anton and Oleg are troubling . . ."

"As a devil's advocate, I'd argue they actually went quite well . . ."

"I know. That's exactly my point. Wouldn't you say they went too well? Anton's off-the-cuff comments and his subsequent report to Oleg seemed too perfect."

"What troubled you the most?"

"The fact that Oleg seemed non-plussed."

"Non-plussed?"

"Yes, David. Non-plussed as he found out that people were after him. Shouldn't he display if not panic at least some serious concern."

"I see that, but I'd argue that there is an opposite rationale you could craft. What about the belief that an illegitimate set up would surely have anticipated the call to Anton. Couldn't they?"

"I see where you're going. Anton would have been briefed and he probably would not have reported back to Oleg. Right?"

"Correct."

Mark added:

"Now, what about this wrinkle? Anton places the call to make certain we are led down the wrong path."

"Believable, but doesn't that assume that Oleg knows that the *Volga's* phone systems are bugged?"

"Damn! Should have thought about that. However, is there a way we can verify that Oleg doesn't know?"

"Absolutely. How does that play with Cristian being on board?"

"Cristian doesn't know about the bugs. Only you, me and the people who placed the bugs know."

"Has Anton informed Oleg of the Cristian situation?"

"No. They have talked. They tend to talk twice a week or so. Anton mentioned the sailor that was incapacitated and preempted any question saying that he had found a temporary solution."

"What was Oleg's reaction?"

"Just as you would expect. The only question he asked was when Anton expected the sailor to be back onboard and how would he send the replacement back ashore."

"And?"

"Anton simply replied that he would use a helicopter, adding that there would be no distance problem for as long as the *Volga* stayed in the general vicinity of Spain. He also said that he would be able to use the same helicopter to bring the sailor back on and to return the replacement to Marbella."

"The plan sounds reasonable. You control the situation on the sailor front?"

"I do. He believes he is in a private clinic because the hospital was full. Our only issues are related to how long we keep him in the dark. I'm told they use sedatives any time he seems to be too full of energy. They don't want him to go snooping around."

"Understood. Great. Let's ensure we keep everything under very close control. In the meantime, let's remain as careful as possible on Oleg. In particular, I really don't want him to find out anything of the cooperation between Hai Chock and Nathan.

■ ■ ■ ■ ■

With Hai Chock and Nathan having separately obtained the green light to share as much information as needed provided any actual use of whatever application they developed be also approved independently by both groups, they decided to focus on the simplest initial system disruption.

They chose missile launchers currently in Khmeimim Air Base, located south-east of Latakia, Syria. That base, though in Syria, was currently operated by Russia. The idea was to find a way to trigger the missiles and to get them to hit other targets than those for which they were initially programmed. The strategy was relatively simple, though, as usual, the devil was in the details. Eventually, they really did not care much for the ability to control the firing by Syria's or for that matter Iran's missile launchers. Rather they wanted to be able to "freeze" them, rendering them effectively useless. However, they could not know that they had succeeded in that endeavor, as they would not be aware of when the missiles would be fired and failed to operate. This was the genesis of the idea of making them fire when not intended to fire. In that case, they were in control of all factors. That would tell them what they needed to know of the impact of their action.

Using Nathan's insertion innovation, which was made easier by the earlier discovery of the weakness identified by Yuri, they were

able to sneak a virus into the computerized controls. They did not attempt to control all the various batteries, as one proof comprising at least two missiles would be sufficient for them. So, they focused their efforts on a single battery, and even there on only two missiles.

The most important element of their work involved the ability of the virus to vanish once the job had been done. Indeed, they fully anticipated that once the Russians had discovered that a couple of missiles "auto-fired" they would immediately suspect some cyber invasion. Yet, the way the attack was designed, both the virus and the way it had entered to system would be totally erased, including from any audit trail if there was one. Hai Chock and Nathan were laughing like young teenagers as they went ahead with the actual application of their invention.

■ ■ ■ ■ ■

Major Kolovski was shaken out of his sleep when the phone by his bed rang. Lieutenant Fedorov was at the other end of the line:

"Major, a couple of missiles just launched."

Major Kolovshi was almost screaming as he replied:

"What?"

Visibly embarrassed, Lieutenant Fedorov repeated the earlier observation, arguing that there was no one anywhere near the launcher when the two missiles went off. He added:

"This was a twelve-missile launching truck and only two went off."

"Where did they go?"

"More crazily, they seemed to be headed toward Southern Lebanon."

"What, Southern Lebanon? They weren't programmed for that, were they?"

"No, sir. They had Israeli targets."

"I see. What did you do?"

"I killed them in flight"

He paused for a second and with a somewhat embarrassed expression in his voice, he added:

"Standard practice as you know, Major, since I had not been notified of an impending launch."

"Excellent, Lieutenant. You clearly did not have the time to call me. Way too short an expected flight time for the missiles."

One could literally hear the relief in Lieutenant Fedorov's voice when he simply replied:

"Absolutely, sir. I would normally have called you."

Before hanging up, Major Kolovski added:

"Please be in my office first thing this morning. I need a total debrief. Be ready with all possible details."

■ ■ ■ ■ ■

Lieutenant Fedorov did not get much sleep after the phone call. He knew that Major Kolovski was a fair individual, but one who would unquestionably push very hard for all facts that could reasonably be expected. He therefore asked a couple of his soldiers to help him do a complete postmortem. Especially, he spent a considerable amount of time looking at the audit files of the computer controlling the particular truck. Out of a concern for completeness, he actually had the audit file printed, and did the same exercise with the computers controlling all other missile launchers. He then compared the printouts and was eventually satisfied that no command was passed through to the launchers; at least none showed up on the audit file.

He called one of his direct contacts in Russia to find out whether there could be any cyber-security explanation. He had sworn his counterpart to secrecy, arguing that he did not want anyone to know about the development before Major Kolovski made his own report. The official's view was that there should be either an indication that there was some entry into the system or some evidence that a virus

had penetrated it. Neither condition appeared to apply. What could it be?

He then woke up the engineering crew to check for any form of electrical malfunction. He started with the "offending" launcher, asking for all electrical contacts to be checked, particularly in terms of any discrepancy between the two tubes which fired and all the others that did not. Out of an abundance of caution, he had them dismantle another launcher to check that the electrical contacts looked exactly the same across both pieces of equipment. Again, the investigation yielded no satisfactory explanation to the unexplained firing.

■ ■ ■ ■ ■

The following morning, Yuri called Oleg on his cellphone. He brought him up to speed on the distressing development, which had by then been reported up the chain of command by Major Kolovski and had thus eventually reached Visla Cybersecurity. The point of Yuri's call was the question that has been put to him by the cyber analysts within the Russian Defense Department. He added:

"I heard from them that they had found absolutely nothing. They looked for both electrical and computer failure and found no anomaly."

"No anomaly?"

"None. No trace of any virus. No trace of entry into the system. No electrical issue. Nothing."

Somewhat incredulously, Oleg asked:

"But they did fire didn't they?"

"Yes. They did. That's the mystery."

"Are they asking us to investigate?"

"They are, but they might want to hear from you directly."

Oleg was at that point fully "onboard." He understood the situation and was ready to play his usual CEO role. He replied:

"No problem. I assume that they want me to go directly to the Minister of Defense. Correct?"

"Absolutely."

"Keep me in the loop. I can only relay the message that we are looking at the problem. Let me know if I am wrong, but my plan is simply to say that it does not look like a cyberattack. Certainly not one that we have so far been able to identify. I'll add that we'll investigate whether or not it is a new approach. Nobody we know can attack without leaving any trace."

"That's correct. But one thing I'm gonna do, Oleg, is set up a project team to find out whether this would even be conceptually possible."

Mechanically, Oleg asked:

"What do you mean by "this?"

Without giving Yuri the time to respond to his question, Oleg immediately went on:

"No worries—I get it. You are referring to triggering an attack without leaving any trace. Correct?"

"Right on."

"A suggestion though: if you don't mind, can you ask the taskforce the question a bit differently: what would one have to do for such an attack to be possible?"

"Excellent suggestion, Oleg. Excellent. Makes a lot more sense and "no" is not an acceptable answer."

■ ■ ■ ■ ■

A few minutes after that phone call was completed, Mark was calling David:

"Our first attack worked like a charm. We triggered two missiles. They exploded them before they hit their target, but we could verify that they were flying in the direction we intended them to fly."

"That's excellent."

"That's not all."

"Got a tape of a call Oleg got from Yuri. They can't figure out what happened. His company is presently working on the feasibility of a cyberattack that leaves no trace . . ."

"How did he behave on the call?"

"Nothing special to report. He was surely surprised. He seemed very interested in what they did and did not know. And he's going to call the Defense Minister to assure him that the whole company is on the issue. He even offered a useful suggestion near the end: classic CEO work."

"An average day at work, then. Right?"

"Absolutely."

■ ■ ■ ■ ■

The "hole" which Nathan had recently discovered in the safety of the Internet was related to the Internet Protocol, or IP address. That address is crucial as it is attached to each packet of information that circulates; it is that address that helps routers send those packets to the right place. In practice, every computer or domain which connects to the Internet is assigned an IP address, though that process uses an intermediary, the Internet Service Provider. More realistically, and accordingly bringing in more complexity, any device may connect through a variety of networks, be they private networks, corporate networks, hotel or coffee-shop provided-networks and many others. Nathan's idea, which he was successfully able to develop involved looking for a possible entry point in some broad network or even collection of networks. Once that was done, he was able to reach any specific device using its IP address.

In order for the "trick" to succeed, a number of specific parameters had to all be aligned, as all of these networks have their own safety protocols. Still, his major discovery was an ability to establish routine and innocent-looking communication with any

network and to use what he was learning through the innocuous part of the communication to penetrate ever deeper into the layers of the security protocol. As the communication did not comprise any specific instruction, there was no need for the target network to record any action, ergo to make an entry in its audit file. However, eventually, when the appropriate "hole" had been identified, Nathan was already inside the system and ready to insert his virus or worm.

In short, the Russian investigation was not focusing on the right entry point, looking for something specific that would have happened to the one computer that was infected. Nathan had simply penetrated the network, using the computer's Ethernet card. Hai Chock's ability to hide his virus, and more importantly, to erase any trace that it had been there, was the equivalent of the Hansel and Gretel fairytale, as they were dropping the breadcrumbs to find their way out of the forest and back home, only to have birds pick them up and eat them.

■ ■ ■ ■ ■

Having confirmed that their initial attack had worked exactly as planned, Hai Chock and Nathan were getting ready to execute their second phase when Hai Chock received a phone call from Countess Renate:

"Congratulations. Everything seems to have worked like a charm."

"Indeed. The combination of Nathan's discovery and of my self-disintegrating virus proved its worth. We're getting ready to repeat the exercise, but this time we won't be sending missiles off. We going to make it impossible to order the launchers to fire."

"That's what I wanted to talk to you about my friend."

"Is there a problem?"

"Not a problem. Just a question of timing. We found out through the tap on Oleg's phone that his firm has been hired to investigate the incident in Syria. I'm not worried that they will find out anything as things stand at this point. However, I think it would be better for us

to wait a few weeks, just to be sure the inquiry does not stumble on anything."

"Excellent idea. Good intelligence. I'll talk to Nathan, and we'll identify another target."

"Could you try something similar on Iran?"

"I'm sure it can be done. Let me get to it."

CHAPTER.12

TEL AVIV AND BEERSHEBA, ISRAEL, ST. PETERSBURG, RUSSIA, SINGAPORE AND SOMEWHERE IN THE AUSTRIAN ALPS

Mark was quietly sipping his second cup of coffee, the first since arriving at the office. The day did not look like it was going to involve anything drastic as he felt all the various subprojects within what he called the "Oleg Escape from the Bear" were well in hand. Was complacency setting in? The cell phone which he always placed on his desk when at the office rang. Mark quickly glanced at the screen to see who the caller was. He jumped up and picked the phone up immediately: Oleg was calling. *This is bound to be important* he thought. Actually, Oleg seemed somewhat excited. He said:

"I need to see you and David, quickly."

Though not typically in character, Mark interrupted:

"How quick is quickly?"

Oleg ignored the question for a second and simply replied:

"Something important has cropped up."

By then, Mark's analytical mind had recovered its full concentration. He asked:

"Do you want us to come to you?"

"I'd prefer that. I'd feel more secure."

"Let me talk to David to find out when he can be free. And I'll send you a text message. How's that?"

"Fine. Thank you. But still make it ASAP."

David was away from his office that morning and Mark knew he could not disturb him. After all, Oleg seemed to think that his issue was quite important, but from Mark's standpoint, the most important issue, Oleg's safety and that of his family, was not in doubt: he was still in the penthouse, with his *Mossad* "caretakers." He still elected to send a text message to David stating Oleg's request and incorporating words that conveyed Oleg's sense of urgency. David saw it as soon as his cell phone vibrated in his pocket. He pulled the phone from his pocket and glanced at the screen. Seeing that it was from Mark and as the meeting was with Simon, he excused himself and chose to read the message. Though Mark had phrased the request such that David understood that there was a sense of urgency, he had made sure to say that the urgency was felt by Oleg and not as much by himself. David told Simon what the message was and said that he would make himself available just after lunch. Though he was prepared to reply quickly, he also wanted to "communicate" to Oleg that he could not always drop everything to satisfy his own needs.

Mark and David arrived at Oleg's penthouse apartment just after lunch. They were buzzed into the elevator and met Oleg at the door to his office. They could hear children's voices in the background. Oleg smiled and noted:

"They have no idea what's going on."

David replied:

"That's good, isn't it?"

"Certainly."

"How about Irina?"

"She's fine as well, although she cannot hide that she is worried."

They had by then sat down in the sofa in Oleg's office. Coffee and biscuits had been set on the Chinese-style table in front of the sofa. David started the conversation asking Oleg what the problem was. Oleg looked excited again and asked:

"Did you try to get into Russian systems recently?"

David looked quite serious though still charming and replied:

"Oleg, I can tell you many things, but I cannot disclose to you what *Mossad* is doing. I'm sure you understand. Don't you?"

"Oh, sure. I understand. But I'd like to know if you used any of the information which Yuri gave me on a call two weeks or so ago to penetrate Russian systems."

David did not hesitate, and did not have to as it was the absolute truth:

"You're right. I can answer that question. It's a clear "No." We surely didn't. The only people within *Mossad* that know about it are Mark, our consultant and me. It hasn't gone any further. Why are you asking?"

"Well, I'm told that there was an issue with a couple of missiles in Syria,"

Admittedly somewhat disingenuously, Mark blurted out:

"Syria? What does that have to do with Russia? What happened?"

"Well, We're involved with a base there. I'm told that the missiles fired in the middle of the night, without any command to fire. Yuri tells me that the missiles were aimed at Southern Lebanon."

Somewhat mischievously and matter-of-factly David observed:

"Haven't heard about any explosion . . ."

"They were destroyed in flight."

Mark interrupted:

"Ah. By whom? Anyway, that's got to be good. But why would you even think that we were involved?"

Oleg surely was not totally convinced by the earlier denial. Still, he could not but note that the conversation, at least on Mark's and

David's side sounded totally normal. Their questions displayed real surprise and were perfectly reasonable. So, he was beginning to wonder whether he had come to the wrong conclusion when he had assumed that *Mossad* was behind the mishap. But, if not *Mossad*, who could it possibly be? Suddenly, he felt that he needed to defuse the potentially tense situation. So, with a smile, he offered what he viewed as a compliment:

"I assumed that only you and maybe one or two others would have the capability . . ."

He continued his description of the incident and then recapped for his hosts all that he had been told; the missile launcher was inspected through and through, the computer driving it compared to other computers in the same area and fulfilling the same function. He concluded:

"Well, no trace of forced entry into the computer system; no trace of virus. Nothing on the electronic front. To top it up, I was told that the users went through the electrical and mechanical systems, and everything looked exactly the way it should."

David was containing a smile as he asked:

"You mean to say that they don't know how or even why the missiles were fired."

"Absolutely. Crazy but true. More importantly, the whole bit about the targeting of the missiles makes no sense . . ."

"What do you mean?"

"Simple, David. These missile batteries have preset targets; and though I don't know the targets they have set, I'm pretty sure southern Lebanon isn't one of them."

Seeing that David had a visible quizzical look, Oleg rephrased his point:

"The way they're set up, we're told, is that the missiles have preset targets though these can be changed at any time. This makes it easier and faster for them to react to any attack. Whenever a target

is changed, there is a log item in the audit file. However, this time and for both missiles, we don't understand how these missiles could have flown in the direction of Southern Lebanon. We don't target Hezbollah . . . You won't be surprised to hear that the targets are typically in Israel."

David saw an opening for a bit of disinformation and decided to play it. He asked Oleg whether it was possible for someone at the base to have found a way to get physically into the systems rather than through cyberspace as seems to be the assumption. Then, once inside, he asked whether there was a way the individual could have triggered the firing, adding:

"And doing that without leaving any trace? Is that what you said? No trace in any audit file?"

"Yep. That's what I said. We don't see how this is possible, though you just gave me an idea. A spy operating within the base?"

Oleg paused ostensibly thinking and then, though refusing to share the whole thought, offered a simple outline:

"Something which would be very hard, even maybe impossible from a remote location, may be easier to do if that person is physically next to the computer . . ."

David nodded and asked:

"By the way, Oleg, we need to plan your next call with Yuri, don't we?"

"We should, but with this current mess, I'm not sure we'll have a regular call. We're likely to be talking every day. I need to report to him on my conversation with the Defense Minister and I want to learn from him how much they have been able to dig and what have they discovered."

"When you do that, you don't use a video conference set up?"

"Good point. No. We didn't the last time we talked. It was a totally unplanned emergency. Let me send him an email to find out whether he wants our next call to be video or just phone."

"Sounds perfect. Keep me in the loop. I have a couple of thoughts which I will share with you when the time comes."

"You're sounding intriguing David . . ."

"Nothing fancy. I'm just wondering whether you should not officially be in your French property."

"Would rather not. I know we have pictures of the inside and that I've had meetings from there, but this is truly on the other side of the Nichakov/Godunov divide, and I'd rather keep it that way."

"Understood. Suit yourself."

■ ■ ■ ■ ■

In the car on the way back to *Mossad* headquarters, Mark could not help himself:

"Super well played, sir. They're going to start looking for a spy at the Khmeimim Air Base. Should we confirm that any resource we have there is warned?"

"Excellent idea. In fact, that's what I am doing right at present. I wanted to wait until we were in the car to send a text message to warn our one guy there. He should go under deeper cover. I'll suggest he should find an excuse to leave the base for a short while, if he can. Having said that, I am not worried too much for him, because he is not directly involved in firing the missiles. He's more a general information guy."

Mark surprised David when he asked:

"You didn't want to send it from there, and I understand, But do you really want to send it from here? It's easier to pick messages from a car than from our headquarters . . ."

"Funny; we're on the same wavelength, but you've beaten me. Just as you probably were, I worried that Oleg could be a plant and therefore have installed cameras and recording equipment in his office?"

"Absolutely. Having said this, I do realize that would require complicity with the people that work for him in the apartment, and you know they work for us. So, at this point, I suspect that it's not a major issue, but, as always, better safe than sorry."

"Anyway, I had not thought of the intercept from the car, though with the Russians, everything is possible. So, you're right. I'll wait until we are at the office to send it."

■ ■ ■ ■ ■

Though this time they did not work from the same office, Hai Chock and Nathan were preparing their next cyberattack. The plan which they had vetted all the way up to Simon was not too dissimilar from their Syrian attack; they were going to fire a couple of Iranian missiles. This time, however, the plan would involve two distinct differences with respect to the earlier attack. First, the missiles would have a longer reach as they would be fired from Bakhtaran, a base in Kermanshah, western Iran, about 600 miles from Nabatiyeh in Southern Lebanon. The base is controlled by the Revolutionary Guard Corps, and it is defended with Hawk and SA-2 air defense batteries. It is designated as the place from which ballistic missiles could be fired at Israel, the Gulf States and Europe. Second, the virus would both trigger the firing of the two missiles and prevent anyone from aborting them in flight. They would be redirected to Nabatiyeh, reach their targets, and cause damage there.

The challenges which our duo faced were more complex, but not necessarily more difficult to execute. Indeed, the difference only revolved around short-circuiting the ability for a ground station to control the missiles. Hai Chock applied a solution which he had used earlier with laptops which he instructed to conduct millions of operations in a loop, at a speed faster than they were designed for. Eventually, the laptops overheated, and their batteries exploded. The approach here was similar and simply involved the virus allowing the

instructions from a ground station to reach the missile but required the internal triggering system to go through a virtually endless loop. The system should fail before the missile reached its target, though the operators in the ground station could confirm that the instruction had been received. They were betting that the operators would focus on stopping the missiles which they would think were fired in error and not focus on the fact that the targets had been changed as well.

They had been extremely careful to select two missiles that were only armed with weak explosives: the kind of missiles which might be fired first in a bid to impress, deter or intimidate the enemy rather than to inflict massive damage. They were, however, aware of the risk that the coding telling the operator which missile should be fired for what purpose might be faulty, accidentally, or even devilishly intentional. Thankfully, the two missiles that were fired did reach their revised intended destination, a Hezbollah training camp, and inflicted material damage, but only limited human casualties. Nathan and Hai Chock had been careful to pick the time of the day where the human quarters surrounding the military installations and intended to serve as human shields would most likely be deserted.

The plan worked perfectly. Hai Chock was able to remove any trace of entry into the system. Similarly, the virus self-erased, leaving the enemy wondering what had happened and how it could have happened. There again, the scenario which had played itself at Khmeimim Air Base was repeated at Bakhtaran: serious worry, twin engineering audits focused on electronics and mechanicals, search for a potential inside spy, and so on. These producing nothing, the next step had to be a conversation with Moscow which had supplied the weapons to Iran.

■ ■ ■ ■ ■

Eventually, what had to happen happened; Oleg received another phone call from Yuri. His first reaction was total surprise again. First

of all, though there had been reports in Israel of the apparent missile attack of a Russian base in Syria, the news seemed to suggest that the only possible explanation had to be that Israel had fired at the camp. The Israeli Minister of Defense promised solemnly that the missiles did not come from Israel. He produced radar images that demonstrated that the two missiles had travelled from due East of their target, which made it impossible for them to be of Israeli origin. Israel is due South of Lebanon, and if anything, more southwest than southeast. In sympathy with Syria, Hezbollah had fired a couple of retaliatory missiles into Israel—missiles that were intercepted by the Iron Dome. The final nail in the coffin was when pieces of the exploded missiles were recovered in the camp; they revealed Iranian markings.

The news died down as quickly as it had arisen, as the rationale for an Israeli attack was so demonstrably weak as to not deserve any more than a few seconds of attention. The question of whether the attack could be traced to Israel was one of the main agenda items when the attack had been discussed. While neither Hai Chock not Nathan had been made aware of that detail, Simon had agreed with the Prime Minister that a meeting of the War Cabinet should be called to approve the attack formally. Ariel Landau smiled when he heard that detail, thinking: *Simon is learning the politics of the game pretty fast*!

Oleg had therefore not focused on the incident until the phone call from Yuri. More to the point, he had not even asked to have a talk with either David or Mark. Yuri brought Oleg up to speed, arguing that, to him at least, the attack seemed to be the same as the one that hit the Hezbollah training camp from Khmeimim Air Base:

"Exactly the same?"

"Well, if not exactly the same, it's certainly quite similar."

Yuri paused and then blurted out:

"The only significant difference was that the Iranians tell us that they tried to abort the missiles and were unable to do so."

"How come. Had they lost radio contact with the missiles?"

"No. They said they had radio contact. They said that the missiles acknowledged the instruction they had received. However, the commands went unanswered."

Oleg thought for a couple of seconds and replied:

"Did you say that there were no trace of cybersecurity breach or virus intrusion?"

"None. That's just the same as last time."

Oleg was trying to understand what was going on and failing to make any progress. He had understood David to have denied that Israel had anything to do with the cyberattack against Syria, though David had left open the possibility *Mossad* might have had a hand, in the normal course of events. Putting one and one together, he had even convinced himself that *Mossad* might have a spy at the base. But, he was pretty sure that David had clearly indicated that nothing in the information which he had learned through him was related to the attack. Oleg viewed what Yuri had described as "the new twist" as a very serious development. Thinking out loud he ventured a hypothesis for Yuri:

"I'm still focusing on what you call the "new twist." I don't know about you, but there's only one explanation that comes to mind. The attack managed to disable the internal command systems within the missile. That is quite a step up from getting a couple of missiles to fire without being commanded to."

Yuri agreed, arguing that their own analysis of the first incident had come to the conclusion that the only two explanations for the Syrian missile strike had to be either a cyber intrusion or a human attack. He added:

"At this point, just as you seem to imply, we're leaning in the direction of a human intrusion, as I don't see how a cyber enemy could hide as well as this one would have had to. The thing that bothers me now is that this new attack reverses the earlier conclusion.

A physical intruder could have triggered the launch of the missiles, but I don't see how he, or she for that matter, could possibly have disabled the internal command systems. That shifts the balance of probabilities for both incidents to a cyberattack."

Yuri paused briefly and point-blank asked:

"Do you see any other explanation Oleg?"

Oleg was desperately trying to think of possibilities, but in the end simply replied:

"Unfortunately not my friend. After all, you're the technical expert. How could I think of something if you haven't been able to discover it?"

"I can't disagree with you Oleg. But the question is how do we, as Visla Cybersecurity, deal with that?"

"Have you been asked?"

"The usual phone call just came in. Just like you did the last time, you should call the Defense Minister. He may ask a few more questions, but you seem quite well-briefed and your last phone call on the Syrian incident seemed to have done the work."

"OK."

Yuri then threw a curve ball to Oleg:

"One issue, though. Isn't this a serious enough issue that you should meet face to face rather than on the phone?"

"Good question, Yuri. Yet, as you know, first I suspect that the Defense Minister has a few other things on his plate. Second, I have a number of issues on which I am working, and I prefer to carry out this work from here."

"By the way, Oleg. Where's here today?"

Oleg replied what he had been told by Mark:

"A hotel room in Palma de Mallorca . . ."

"Why aren't you using the yacht?"

"So many questions, Yuri. So many questions . . ."

CHAPTER.13

TEL AVIV AND BEERSHEBA, ISRAEL, ST. PETERSBURG, RUSSIA, SINGAPORE AND SOMEWHERE IN THE AUSTRIAN ALPS

Mark reported to David the full contents of the call which Oleg had had with Yuri. They were delighted that the Russian duo did not seem anywhere closer to understanding the events triggered by Hai Chock and Nathan. David however observed:

"They are at this time taking the cyber warfare route more seriously than earlier . . ."

"Yes, but they don't seem to know where to look. Have you heard anything from sources on the ground in Iran or Syria?"

David quickly said he had not and then added:

"Wait, I have heard the usual report from their controllers, you know the agents that are responsible for keeping us informed and for our activities around there when we have them. My read, which by the way is their read as well, is that it does not look as if either country has any idea what is happening. One thing is for sure, neither is officially at least pointing the finger at Israel."

Their meeting was interrupted by an unexpected phone call. Oleg wanted to discuss the latest development with them. Without missing

a beat, David offered to send a *Mossad* car to bring Oleg to his office, arguing:

"After all, we are here, and we were indeed discussing what we know of the latest incident. You might be able to shed some additional light . . ."

Oleg was initially reluctant to leave the penthouse, but he finally agreed when David offered to add one bodyguard in the lobby of the building to check on anyone asking to go to the penthouse while Oleg was away.

Oleg did not waste any time when he arrived in David's office at *Mossad* headquarters:

"What's going on here? I had a call from my technology guru, and he told me of a new attack. What's going on? Who else but Israel or the U.S. has the ability to do what's being reported. I'll grant you I am thoroughly impressed, but I don't understand anything . . ."

David provided the inevitable official answer, with an important preamble:

"Oleg, I appreciate your position. I'm sorry I'm going to disappoint you, but we don't know much; you probably know more than we do. The only thing I can tell you, and I've already mentioned it when we were discussing Syria is this: the attacks are not related to anything you have told us."

Oleg was motioning as if he was going to reply, but Mark came into the conversation ahead of him:

"Practically, is there anything in what you know that you can link to anything you said?"

Oleg had to concede that he did not have a smoking gun; not even the shadow of one. But, he added something which concerned both David and Mark:

"Guys, I didn't comment on this thought to Yuri because I am still ready to try and help you. But one thing is running around in my mind."

David and Mark looked suddenly more attentive. Oleg continued:

"I am pretty sure I know that the best cyber experts in the world are in Israel, Singapore and possibly the U.S., although I am not so sure about the U.S. They have the brains, but they don't seem to have made cyberspace a top priority as Israel and Singapore have."

David replied laconically:

"So?"

"These two attacks seem quite sophisticated. In actual fact, they both call upon at least two, possibly three features which we did not believe anybody could yet exploit."

Mark asked:

"You're losing me. Which ones?"

"The first is this remote insertion. I cannot believe that someone was able to go physically first to Syria, in a Russian Base, and second to Iran, in a Revolutionary Corps base too. To top it up, how could they exploit some normal entry such as an email or a thumb drive. Way too much and too precise targeting to assume that it was not something done remotely."

"Do you know anything on that?"

"Well, Mark, that's the problem. I don't. Anyway, back to my earlier point, the second feature is that ability to erase all traces."

Mark did not miss a beat:

"What's that?"

"Well, the key is that I don't know and neither does Yuri by the way. As I said, we are virtually sure that this is a remote attack. It's not physical. Rather we won't believe it's physical until we find at least the trace of a smoking gun."

Oleg paused and continued after having sipped some water:

"So, a remote attack requires, as I just said, a way to get in. We don't know how the enemy does it, but we think we know, theoretically at least, what that should look like. Once in, so far, we have heard of viruses which self-destroy. We even know how to do that. But,

and that's the key, we have not seen any virus which manages to erase traces of its presence on audit files. We had never heard of that capability and didn't even think it could be done."

David smiled and replied:

"You're beyond our depth here, I am afraid."

Oleg nodded, but was not through:

"The third feature is this ability to mess up a control system allowing it to receive instructions but preventing it to act on them, all the while seeming to reply to the external operator as if it was functioning normally."

Mark could only repeat David's point:

"I'm not sure I am even following the facts you are mentioning. More to the point, as to understanding what they mean, I'm lost."

Oleg appeared somewhat disturbed and blurted out:

"I'm not sure what game you guys are playing, but I'm starting to worry."

David ignored the potentially insulting tone; he understood that Oleg was stressed and felt his life and those of his wife and children on the line. He wanted to sooth Oleg and at the same time make a crucial point:

"Oleg, I understand your frustration. I think I'd react that same way if I were in your shoes. Let me be very clear: you can be sure that we would never do anything which would put your safety and that of your wife and two children at risk. Makes sense?"

"Does. Thanks, though . . ."

David waved off Oleg's further comment and continued:

"At the same time, you must understand us as well. Our bargain was that we were going to help you if you agreed to help us. We want to find ways to penetrate Russia's communications with its two largest client states in the region. We don't seem to have made much progress on that, have we?"

Oleg disagreed:

"Hold the phone. Wouldn't you agree that these two incidents would suggest that someone has that capability?"

"I would agree if it were our doing. But what if we're not involved?"

Oleg was still emotional, but he did realize that he did not hold any trump card at that moment. He calmed down and simply asked:

"What do you need from me that I haven't provided yet?"

Mark took the lead:

"Well, it seems to me that you were going to help us find out, via your friend Yuri, where the main weaknesses were and how they were to be exploited. So far, we've only had two formal calls with Yuri. Nothing in the last ten days . . . Why are we falling behind?"

Oleg actually smiled and explained to Mark and David that the two cyberattacks, if that is what they were, have changed the focus of his communications with Yuri. He added:

"Simply put, we're in a crisis mode. We're not managing the business as usual. We have to respond to serious security breaches in two very important installations. The first, as you know is a bona fide Russian base. We are, I mean Russia, is in control. So, the ball bounced directly into our camp. The second may well be the most important operational ballistic missile base in Iran. We don't control it, but without us, I mean without Russia, Iran would not have these capabilities. So, again, the ball was immediately thrown into our camp."

He paused to take a quick drink of water and concluded:

"You could argue the future of our company is in play. After all, we are supposed to supply all defensive tools to ensure that the cyber environment surrounding these installations is kept safe. Doesn't look as if it is. Wouldn't you agree?"

Mark smiled and replied, still trying to help Oleg on the one hand, but moving further on *Mossad*'s own agenda on the other:

"You've told us you're not considering the possibility that either or both jobs were done by physical intruders."

"As I told you, Yuri and I batted this one back and forth; we're stumped. I don't think we're excluding anything. We're simply focusing on what seems the most likely."

It was very clear in his eyes that Oleg hesitated before continuing on his current line of thought. However, he did, feeling that he did not have any choice:

"Again, I don't want to point the finger. But, please, remember when we first met in Tel Aviv, in this office. You told me that Israel did not want to take side in any of the conflicts in which Russia was involved, except for as long as they affected its own security. I understood you had no desire to do anything to Russia. You wanted to deal a blow to Russia's major clients in the region. Remember?"

David conceded that this was the gist of the conversation. Though he added:

"Where are we down that path, Oleg?"

"David, I don't want to presume, yet wouldn't you agree that the two developments which we have been discussing suggest that you already have plenty of capabilities?"

David repeated, almost verbatim his earlier point:

"That would be true if we were behind them. However, what if we are not?"

Oleg clearly understood that this avenue of logic was closed to him, though deep down he remained convinced that Israel had to be in on it. He played what he saw as one of his last cards:

"I need your help. Yuri asked a perfectly reasonable question on our last call. He asked why I was doing all this business by phone or video conference rather than in person . . ."

"Ah. What does that mean?"

"Well. Mark, what I think it means is that pressure is going to rise for me to be in Russia soon, if only to help on this crisis. However, I don't know the state of mind of our President, and I don't want to take any risk. I don't know what they know. I don't want to finish as

a few of my peers. Or even worse, I don't want Irina or the children to be hurt."

Mark let David take over the conversation:

"Oleg, I fully understand your worries. So, at this point, don't accept any invitation to go back. But at the same time how do we move forward?"

"I can try and organize a video conference with Yuri. I'm sure we'll be focused on the recent incidents; it'd be totally unnatural to ignore them. I'll try to steer the conversation toward communications between Russia on the one hand and Syria and Iran on the other. But please realize that I'm not terribly optimistic that it'll yield anything of interest."

"At this point, Oleg, that's the best we can do. So, where will you officially be?"

"The safest route is the *Volga*. I told Yuri that I was in Palma in Mallorca on one of our last calls. I don't want to go ashore, particularly so far from here. But I need to contact Anton to warn him that I'll be "using the boat" without really being there. I'm sure there'll be a phone call to him with questions quite soon."

Mark concluded:

"Makes a lot of sense. Let us know the date you pick. You won't be there, but I want a helicopter to land on the *Volga* before the call and to take off soon thereafter. Where will the closest land heliport be?"

"Palma de Mallorca as I said a minute ago."

"Countess Renate? Mark here."

"Great to hear you voice, Mark. Anything I can do for you?"

Mark proceeded to take Countess Renate through the conversations which he and David had had with Oleg. He shared their continued concern with respect to Oleg, given both the fact that he had not delivered much on the cyber warfare front and his apparent sharp

focus on the impact of the excellent work of Hai Chock and Nathan. Countess Renate interrupted:

"Truthfully, Mark, there are times when I wonder whether you all really need Oleg."

"Up to a point only. Up to a point. The work which our colleagues have done is absolutely top class. But we still do not have any capability to interfere in the communications between Moscow and Syria or Iran. The only thing we can do is take control of both firing stations and the missiles themselves. Just as an example, Hezbollah is reputedly controlling 150,000 missiles. Imagine what it would take for us to control that."

Countess Renate readily conceded the point, though she probed a bit further:

"You're not trying to go after Russia on your own, are you?"

Mark's voice went up a few decibels when he replied:

"For sure not!"

Calming down a bit, he however added:

"It's not that we want to interfere in Russia's internal affairs or even in whatever they do on their own, including their attack on Ukraine."

He paused and added:

"Not that we wouldn't wish to. It's just that it's too big a bite. However, what we want to be able to do is to have weapons located in Syria and Iran malfunction in a way that could be traced to Russia."

"I see the subtlety. Currently, Hai Chock and Nathan can create malfunctions, but they cannot be traced to anyone. So, naturally, I've heard people assuming that Israel was involved."

"That's absolutely right. We want to use Hai Chock's ability to hide or not hide his viruses so that the problem is visibly traced to Russia. That would create tensions between Russia and its clients, and it couldn't hurt our cause."

"And that's where you need Oleg."

"Exactly. We need to be able to penetrate Russian systems and have them visibly send faulty instructions. And to penetrate Russian systems, we need Oleg and the knowledge within his company to know what to target and how to get there."

"Got it! When are you next meeting with Oleg and Yuri? Actually, I should say when are Oleg and Yuri next meeting with you and Hai Chock eavesdropping?"

"Excellent question. The day after tomorrow."

"Where will you be?"

"Here, in Tel Aviv. But Oleg will look as if he is onboard the *Volga*."

"Can't wait to see what happens . . ."

"We know it's not gonna be easy. We assume that Yuri will want to discuss the Syrian and Iranian weapon malfunctions, and still we need Oleg to find out more about the Russian systems weaknesses."

"I'm sure you have a plan."

"We do, but we will need to have a more direct help from Hai Chock. We'll have the usual interpreter, but we'll need Hai Chock to use two lines: one, the main conference audio and the other going directly into Oleg's ear. Is he briefed?"

Countess Renate noted:

"He is, but I'll go over everything again. By the way, he has asked for Nathan to receive the audio as well, so that he can connect with Hai Chock."

David had to ask the obvious question:

"Oleg won't know any of that, correct?"

"Absolutely. He doesn't know who Nathan is or that he is involved. By the way, in what time zone will Oleg be supposed to be?"

"Still off the coast of Spain, but this time it will be off Palma de Mallorca rather than Marbella."

CHAPTER.14

TEL AVIV AND BEERSHEBA, ISRAEL, ST. PETERSBURG, RUSSIA, SINGAPORE, MALLORCA, SPAIN, AND SOMEWHERE IN THE AUSTRIAN ALPS

At about 9:45 a.m., Mallorca time, anyone who was watching the *Volga* from shore could see a helicopter approach the bow of the ship. At the same time, a careful observer might have noticed that a few sailors comfortably sitting at the terrace of a coffee house on the promenade that connects the entire Port of Palma from one end to the other seemed to look at the helicopter more intently than others.

Port of Palma is one of the five ports managed by the Port Authority of the Balearic Islands and is viewed by many as the most scenic. It is located in the middle of the city, just in front of the old streets which make up the Old Town. It caters to all kinds of vessels, from commercial traffic, to fishing boats or to cruise ships, being for instance one of the most important cruise ports in the region.

Locals as well as tourists were seemingly not surprised by the fact that one of the five men seated on the terrace and sipping coffee was frequently looking out into the distance with binoculars. They must have assumed that the sailor was fascinated by the relatively large white yacht that appeared to have cast anchor. The men could see a

helicopter approaching the bow of the yacht. It seemed to be diving as the front of the aircraft appeared to be quite a bit lower than the tail rotor. Suddenly the man with the binoculars blurted out:

"Fuck it! They've outsmarted us!"

He paused and went on, turning more specifically to the man seated to his right:

"Finish your coffees and pay the bill. Change of plans. He's not coming ashore. We'll have to go get him. Angelo, get us a Zodiac. We'll meet you at the top of the jetty there."

■ ■ ■ ■ ■

A Zodiac is often called a "rigid hull inflatable" or "semi-inflatable" boat because it has inflatable tubes on the sides with a rigid, "deep Vee hull." The boats' very low center of gravity, due to the fact that the buoyancy is distributed to the inflatable tubes on the side, gives them a stability such that boats of its type are known to be virtually impossible to capsize. These boats are frequently equipped with quite powerful single or even twin outboard engines. They are highly maneuverable and can usually outperform virtually any kind of vessels in the same general class.

■ ■ ■ ■ ■

The helicopter eventually settled with the tail rotor quite visible, not quite sticking out over the tip of the bow, but close. A man stepped down from the helicopter and was met by someone who looked like Anton. The two men walked quickly to the door opening on the suite of reception rooms that made up the promenade deck. The helicopter remained on the ship, which resumed its slow cruising speed: it had to be stopped for the helicopter to land on her, as the up and down movements of the bow of a moving ship would make the actual touchdown too dangerous. Unknown to the pilot of the helicopter

was the fact that the helipad could be slid back to reveal a pool, which sat directly in front of the owner's stateroom, down one deck.

Fifteen minutes later, the zoom conference between Oleg and Yuri started. Yuri looked drawn. Oleg greeted him:

"You look quite tired, my friend . . ."

"Well, as you know, we have been working overtime to address the two incidents in Syria and Iran. I'm looking forward to this problem being resolved. I need more sleep. Oh, and by the way, why are you in Mallorca if it's not too much to ask."

"A golf tournament as you would have guessed. But I've been thinking a lot about the two issues incidents as well. Any progress report?"

Yuri went through a somewhat lengthy discussion, of course totally unaware that Hai Chock and Nathan were listening in. They were delighted to hear that the investigations had not yet produced anything concrete. The only progress seemed to be in the direction of being more concerned that some physical rather than cyber penetration was involved, not because they had found anything special, but simply because they could not explain a cyber incursion. Yuri specifically argued that they could not understand how a cyber penetration could occur without leaving any trace. Though nobody could see him, Hai Chock was smiling. He invited Oleg to ask a question on the topic, in the process intentionally leading Yuri in a wrong direction, effectively leading him to give more credence to the theory of a physical intrusion.

A few minutes later, Hai Chock's next suggestion to Oleg was to ask whether there was any reason to believe that their own Russian systems would be harder to penetrate, if the two incidents were due to an external intrusion. Oleg grimaced briefly but did as he knew he had to and relayed the question to Yuri. Yuri's reply warmed the hearts of most people in the room, Oleg being probably the lone exception. He simply said:

"I can't think of what we have in Russia that's any different from what we have put in place in Syria or Iran. So, if someone was able to trespass into the systems there, they should be able to do the same in Russia. But I thought we were going toward the physical intrusion, and it looks as if you're back on the cyberattack."

Oleg replied wincing but still appropriately prompted:

"Don't we have more firewalls and other related protections for our most sensitive systems?"

"We do. We do. But the point is that, in truth, these really cannot stop a hacker who knows what he's doing. They make his task more complex and time consuming. They increase his chances of being detected before he gets to the most sensitive stuff. But that's about it."

Hai Chock had a quick offline conversation with Nathan who concurred with his assessment: they next step should involve hacking into something in Russia. Hai Chock smiled and simply said:

"Why don't we try a local electrical grid somewhere at the periphery?"

"Crimea?"

"Why not?"

Mark suddenly brought the videoconference to an end by closing the meeting for all Zoom attendees. Just before he decided to end the video conference call, Mark fielded an emergency call from Cristian who was still on the *Volga*. Mark did not allow his face to reveal anything, but the news was quite worrisome. Oleg was quite surprised, but Mark quickly calmed him taking him through the crucial information from the call.

■ ■ ■ ■

A Zodiac with five people onboard had closed in at fast speed on the Volga. A few of these men were attempting to board her from the lowest deck at the stern. Coincidentally, Cristian who had just completed his tour of duty near the engine room was climbing up

the stairs leading to the lowest deck with an open-air access, the main deck. He saw a couple of men dressed in black and wearing black face masks as well getting off the swimming platform that protruded at the stern right at the level of the water. They were climbing over the back gunwale and stepping onto the deck. They were brandishing automatic weapons and yelling:

"Hands up and nobody will get hurt."

Cristian could only see one of his fellow crewmembers near the men, who duly complied with the order. Cristian further noted the Slavic-accented Spanish. He immediately picked up the interphone at the top of the staircase from the floor below the main deck, and warned Anton, speaking in a low voice to avoid calling attention to himself. Anton called an emergency and asked someone to call the harbor police on the ship-to-shore radio. Racing down two decks toward Cristian, Anton asked:

"Can you use a gun?"

"Sure can. I was in the army you know . . ."

He handed him the extra handgun he was carrying and an extra magazine. He kept going further downstairs in the staff quarters, looking for more help and additional ammunitions. Cristian cautiously maneuvered himself toward one of the columns on the port side of the vessel. There he hid and waited for further instructions. He knew very well both that he did not have the firepower needed to win a battle against the pirates and that he was safe for as long as they did not see him.

Anton reappeared and invited the few of his crewmen to walk with him to the back of the main deck. Of course, those sailors that were needed to steer the boat, which had, by then, lifted anchor and as such was still moving, kept focusing on the ship. He walked toward the pirates that had walked inside the sitting room opening on the terrace at the back of the deck and simply asked:

"What do you want?"

Though he had no idea what the whole thing was about, he was hoping to keep the pirates busy for a long enough time to allow the marine police to arrive, or at least to be close enough to scare the pirates away. He had spoken in his own brand of Spanish. The pirate who looked like he was in charge replied:

"Where is the person that came by helicopter?"

Anton smiled and simply said:

"Back in the helicopter. He's about to fly back to Mallorca."

The pirate stopped talking and listened carefully. He could indeed hear the sound of the helicopter engine running at the bow of the yacht. The helicopter took off, first vertically and then rotating onto its own axis, flying away from the bow of the ship. The maneuver would minimize the risk that it would be in the pirates' line of fire. The pilot was rather working so that the helicopter would be too high up by the time the pirates would have a clear shot at it. Mark had indeed planned the move that way based on the assumption that the pirates would surely, if they manifested themselves, want to avoid killing Oleg.

The pirate who appeared not to be sure what was happening and who by then had still not seen the helicopter, asked probably more out of habit than because the request made sense:

"Show me."

Anton took him along with two of his associates up a flight of stairs to the front of the promenade deck. The helicopter was climbing out of range and crew had started the process of uncovering the pool. The three pirates swore in Russian, forgetting they were supposed to be speaking Spanish. They surely would have liked to take some revenge on Anton and the crew, but their orders were absolutely strict:

"Bring back the man who landed with the helicopter. Do not harm anyone else, unless your own safety is compromised."

The three men were walking back toward the stern deck when they saw the comrade they had left in the back living room on the

main deck on which they had boarded; he was lying down on the carpeting, his gun still in his hand. There was no blood. He seemed to be breathing but was otherwise totally unresponsive.

The pirates could not know that the pirate had walked around the deck and found himself quite close to Cristian. Cristian had jumped out of his hiding place and pistol whipped the pirate on the right temple. Before the man could move, Cristian was sitting on top of him. Using the same sedative he had used on the sailor he "treated" in Puerto Banus and ended up replacing, and the same needle set in his pinky ring, he had inoculated him with full dose of the drug, a variant on the propofol theme. The man would be sleeping for a couple of hours, unless he had drunk alcohol earlier in which case the sedation would last longer, potentialized as it was by the alcohol. The leader and one of his men picked the man up by the shoulders and started walking back to the stern. They clearly intended to take him onboard their zodiac with them.

However, the other man accompanying the leader had reached the swimming platform first and yelled, still in Russian:

"Harbor police boat incoming; quite fast speed. Closing in quickly."

The leader unceremoniously dropped his "indisposed" comrade on the aft terrace and jumped into their Zodiac. He yelled to the pilot of the boat to get ready to take flight. His two comrades jumped aboard as well while the leader was untying the mooring rope that kept the boat attached to the yacht. As soon as he could, the driver threw both engines into reverse to create some distance between him and the yacht and then quickly yanked the port engine into a forward gear, while keeping the starboard engine in reverse. This made the boat virtually spin on its own axis to the right. The pilot then switched the starboard motor to forward, and the Zodiac sped away in the direction of the island.

The police boat could clearly see that the pirates were escaping. Still, their first priority was to go and respond to the emergency call from the yacht. The captain of the police boat, coincidentally a Zodiac as well, called for help on the radio, hoping that one or two other boats could race after the pirate's vessel. Unfortunately, it turned out that the pirates' boat was never caught. The area around that part of Mallorca Island comprises indeed many, many fjords. They provide a huge number of places around the island where a boat could hide, particularly given the fact that Zodiac are prevalent in the area and rarely have a look customized to each user.

The police initially focused on the sleeping sailor. They were quite surprised that nobody could offer any sort of feasible explanation for why the man had lost consciousness. The bump from the pistol whip on his temple was the only visible mark that something had gone wrong. The police officer in charge was left assuming that the sailor had lost his footing and hit his head against a blunt object: the wooden arm of an armchair? Anton tried to help find the object showing the police officer where they had first found the man lying on the ground. But there was no trace of blood nor any hair sample which could be found. Cristian was smiling interiorly but was certainly not ready to claim any form of official responsibility; the only place where traces of blood or hair might be found was safely in his right pocket—the grip of the handgun. The police took the sleeping sailor away and invited Anton to come ashore at his earliest convenience so that his deposition could be duly recorded.

■ ■ ■ ■ ■

As soon as the police had left the Volga, Anton placed a call to Oleg to bring him in the loop. Oleg was still in the conference room with David and Mark, as Mark had started explaining why he terminated the conference call. He had started with the punch line:

"The *Volga* was attacked by pirates. We think they were looking for you Oleg. So, we organized to have you flee by helicopter."

Oleg, with an unmistakable look of surprise on his face, managed to ask in a meak voice:

"Anything else?"

Anton who was still on the phone with Oleg gave a few more details:

"One of the pirates had somehow knocked himself out on the boat. His colleagues abandoned him in their rush to get away from the police. The police took him away with them and said they would share with me any intelligence they find relevant. Oh, and a last thing: I definitely heard the senior pirate as I'll call him swear; it was in Russian."

Oleg gave a quick translation to David and Mark and asked them if they had any question they wanted to ask. Mark could not resist probing the accident that knocked the sailor out. Oleg relayed the question, and Anton's response was totally vague. The only element he was able to add to what he had already said was that one of his sailors, actually the individual who replaced a sailor that got sick in Puerto Banus, was in the stairwell leading to the deck where the victim was found.

Mark smiled broadly while David nodded he understood. They both were thinking: *Cristian did his job*. Oleg thanked Anton and said he would call him back if he needed more. David let go of a short laugh and then said:

"Whoever was looking for you will not have found you. However, if Yuri was behind the attack, he will have no reason to believe you were not there . . ."

Oleg looked totally stunned. He mumbled:

"Why are you blaming Yuri?"

Mark replied that nobody was blaming Yuri since there was no proof. However, turning the tables on Oleg, he asked:

"Who knew you were NOT going to be on the boat?"

"Why, only Anton. He even told me that the crew did not know anything."

Mark continued:

"Now, who knew that you were taking the call from the *Volga*?"

"Yuri . . ."

"And who knew where the Volga was going to be?"

"Yuri . . ."

"See why we should at the very least suspect him?"

Oleg nodded. David added:

"Hold it, who else could it be?"

Oleg mumbled:

"I really don't know. But I still think it's totally possible that Yuri might have mentioned both the conference call and the location of the boat to any one of his direct reports."

Mark conceded that it was possible. Yet he asked:

"Why would anyone other than Yuri try to kidnap you?"

Oleg smiled and said:

"My dear Mark, you don't know how a communist regime really works do you?"

Oleg's comment stunned Mark, but he elected to let him finish his thought rather than interrupting. Oleg's explanation continued:

"I have always assumed that there are at least one or possibly two additional "plants" from the Foreign Intelligence Service in Visla. OK, let me tell you something about me which you don't know. I was originally working for the Foreign Intelligence Service . . ."

Mark could not restrain himself. He jumped up and interrupted:

"What? Are you a spy?"

"Don't jump to conclusions, Mark. I said I was. That was the only way the state was going to help me with the development of the company. Actually, this is where I met Yuri."

Oleg was starting to have second thoughts on his sudden impulse to divulge a bit more of his past. He mumbled:

"Wait a minute. Wait a bloody minute. That's how it was. Still, as time passed and our company prospered, we formally left the employ of the Foreign Intelligence Service. The state could clearly see that we would be way more useful in our new endeavor if focused entirely on our corporate goal. That was how we would be serving Russia and build the wealth the government allowed people like us to build."

Mark could only reply:

"Carry on with your explanation, but I will want to come back to this part of your life."

Oleg continued:

"So, we're not part of FIS, but I'm sure that we are closely monitored. After all, our work is quite sensitive, you know that. So, it wouldn't be hard to imagine a scenario where the regime is starting to get quite upset with me for instance because I am not vocally and otherwise visibly supporting our President. There are lot of other possible reasons."

Oleg paused for a second and went on:

"We know that someone called Anton, my captain, was on the phone looking for me when I was supposed to be in Marbella. That might have been the first attempt at kidnapping me. We know it failed. This time, you organized for the call to take place at sea rather than at anchor in the harbor. The helicopter trick was quite smart by the way, congratulations."

He paused to acknowledge Mark's nod of the head. He then continued:

"So, the logical thing is for them to try and get me at sea. I would even think that the reason why they might have arrived somewhat late in the call is simply that they had not anticipated the helicopter trick as I just called it. They might have expected the *Volga* to sail into the harbor. So, it might have taken them some time to get organized . . ."

Mark congratulated Oleg conceding that his scenario held together very well.

■ ■ ■ ■ ■

Two days later, Anton called Oleg again to report on his short trip to the police station. The victim had said a few things but did not really talk. He was seemingly quite upset that his comrades had let him hang high and dry. But, the same kind of "Omerta" which exists within the Sicilian mafia took precedent on his sentiments. He refused to say more than the fact that he was a Russian citizen currently vacationing in the area. He was able to point to a hotel reservation which suggested that the man was not super well-off, but certainly more affluent than the average tourist. But then again, hit men typically receive generous compensation. He added that the police booked him on a trespass charge, and he would be out of jail within a week.

CHAPTER.15

TEL AVIV AND BEERSHEBA, ISRAEL, SINGAPORE, AND SOMEWHERE IN THE AUSTRIAN ALPS

Oleg was sitting in his office in the penthouse in Tel Aviv. He was surprised to say the least to see an incoming email from David. He thought: *What can he possibly want to tell me that he could not do using the phone?* Yet, he knew David and he therefore opened the email. He immediately understood why David was sending him an email. He was forwarding an email from Hai Chock; Oleg thought: *He needs me to verify his thought process . . .*

Hai Chock and Nathan had indeed spent the prior few days putting together, and on paper, or at least on "virtual paper," a document which listed what they thought they knew, what they thought they did not know and what they were unsure about, all focused on the two incidents that had occurred in Syria and Iran. Ostensibly, the paper only bore Hai Chock's name, as Oleg had no idea who Nathan was. The email had a short executive summary to outline their thought process and the reason why the three categories were required. It said that the attached document developed all the various thoughts in more detail. Oleg surely could not disagree with any of the logic in the executive summary. He still paused for a few

seconds, as his experience told him to avoid all emails which could be suspect. *Why would David send me a suspect email?* His training won out and he decided not to open the attached document before he had called David to verify that the email he was receiving was really from him. David was happy to confirm that the document had come from him and was genuine. Oleg read the more detailed analysis and concluded that he was in broad agreement with what the document concluded. At the same time, he was mildly disappointed that he surely had not learned anything new.

■ ■ ■ ■ ■

Ever since the conference call with Yuri had been interrupted by the pirate attack on the *Volga*, David, Mark, Countess Renate, Hai Chock and Nathan had met a couple of times to regroup. Their initial conclusion was that the attack had prevented them from getting further into their plan to attempt to find entries into various Russian government systems. The focus on the two successful attacks on the Russian base in Syria and the missile installation in Iran had taken over the carefully laid out agenda of the video conference call between Oleg and Yuri. While they still had every hope that they would eventually get to their goal, the pirate attack and the need to abort the call had changed everything.

Countess Renate had asked Hai Chock and Nathan whether they could go any further based on what they had. Hai Chock's reply had been both laconic and brief:

"No! The only thing we could do is a repeat of what we've already done."

Nathan concurred adding:

"And, frankly, I don't see what insight we would gain."

They were going back and forth on the topic when the proverbial light bulb went on in Nathan's mind. Suddenly, he exclaimed:

"Sorry to interrupt the conversation you all, but I think we're ignoring the obvious."

Hai Chock was the first to react. He had over the previous few weeks developed a very healthy respect for Nathan and his bias was always first to believe that he had the solution, or at least that he had the solution until something proved him wrong. He asked:

"What have you again discovered?"

"I hate to say it because every one of us ought to have thought about it. Is Oleg's computer connected to his company's network?"

Hai Chock had figured it out:

"We are indeed all pretty slow on the uptick. Yes, Nathan; yes. He told David so. That's the entry point. His computer must be linked to his company's network if only to access their email system and probably quite a number of files that he would need to do his job."

Nathan continued Hai Chock's train of thought and with a fake tone of revealing the latest secret said:

"Therefore, we can penetrate his company's network if we can bug his computer."

He paused and with a smile and a modest hand gesture added:

"Simple as that!"

Countess Renate was the first to react, although an observer of the scene on the video screen would have argued that David and Mark were so close behind her as to justify probably calling it a tie. She said:

"This is brilliant. I'm glad we have your team set up; individually you're obviously very good but put together you're deadly!"

She smiled broadly and asked:

"How would you propose to bug his computer?"

Mark saw David's sign with his eyelids and interrupted:

"Before Nathan or Hai Chock reply, there is something which you both need to know. Countess Renate already does, but we haven't shared it further to maximize the chances that everyone behaved as naturally as possible. By the way, that doesn't apply to you, Nathan,

as you have never interacted with Oleg, at least officially. We have a fear that Oleg might be a plant rather than a genuine fugitive ... Further, after we interrupted the last zoom call, he confessed that he was once a spy."

He let that sink for a couple of seconds and continued, waving aside what seemed a question from Nathan:

"Just a second, Nathan, let me please finish this thought. We do not have any proof whatsoever that Oleg is anything but genuine. Nonetheless, a number of plausible coincidences, but coincidences none the less, suggest that we should at least not let our guard down. So, while I like the idea of using Oleg as an entry point into his company, I would prefer for him not to be aware of our effort."

Nathan smiled and replied:

"It's funny you should say this Mark, because Hai Chock and I had been asking ourselves how Oleg would behave if he was a spy."

He paused for effect and concluded:

"We came to the obvious conclusion that he would do exactly what he is doing."

Hai Chock could be seen on the screen nodding. Nathan suggested that the easiest option would be to find a way to get Oleg to open a document containing a virus. Mark countered:

"You must be talking of someone sending him a virus or a worm in an email."

"Absolutely. By the way, the email could well contain both virus and worm and anything else we can think of."

David asked:

"But, I've only used an email with him once, to send him the "paper" which you guys prepared on the incidents. He was very careful and did not open the attachment until he had called me to verify that I had indeed sent the email. Remember, that was the time you and Nathan created your "progress report" on the two incidents and sent to him to ask for his thoughts."

Mark smiled and added:

"That created a useful precedent . . ."

David's eyes widened quite a bit and he started to nod furiously. Mark continued:

"Is there anything which we can think of which would be better communicated by email rather than orally."

Hai Chock piped up:

"How about an academic paper?"

Turning toward Nathan, he added:

"Not something sensitive or requiring new work. Just some rewrite of some paper . . ."

David congratulated Hai Chock for the idea, beating Countess to the punch this time, but asked what had to be one of the two obvious questions:

"What about any anti-virus software he may have on his computer? After all, he heads up a company specializing in cybersecurity. Wouldn't it be odd if he didn't have the top of the top?"

Hai Chock interrupted:

"There are at least two replies to your question, David. The first is that Nathan and I are pretty sure that no software has stopped us yet; so there's quite a bit of room. I know this is kind of pretentious, but that's our reality."

He paused and quickly continued on his thought noticing some measure of incredulity in the faces of the people on the video conference:

"The second is much more powerful. Remember, in our first conference with Yuri, Oleg asked about a weakness in their systems. We noted it. We surely did not want to seem to capitalize on it directly then and there as it would have pointed the finger directly at Oleg. But that weakness can be used at present, particularly as it involves bugging Yuri's computer . . ."

David was still not totally sure:

"I think I see what you're saying, but I need more. Let me be the devil's advocate. How does that not point the finger at Oleg? Couldn't someone argue that he allowed his computer to be bugged to let someone into the company's systems."

Hai Chock replied:

"Totally valid concern David. But remember that we can make our viruses disappear. So, if we went ahead with the plan, the first thing we'd do would be to send a bugged email to Oleg. Then, once inside his company's systems, we would erase any trace of the bug in the email we had sent to him."

Nathan added:

"Practically, and that's yours or Mark's call, we should probably tell Oleg to delete both the email and the document from his computer. We could argue that it would not look good if our document was found. We might actually use the opportunity to give him another email address to communicate with us in a safe manner . . ."

David exclaimed:

"You should have my job, Nathan. It makes a lot of sense. Now, let me ask you and Hai Chock the same question, but differently: What could go wrong?"

Hai Chock and Nathan could be seen thinking through the proposal, which, in fairness they had not had a chance to dissect. Nathan was the first to reply:

"Subject to Hai Chock's agreeing, I don't think that I can answer that question right away. The idea is new; in truth, we've been making it up as we went along. Could we have . . ."

He paused to think and went on:

"Say, 24 hours to think it through?"

Hai Chock cheerfully agreed adding:

"I hate to do things under unnecessary pressure. Twenty-four hours is plenty of time and I am pretty sure that between the two

of us we'll figure it out. Let me offer one note of caution. Let's ask ourselves a question:

"What if Oleg decides not to open the document, precisely because he does not trust it?"

Mark could only reply:

"We know what he did the last time. Let's hope he does the same or dispenses with the step thinking that he knows how you're going to answer, David. So, one thing is clear to me: the email with the bugged paper should come from David."

▪▪▬▪▪

While Nathan and Hai Chock were working on the plan to try to invade Oleg's company systems, David and Mark had had another conversation with Countess Renate. A perspicuous outside observer would correctly observe that the topic of their discussion surely did not require the participation of Countess Renate. However, though the logic would be true on the surface it would be missing an important element: the trust and respect relationship which had been established between *Mossad* and The Shadow Experts was deep enough that they would try to work together whenever it was both appropriate and feasible. In this instance, David and Mark wanted to check their logic. David would in the end surely need to discuss the matter with Simon, but, as David was gradually growing in a role which after all was still relatively new to him, having a couple of advisers could not hurt him.

The issue they were discussing concerned the location of the *Volga*. They could clearly see that Oleg did not want any of the homes he owned under the Godunov name to come anywhere near the current environment. After all, his logic on that point was absolutely perfect: assuming that he could manage to escape the bear hug which he felt was being placed on him by the Yushin regime, his future peace of mind relied entirely on his being able to fall back into the Godunov identity and as they used to say, "live happily ever after." Indeed, from

time to time, he could be seen contemplating a scenario which could have Oleg die while Dimitri would stay alive . . .

The *Volga* being in close proximity to the coast of Spain made any support by Israel absolutely inconceivable. Intervening in the territorial waters of a country within the European Union would be just what was needed to bring closer to the surface the rampant antisemitism which many believed prevailed in a number of European countries. Whether that was because of the influence of heavy Muslim immigration, or the remnants of historical conflicts was really not the point. So, after having heard the logic of Countess Renate and Mark on what might be considered, David summarized what he thought he heard, adding his own editorial comment here or there:

"It seems to me we agree that it would be better if the *Volga* was less than a full day sailing distance from Israel, assuming that our vessels are going nearly full speed."

Mark noted:

"Makes a lot of sense, though we probably ought to be sending a tanker ahead as soon as possible as we're going to need refueling and it may or may not be available in local harbors."

David agreed and continued:

"Good. We should probably ask Oleg to have the Volga sail to somewhere abeam Matala in Crete. It's about 75 miles almost due south of Crete's capital, Heraklion. I see it as a better destination than Heraklion, or at least better at present, as Heraklion sits on the north side of the Island, while Matala is on the southern coast. We'll always have a chance to ask Anton to change heading if we want the Volga to get into the Aegean Sea."

Mark noted:

"Couldn't agree more, David. After all, the Aegean Sea extends to the south of Crete. So, you're still in Greek territorial waters, south of Crete. But the north of the island is so much smack into the Aegean Sea that it adds a number of degrees of difficulty. Being near

Heraklion could be very good for the *Volga*, but less so for us in our effort to protect her if we agree on the second leg of the plan."

The second leg of the plan involved sending at least one and possibly two of Israel's special spy boats.

■ ■ ■ ■ ■

Though they looked like regular boats with the bridge toward the front half of the boat and the middle and aft sections above deck suitable to carry many different loads, these were fast boats which could transform into hydrofoils with a couple of simple maneuvers.[5] The foils, which at rest were folded into the hull at the bow of the boat, could be extended; at speed, the boat riding on these foils would rise higher on the water and have both less friction and more speed. Another series of modifications would never be visible except to those who knew where to look. First, the vessels were equipped with an air lock which allowed the boat to pick up or deliver loads underwater. Usually, this feature was used to transfer loads from one to another boat, but it also allowed the boats to be resupplied in food or water from a submarine without the operations being visible to anyone not underwater. Also, the lower level of the front deck, under the bridge tower, hid a full gamut of electronic surveillance equipment; it offered space for a couple of operators to work all the while allowing them to move from that space to the modest living quarters on the bridge without being required to step out in the open.

Finally, the boats could readily change "identity." First, they could rotate the support bearing their names on each side of the bow of the ship: that would allow them to "change name." However, that would not have been enough. So, each of the names corresponded to a country of registration. Currently, they were using Malta, Panama, and Gibraltar. Thus, the flagpole at the very aft of the ship would

---

[5] By the same author, see "Below the Surface," Barringer Publishing, 2022

display the correct flag through a clever mechanism inspired by the multi-color ballpoint pens of the past: each flag would roll around its own axis and the whole retract into a sheave. The captain could therefore "dial up" the flag he wanted." The cherry on top of the cake dealt with the colored middle section of the hull. The top of the hull would always be white, while the bottom, the part most often immersed into the water would always be black. The middle section, however, comprised vertical rotating triangles which could display one of three colors: red, dark green and white.

▋▋■▋▋

One or two of these ships had participated in a number of earlier *Mossad* missions and the surprise caused by the ships seemingly appearing or disappearing almost at will, and potentially sailing at speeds comfortably two or three times faster than other boats was at times enough to overwhelm the enemy. In this instance, given who the enemy could be, David had asked the two ships to carry twice as many sailors as usual: six instead of three, not counting the electronic surveillance officers.

Once the *Volga* would be in the general area south of Matala and possibly even a bit further west, one or both of the Israeli spy ships would take position less than an hour's sailing distance away. This would allow their electronic surveillance equipment to identify any threat to the *Volga* before the enemy even got there and to close in rapidly if some firepower was needed. In the early stages of the operation, it had been decided that only Cristian, the *Mossad* agent onboard the *Volga*, would be made aware of the support that was available. David and Mark indeed agreed that Oleg should not know what the specific defenses were, though he would be told that the *Volga* would be under close surveillance. Finally, *INS Dragon*, a Dolphin class submarine, would be submerged in the general vicinity, equipped with two Orcas submarine drones. To complete the picture,

an unmarked tanker would be in the vicinity as well in the event there was a need for refueling.

Countess Renate chimed in:

"I know that all plans are liable to fail here or there. But, to me, this one is as carefully thought through as I can imagine. The key will be in the interaction between the various parties. I don't have any worry as to the communications within your own fleet, but I wonder how things will work in an emergency."

David simply replied:

"Couldn't agree with you more, Countess. These guys are used to working together. The key is to ensure that the folks on the *Volga* and Oleg have no idea what is going on."

CHAPTER.16

TEL AVIV, ISRAEL, AND OFF THE COAST OF MALLORCA, SPAIN

A few days earlier, Mark had called the team who was holding the *Volga*'s sailor who had "fallen sick" in Puerto Banus.

The sailor had been kept in a state of semi-consciousness, in that he was fully able to eat and drink and to talk to the "medical personnel" assisting him. The sailor had been allowed to receive a couple of phone calls from Anton inquiring about his condition. Each time Anton's call would come, a "nurse" would race to the sailor's room and administer him a fast-acting sedative in the permanent drip line attached to his right arm. While he would therefore still be able to speak and answer his captain's questions, his voice would be sufficiently weak and his speech sufficiently slurry that Anton had no trouble believing that he was not ready to come back onboard.

With the decision to ask Anton to sail the Volga into the Eastern Mediterranean, the issue of the sailor, and secondarily of the role and availability of Cristian, were bound to crop up. After having talked to David about it, Mark decided that the best approach would be to release the sailor all the while ordering him to rest at home. Ari, the

senior *Mossad* agent in charge of caring for the sailor, Daniel, called Anton:

"We believe that Daniel is probably ready to be released . . ."

"Ah! Excellent news. There's a small problem though. We have sailed away from Marbella and are as we speak just off the coast of Mallorca. Can we get a helicopter to fly him back?"

"Well, not quite. You see, he is well enough that he no longer needs hospital supervision. But, he still occasionally loses consciousness. So, we would recommend that he be sent home to rest, staying there until he has been a full month without a fainting spell."

"A full month?"

"I'm afraid so. If he was working onshore, we would probably be recommending nothing more than ten days to two weeks of observation. But, as I'm sure you realize, on a boat, there is always a danger that a fainting spell causes him to fall overboard."

"I see."

Anton remained silent for a few seconds afterwards, but immediately understood his personnel challenge. His mind was racing as he was wondering whether Cristian would remain available for such a long time period. Focusing anew on the problem at hand, his sailor, Daniel, he asked:

"Can you help us organize transport to his home? He is from Rumania, you know?"

"Do you have insurance?"

"Sure do, including medical repatriation."

"No problem. We'll take care of it. Can you send me an email with all the various details, things like his home address, your insurance policy number and the like? We'll bill the insurance company directly . . ."

Anton was delighted and realized that his next step had to be to have a talk with Cristian. Ari, on the other hand, knew very well both that Daniel's transfer would not involve any more expense than his

"hospital stay." Where would he find a bona fide doctor to sign the various medical papers? *Mossad* would take care of getting Daniel back home to Rumania. Ari knew very well that Daniel would not have any fainting spell any time soon, unless he caught some bug, as he had been in perfect health the whole time.

▎▎■▎▎

Oleg was simultaneously surprised and elated by David's recommendation that the *Volga* should be asked to sail toward the Eastern Mediterranean. Though David did not discuss in any detail the security apparatus *Mossad* was putting in place, he felt he needed to reassure Oleg. He told him that the risks of anyone attacking the ship any time soon should not worry him. After all, why would anyone want anything to do with the *Volga* if he, Oleg, was not onboard. So, he had calmly mentioned:

"Don't expect any form of visible protection. That would probably be counterproductive."

Noting the quizzical expression on Oleg's face, David explained with a wry smile:

"Nobody knows you're in Israel. Nobody knows that *Mossad* is protecting you . . ."

Oleg's face lit up. He had understood. He had no difficulty realizing that *Mossad* surely would have a much more difficult time protecting him if anyone knew that Oleg was in their care. As it stood, no protection that looked directed by Israel would make any sense, other than suggesting that Oleg had sought that same protection for himself, and therefore quite likely for his family as well. The particular focus which Israel was known to have with cybersecurity would be one more reason to assume that he was betraying Russia: he had found a way, people would argue, to exchange his knowledge for citizenship or at least a residency permit. From that point on, Oleg was quite conscious that the next steps that would logically be taken

by his enemies would involve actively looking for him, potentially going after someone close to him, or even trying to take his company from him, though that might be a bit too rash unless there was no other option. Consequently, the best route for him had to be to keep hiding the Israel connection and still ensure that he and his family were totally safe, protected as they were by *Mossad*.

David suggested that, at this point, he was probably assumed to be traveling within southern Europe, though he asked:

"Is that indeed the way you spend most of your winters?"

"I do travel a lot, or rather I did. You know, I always tried to be in Switzerland at least weekly and would travel through Russia, Europe and occasionally Africa and the Middle East the rest of the time."

David had anticipated a question which Oleg had admittedly not asked yet: what if he was officially on business in Israel? He asked:

"Any visit to Israel?"

"Sure, but usually when there was some conference taking place. Otherwise, we do not have any client here."

"So very little business in Israel ever?"

"Absolutely. Never sold anything here, but we have tried to see if we could buy this or that. So, say that on average I would not have more than a trip or two to Israel each year."

David offered a simple non-sequitur:

"And since there is no conference taking place currently or scheduled to take place in the near future, . . ."

"Couldn't agree more. There is no reason for me to be in Israel. I'm still wandering within Europe I guess."

■ ■ ■ ■ ■

Oleg's call to Anton was also relatively uneventful. Oleg did not need to invent any reason for wanting the *Volga* near Crete. It was standard practice for him to fix "rendezvous" with his yacht in various places. *Why not Crete* was all that Anton would have thought.

While still on the phone with Oleg, Anton turned on his navigating computer and opened the software he would normally use. It would allow him to look at the possible route, compute the likely fuel consumption at various speeds and plan for the necessary stops along the way. Oleg asked:

"How long should it take you to get to Matala?"

"Probably a week or so unless we need to go faster. My guess is that the route is about 1,100 nautical miles, so, assuming we'll average 150 miles per day it comes out to a week."

"150 miles a day? Is that all?"

"Well, we'll need to make at least one refueling stop, probably in Malta . . ."

"Refueling stop?"

"Well, as you know, unless we have to, I prefer not to fill the tanks up to the brim. After all, it takes fuel to move fuel. So, I prefer to carry the fuel I need plus some reserve. So, here I would guess that we would use about 600 gallons an hour sailing around 10 knots, if we carry no more than a half load of fuel. With that, we can sail to Malta without any trouble, use the stop to refuel and while it's being done have a couple of the guys go onshore to buy provisions. Am I making sense?"

"You are Anton. You are. As always, I am a bit impatient, but I know you're right. Tell me what would happen if I needed you to go faster?"

Anton replied that it would depend upon the circumstances. Ostensibly, if a higher speed was agreed upon at the outset, then he would need to have more fuel in the boat. All the while looking at his software app, he added:

"With full tanks at the start and a cruising speed of 15 knots, I would plan on an hourly fuel consumption of 1,000 gallons depending on prevailing winds, sea conditions and the like."

He paused and noted that the situation would be quite different if the higher speed was requested after he had left port, explaining:

"In that case, assuming that I would have only taken a half load of fuel, I would need to stop earlier. I would consume a bit less fuel, because the Volga would be lighter, but I would not want to take the risk of running out of fuel. I guess I would aim for Sardinia or the west Coast of Sicily. Unfortunately, that would require me to navigate a more northerly route than needed and add distance to the trip."

He stopped again and simply concluded:

"As you know, we have a lot of flexibility, but it would be best if any change of speed only occurred in an emergency. I always plan for an extra 10-15% fuel reserve to deal with those circumstances."

"Understood, Anton. Let's stick with your 10-knot target and hope we do not need to change it. Or, if I understand you, not change it before you reach Malta. I guess that it would be easier for you to adjust at that point."

"Absolutely, sir."

Oleg shifted topic as asked:

"How is the sailor that fell sick in Marbella?"

"Excellent. The news is good. He was flown to Rumania in a medicalized jet to rest there with his family. The medics told us that they wanted him to spend a full month without a fainting spell before we could let him come back onboard."

"A month?"

"Yes. We don't want him to faint near a gunwale and fall overboard . . ."

"Sure don't. How about a replacement?"

"We've taken care of that. The fellow whom we hired in Marbella agreed to stay with us. His only request is that we fly him back to Malaga when we no longer need him."

"That's good. Very reasonable request. Agreed?"

Mark was back in David's office. He looked visibly excited. David asked:

"Any specific great news you want to share?"

"Not great news, but an idea. Not fully baked I must add, but I have a hunch it might work. I need someone I can bounce it off of."

"Be my guest, my friend. You've never disappointed me, can't believe it's about to happen."

Mark smiled and asked:

"What if Oleg was to buy a cybersecurity company in Israel?"

"Hold it. You've got to tell me more . . . Buy a cyber company here?"

"OK. Let me rephrase it. What if Oleg's company was to buy an Israeli cybersecurity company?"

"Hate to tell you this, but that's not much clearer. Why in the world would it do that? Why does that help us?"

Mark mused on for a few seconds and simply replied:

"Wouldn't it be nice to get Oleg some more of his money out of Russia and in the process weaken his company there?"

David initially did not pick up on the point, continuing as he was on his prior thought. His main question though might be why would an Israeli company sell itself to a Russian-controlled competitor. He was going to continue with the argument, observing it was not very hard for him to understand why Oleg would do it, but Mark realized he had to interrupt. He could see that David was struggling:

"David don't focus on the way we might get there. Just think of the goal . . ."

Mark's comment helped David reframe his thoughts. He then very quickly get to the point. He suddenly paused and started laughing:

"How diabolic! Brilliant. Doesn't make the practical challenge any easier by the way."

David paused and jokingly added:

"*Mossad* should ask for some commission . . ."

They went back and forth on the specifics of the idea, focusing on increasingly arcane details as they developed their scenario. They knew that they would need a believable CEO, which they agreed should not be a terribly difficult person to find, though the context made the search considerably more touchy than might superficially seem. Mark switched to the next practical issue:

"We really need both some operating history and some intellectual property, don't we? That's what is being sold, right?"

David replied that the operating history would not be a real challenge. *Mossad* had experience there, as he said:

"Creating a false document is a basic part of our trade. How far back do you feel you need to go?"

"Don't know yet. I need to talk to a bona fide investment banker. But I suspect that in a new field such as this one to three years would be plenty."

"Would you need a corresponding banking history?"

"More than likely!"

"Facilities?"

"Absolutely, though remember these guys work off laptops and servers. They do not need tens of thousands of square feet to operate."

"Customers?"

"I think we could argue that this must remain secret. We could say that the company got its start with the Israeli government in general and *Mossad* in particular."

"Sounds believable on the surface. But imagine this were a real situation, would *Mossad* allow one of its suppliers to be sold to Russia?"

"Probably not. But what if the entrepreneur offered to split his business? What if he really needed the money? Think of a guy who divorces his wife or vice versa: either one would need liquidities to pay the other his or her share. Wouldn't it be possible for the entrepreneur

to sell the part of its practice that relates to *Mossad* to the Israeli government."

"Insidious, but quite plausible. You've really thought that one through haven't you?"

"I'm sure there's more, much more to do. But I first wanted to confirm there was no gaping hole."

David smiled again and told Mark to keep going with the idea, all the while keeping him in the loop. He added:

"Any resource you're going to need?"

"Not at this point, but I'm sure there'll be some when I get deeper into it. For a start, I'm sure I'll need you to identify our CEO."

Mark paused and, switching topics, asked:

"David, where are we with Gael Orbach?"

Mark was referring to the head of the Israeli Navy, who reported directly to the Defense Minister, Aaron Spielberg. David replied that he had liaised with him, bringing Simon into the loop. There was a general agreement that the strategy with respect to the next steps regarding the *Volga* made sense and that the resources could be freed up if only because the potential disruption which success in this mission could cause in Russia and its Middle Eastern allies was well worth every penny they were spending on it. David added:

"As usual, there's a caveat . . ."

"Yes?"

"We can't be seen to be going after Russia. So, it's critical that we remain focused on Oleg and his company on the one hand and on what damage we can inflict on Russia's Middle Eastern allies."

"Understood. Another red line which we can't see clearly but we sure don't ever want to cross."

"Got it in one."

CHAPTER.17

TEL AVIV AND BEERSHEBA, ISRAEL, SINGAPORE, ST. PETERSBURG, RUSSIA, AND SOMEWHERE IN THE AUSTRIAN ALPS

Nathan and Hai Chock were still working on their idea of sending a virus and/or a worm by email to Oleg. They had a good laugh recalling what they liked to call their "trial run." The whole idea a short while ago to send a report on the two missiles incidents observed in Syria and Iran were but a dry run to get Oleg used to the idea that he might need to open attachments in emails received from any member of the team. Their plan had worked, though, as they had cautioned, Oleg checked first before he opened David's email. This should make their new idea easier to implement; at least it would make it easier for *Mossad* to anticipate what Oleg might do if he received some attachment by email directly or indirectly from *Mossad*. Hai Chock suddenly exclaimed:

"Nathan. There's one element we haven't considered. Something which didn't enter into consideration in the dry run . . ."

"What is it?"

"Well, what if Oleg decided to share the document before opening it with Yuri to have him check it for viruses?"

Nathan seemed for a few second lost in his thoughts. His first reaction was to minimize the risk, replying:

"He didn't do it with the dry run. Why would he do it this time around?"

Nevertheless, he clearly allowed that the circumstances being a bit different, the risk that Oleg would take one more step to protect the integrity of his systems was less irrelevant than he had first thought. He took Hai Chock through his whole logic. He first remembered that the idea of the virus was in order for the group to get a better handle on whether Oleg was for real or a Russian plant. Having said that, if he was for real, he would have to be worried sharing anything with Yuri. After all, he had agreed to "play tricks" with his associate to the extent that they were having video conferences with fake screen backgrounds. So, ostensibly, real or plant, he was playing a role based on the idea that Yuri could not be in the know of where he was and what he was up to. On the other hand, his potential suspicions then might be the trigger that would get him back to his role as a spy if that was what he was in the first place. In short, there was no easy answer. Nathan suggested that they might keep on with the original idea, but it had to be rethought so that there could be no damage to Israel or The Shadow Experts if anyone got their hands on the document that was bugged.

Hai Chock readily agreed. At the same time, another question popped into his mind:

"What kind of document could we send that would have no chance of coming back to bite us in the tail? By the way, I remember David and Mark talking of something academic when we mentioned the idea to them."

He paused and almost immediately exclaimed:

"Nathan, is there one article that you have published that is sufficiently innocuous not to cause damage in Russian hands?"

"I see where you're going. I've got plenty of those. Almost by definition, anything I publish is stripped of all elements which could be reverse engineered."

"Great. Beside reverse engineering, is there anything that could give someone an idea that we think is valuable?"

"Always possible. But the real issue is not there: do we really want my name on the article?"

"By God. Of course not. So, what do you suggest?"

"I can choose something recent, unpublished as it turns out, which I strip of anything really valuable. And the cherry on top of the cake is that I "invent" an associate of mine."

"Invent an associate?"

"Sure. It's easy. I create a name and have the fellow or the lady by the way give credit to all the members of his team without mentioning them by name. Oleg will see something interesting; my name will not appear, and we are home free.

"What if Oleg calls the office to check whether the someone is employed there?"

"Possible, but for security reasons, we always refuse to answer these kinds of queries."

"What if he asks to speak to that person?"

"Same. Official policy is that, if someone asks to speak to someone whose name does not appear on the list, the answer is always the same: the person is not currently here, could he or she call you back?"

"I give up. So, next question on a different register: how long would that take you?"

"A few hours at the most."

"So, why don't we get to it? In the meantime, I'm gonna make a couple of calls just to ensure that everyone is OK with the idea. By the way, as soon as you have the document ready, in Adobe pdf I assume, let me know so that I can prepare a cocktail of viruses."

"Done."

■ ■ ■ ■ ■

Meanwhile, Hai Chock called Countess Renate who conferenced Mark in. He had taken a good half hour to think through every permutation of the new idea and could not identify any major flaw. Nathan's answers to all his hypothetical questions had also confirmed him in the view that he seemed to have a winner. He still rehearsed every possible mishap in his head. They would be totally safe if Oleg was genuinely a fugitive and wanted to help Israel. They would still be safe if Oleg, whether genuine or not, thought the article was worth sharing with Yuri. Practically, in Hai Chock's mind, Oleg sharing the document with Yuri would potentially be even more productive, thinking *that would give me more than one way into their computer systems.*

Mark brought David into the loop to have every available mind focus on the idea for a while. In the end, everyone agreed. The real risk was that the document would lead to a leak of some important information. But, the consensus was clear that if Nathan told everyone that this was not a worry, he should know better. David took the discussion one step further:

"What if they identify the virus early?"

Hai Chock returned to his earlier point that he was pretty sure that between he and Nathan they could construct something that the Russians would not notice. But he took his usual line further:

"It would be a pain because one of "my" cocktails would have become known. However, it would still be a valuable exercise for me at least. It would be a sign that I needed to sharpen my game."

David noted that Hai Chock and Nathan were the experts on the topic and their opinions were the one that mattered.

The actual execution of the plan took another couple of different dimensions. They had all agreed that the email should not come from Hai Chock, but actually from *Mossad*. Initially, the group had defaulted to the idea that David would send it; after all, he had sent the earlier one. The fact that the email containing the document would look and feel exactly like the one David had sent earlier seemed the most logical decision. In the end, it was decided that Mark should still send it, as he had been the one with the most contact with Oleg. He would send it from a generic, public email source, so that no one could ever see that *Mossad* per se had anything to do with it. However, to make certain that the switch in the sender's identity did not create a problem, David sent an email to Oleg warning him that Mark was about to send him something important.

Despite his background in cybersecurity, Oleg did exactly as the team had anticipated. He did not seem to have any concern opening the email and its attachment. After all, Mark had told him that one of his associates had picked up the article and told him that he should read it. Mark said he had read it, understood only a fraction of the contents, but immediately thought of Oleg.

Oleg opened the document and was indeed grateful. The topic was somewhat deeper than what he typically discussed, but his background and conversancy with the language and the concepts made the article readable and moreover interesting. Oleg called Mark back:

"Hey, I read the article. Quite interesting. Thanks for thinking of me."

He paused and then, out of the blue, asked:

"Would it be a problem if I forwarded it to Yuri?"

Mark was smiling interiorly and replied:

"assure yourself that there is no trace of me or anyone else in Israel. If I were you, I would save the document on your hard drive or

in the cloud depending on how you do things normally. Then, erase my email. Then, I suspect it's safe to send it from your own folders."

He paused and with a devilish look in his eyes which Oleg could not see, he added:

"By the way, I scanned it for viruses as per common procedure. You might also want to scan it. I'd hate being the one introducing a virus into your systems."

"Good thought, Mark. Actually, the default setting on my computer is that all attachments are scanned before they are opened. Not to worry, our scan told me that this one was clean!"

■ ■ ■ ■ ■

Mark dutifully reported his last conversation to David, Countess Renate, Hai Chock and Nathan. They all agreed to set the actual effort into motion. Hai Chock explained:

"The first step is for me to see how far we can go into their systems. If possible, I'd like to create some sort of schematic of their installation. Then, we should test if the virus and the worm can allow us to go deeper, possibly into the systems of several of their clients."

He paused for a second and added:

"For the benefit of everyone other than Nathan who already knows, the virus and worm we created can travel from one computer to the next and even auto attach to documents in the right files. Hence, one would hope that within a short week, we should have the ability to access or at least interfere with multiple computer systems in Russia."

Looking at Countess Renate on the screen, he jokingly added:

"Naturally, we are not on the attack versus Russia. We just want to be able to affect what they do or try to do in the Middle East."

Countess Renate had a short laugh. David, always the worrywart, then asked:

"Sorry to be a pain, but it's my job to think of this: what could go wrong in here?"

Hai Chock let Nathan reply:

"Obviously, in this discipline, a lot of things can go wrong. More to the point, everything can go wrong at one time or another. However, the important thing is to remember that we penetrated the systems without being in any way identifiable. The key was the idea that Mark gave to Oleg to save the document on his computer rather than simply forward his original email. So, the worst that could happen from our point of view is that they pick the virus up and neutralize it; the earlier they pick it up the less insight we'll get. The corollary is true as well: the longer the virus remains undetected, the more information we shall be getting."

Hai Chock interrupted:

"A big to-do now is for us to keep track of the virus. I've seen instances in the past where some target manages to send a cyber bomb up the chain. As a matter of fact, it would never get to us, that door is closed. But it could get back to Oleg. So, we need to keep monitoring. I've hired an interim associate, a doctoral student, to help me. He has no idea where the virus is, but he is following the IPs."

"IPs?"

"Yes, Countess, Internet Protocols. I don't know if now is the time to discuss it, but that's Nathan's great find. The more of those we know and can access, the easier it might be for us to interfere."

David had to ask:

"Don't you find it a bit surprising that the top cybersecurity firm in Russia would be so easy to penetrate? One thing I've learned over the years is that if something looks too good to be true it often is . . ."

Hai Chock conceded the point, arguing that things would probably not have worked any differently if Oleg was a spy. He added:

"There are a couple of important points here. The first is that we knew we had a hard-to-detect virus/worm combination. We had a

relatively soft target, Oleg; easy in that once we had picked the right topic getting him to open the document was not terribly hard. From there, him sending the document to Yuri was the cherry on top of the cake."

He paused for a second and concluded:

"The second is that, in my limited experience with Russia, they often tend to display some form of arrogance. They are at or near the top of the leagues when it comes to cyberattacks: super powerful tools, though it's usually brute strength by numbers rather than through sophistication. But on the other hand, they often fail to appreciate their weaknesses. Their defenses are not always nearly as good as their offense."

David conceded the point and asked:

"What is the next step?"

Nathan replied on behalf of the duo:

"We follow the virus which keeps sending us signals via the Internet. We learn as much as we can about the various routes which are available to us. With any luck, we will find an entry point into the network which links Russia to its clients in the Middle East."

Hai Chock completed the reply:

"And then, with your approval, we strike. We'll need to be careful that we do it the right way, but that should not be so difficult. Yet, I am steadying myself for one of the biggest challenges I have ever faced."

Nathen chimed in:

"I'll second that"

❚ ❚ ◼ ❚ ❚

A week later, Oleg was having his weekly call with Yuri, with the usual suspects, David, Mark and Hai Chock "in attendance" and Nathan on the phone. No elaborate set up had been planned for the call, as Oleg simply had said that he was still in a hotel room

in Palma de Mallorca. The group was delighted to observe that the initial part of the conversation was all about the article which Mark had forwarded to Oleg, and which he in turn sent on to Yuri. Though more technical than what David and Mark could easily follow, the discussion did not seem to be bringing in more information. It confirmed that Yuri had read and appreciated the article, so much that he had forwarded it to his direct reports. Everyone on the call, but Oleg and Yuri, understood that it meant that there were plenty of infected computers, and, more to the point, that the virus/worm combination was undoubtedly well into the company's servers, and possibly even into those of certain clients.

Hai Chock and Nathan jumped up from their seats figuratively at least as Yuri was asking the next question to his friend Oleg:

"Have you noticed anything strange on your computer lately?"

"No. Nothing. Why would you ask?"

"Well, we do not know the cause, but we have experienced a couple of instances when it appeared that a computer was quite slow in the shutdown process."

"You're the expert, my friend. What could that be?"

"Honestly, so far, I'm stumped. I've had the whole system swept for viruses or worms and we have not found anything of substance. A couple of innocuous bugs, probably imbedded in cookies or in some game."

"Thought we had a company rule: people weren't supposed to play games with their business computers . . ."

"That's the rule indeed. But, as you know, people are people. These geeks enjoy the odd game. Plus, I've been told that the most frequent infraction is when someone receives a game from a friend while still at work. Often, they won't have the patience to wait until they're home. They try the game and then close it quickly. But, if there is something that looks like a virus, even if it's not mischievous, it's already in by the time they stop the game."

Oleg sighed and simply said:

"I guess we can't manage everything down to individual computers. We'd end up firing everyone or not able to hire any top talent. Creativity, skill and blind obedience don't usually go hand in hand."

He paused and came back to the central topic:

"What are you doing about these incidents?"

"Well, as I said, I had the system swept and got no result; or rather did not find anything explaining the problem. It is a result, a good one, to know that our systems are virus-free."

Nathan and Hai Chock were smiling widely! Yuri continued:

"I also instructed Vlad Kroshenko, the head of security, to run random system-wide virus scans a couple of times during each day, in the hope that something will register. However, so far, still nothing."

Oleg brought to topic to a conclusion saying:

"Well, keep me in the loop. This could be serious. Can't imagine how or where it started, but we've got to get on top of that. After the incidents in Syria and Iran, the last thing we need is for someone to discover that their systems have been penetrated and corrupted by a virus they received from Visla Cybersecurity."

CHAPTER.18

TEL AVIV, ISRAEL, LONDON, ENGLAND, AND SOMEWHERE IN THE AUSTRIAN ALPS

Sir Martin Simson was sitting in the library of his London double-fronted townhouse. It sat at the back of the ground floor of the house and offered a perfect view of the Little Venice Park, right behind it. Two of the four walls of the room were covered with books, while the other two were adorned with traditional British paintings of hunting scenes. Sir Martin's desk was angled in the corner just right of the entry door, allowing him to have a nice view both of the park opposite the back of house and of the fireplace when it was lit in the colder fall and winter months. The library doubled up as his office since he retired from the chairmanship of Overseas Finance Ltd one of the most prestigious financial institutions in the United Kingdom. He did have access to an office in the old headquarters building, but Sir Martin preferred the quiet of his own home. In truth, though quite prestigious, the "firm," as it was known to insiders, and its name were not on everyone's lips: it really never or at most hardly ever dealt with individual customers. Indeed, Sir Martin liked to quip that his firm did not have any customers, only clients.

It had always specialized in merchant banking. Merchant banks and investment banks, as financial institutions, do not serve consumers and small- to mid-sized businesses, who typically primarily seek commercial banking services—deposit accounts and a variety of loans. Technically, the main difference between merchant and investment banking is that investment banks conduct trade finance activities while merchant banks get involved in international finance and underwriting activities. But, in reality, the line has become more and more blurred, and a number of people think, not necessarily too wrongly, that investment bank is the moniker used to cover these activities in the U.S.A. while in the U.K. and the Commonwealth the term "merchant banks" is often preferred, maybe because of traditions.

Sir Martin had risen through the ranks, being one of these very rare, highly talented individuals who succeeded on the London financial scene without having attended Oxford or Cambridge, come from aristocratic families, or been born with a silver spoon in his mouth. He had one of those incredibly keen intellects that allowed him to analyze a problem more rapidly than others, because he could see the various parts distinctly in his mind, and never got lost in detail though he would never overlook them either. He also had this unusual ability to adopt the "code of behavior" of the group of people within which he was circulating. Though nobody would ever accuse him of faking some lineage or pretend he was someone he was not, his mannerism could adapt. That, his incredible wit, and his natural charm ensured that he was readily accepted as a peer within any group, even if his birth or educational cursus would probably be of lower prestige than rest of the members.

His career had taken him pretty much around the world, principally to places where the British Empire had prospered. Eventually, he was called back to London to oversee the international part of the firm's business, from which position he was ultimately promoted to the top

job, Managing Director and Chief Executive Officer. Alongside these responsibilities, came membership in numerous corporate boards as well as leadership positions in many charitable organizations. He might not have been born in the financial gentry of the U.K., but he certainly eventually became an unavoidable part of it. He was considered for and offered a number of prestigious positions when he announced his retirement; among them was an opportunity to be appointed Governor of the Bank of England.

However, none of these positions attracted him. He was not seeking more or newer responsibilities, nor any higher visibility. Neither did he feel he needed more money. Truth be known, though he was touched and grateful, he had told his wife upon learning that he had been named a Knight of the British Empire, a title which would henceforth justify the "sir" in front of his name, that he was not really sure he deserved any additional recognition. As he had put it:

"I did my job and ended up doing pretty well financially. Shouldn't that be sufficient?"

He had indeed done quite well financially. The firm had long remained a partnership, with the more senior partners earning quite comfortable compensation. Additionally, always with the appropriate limits imposed by the law and simple ethical principles, he had been able to invest in some of his clients. His considerable remuneration did not require him to sell any of these investments to maintain the lifestyle he chose. Time and bull markets helping, the value of his various holdings had risen quite substantially. Upon retirement what attracted him the most was the ability to keep his mind active and the potential to help others, whether by mentoring them or assisting them as they looked for a solution to a complex challenge.

The phone on his desk rang. Sir Martin promptly picked it up, answering in the typical style of senior British executives, using his last name, rather than his full name:

"Simson here."

"How great to hear your voice, Sir Martin."

He immediately recognized the voice of Countess Renate.

■ ■ ■ ■ ■

Five or six years earlier, Sir Martin had been introduced to Countess Renate by one of her clients. She had surely met a number of finance executives in her life. She was surprised by the charm oozing from every pore of Sir Martin's skin. Physically, he was not particularly impressive: he was of middle stature, probably less than 5 feet 8, and tipped the scales at no more than 155 pounds: he was trim, but not in an athletic sense; he was just not overweight. His hair which had turned prematurely white had started to thin out, though he did not appear to have any obvious bald spot. He normally did not need glasses and did not wear any except when he was reading something. In that case, a pair of golden half-reading glasses would magically appear from the pocket of his perfectly tailored Saville Row suit, and he would typically place them a bit too low on his nose. Coincidentally, this would be the "pose" which caricaturists would often use when they focused on him, quite a rare event in any case.

Countess Renate knew very well how impressive Sir Martin's career had been and did not feel the need to "test" his knowledge. She kept thinking: *he has probably forgotten more than I ever learned.* However, she was very interested in both his "view of the world" and, almost more importantly, in how he would communicate it. She knew that many financiers enjoy defaulting to jargon; whether it was because they did not know any better or because it allowed them, as it does several other professions such as in medicine or the law, to make themselves look more important. Others would become downright

professorial with the same goal in mind, looking like something more than they were, or, putting it more bluntly, to select those people who were considered "worthy" of having him share his thoughts with them. Sir Martin, however, was absolutely not one to fit in either of these stereotypical categories. He knew who he was, was comfortable with it, and had a genuine desire to help. He would therefore start offering a direct, nuanced but not excessively hedged response to a question and then let himself be guided by his interlocutor in terms of how deep he should go into detail. Renate felt that she was always learning something when she talked with him and yet having what seemed like a totally normal conversation.

She had always felt that one of the disciplines that was missing so far at least in the Shadow Experts was finance, or more precisely, senior corporate financial advisory. She invited Sir Martin to join her for a lunch, which he gladly accepted though he made sure that "the lady should not pick up the tab." She discussed the concept of the Shadow Experts, as usual without claiming that the group existed or that she had any link with it if it did. Nevertheless, a few weeks later, she and Sir Martin agreed that he would thoroughly enjoy being a part of the group, adding:

"I was not looking for more responsibilities or visibility, but for intellectual stimulation. This seems custom-made for me. To top it up, one is expected to remain behind the scenes, in the "shadows" so to speak!"

Sir Martin let go a short, almost "Etonian" laugh at his own joke.

■ ■ ■ ■ ■

Having found out Countess Renate was on the phone, Sir Martin simply asked:

"What may I do for you, Countess?"

Renate started to explain to Sir Martin the mission she had in mind, prefacing her description with a large caveat:

"I need you to know that the transaction on which your help would be so important is not a real one."

She noted that Sir Martin did not react, at least not in an audible manner. She continued:

"It is a trap."

"Who are you trying to entrap and why? I'm surprised that you would even be involved in anything like that . . ."

His voice sounded quite serious, almost as a parent admonishing a child. She let go of a small laugh and said:

"I wanted you to have the punch line first. The client, whose identity you would know before starting the assignment, has an opportunity to do a lot of good, both politically and at the human level."

"Still not sure I follow . . ."

"Let me explain. Suppose . . ."

Sir Martin interrupted:

"You make it sound so hypothetical when I'm sure you're going to present a real situation somehow disguised . . ."

"Certainly can't pull wool over your eyes, Sir Martin. You're right, but let's stay with the scenario for everyone's benefit."

"Go right ahead."

"Suppose that a country's government agency is approached by someone who has a very important skill. Suppose that the skill is well-enough developed to have given birth to a well-respected company, a large share of which he or she still owns. As we speak, what makes the situation doubly interesting is that the individual wants to leave his country, being scared for his life and that of his family. The government agency would love to get their hand on the intellectual property of the company and is prepared to offer sanctuary to the individual."

"If those were the facts, I would think the answer is pretty straightforward. However why would anyone try to entrap anyone?"

"That's where the story becomes less clear. Assume with me that though the agency is tempted to believe that the fugitive is for real, it cannot prove that the gentleman or the lady is not a "plant.""

"A plant?"

"Yes, a spy who would actually be sent by the government of the country the individual claims he or she is trying to escape."

Sir Martin seemed and sounded pensive. His first reaction was to ask:

"Why would that make sense?"

But before Countess Renate could even answer, he added:

"Except I guess if the country to which he is fleeing is known to be a leader in some field about which he himself is knowledgeable enough to pick through the fog."

"Exactly, Sir Martin. In this case, we think that the individual's skills and his company's expertise seem to be quite germane to an economic sector the country my client represents feels it must dominate."

"This is getting more and more convoluted. But I can detect a glimmer of sense in there."

Renate stopped and simply conceded that her description was becoming increasingly unclear. She added:

"It would not seem nearly as complex if I could dot the "Is" or cross the "Ts.""

Sir Martin paused for a few seconds to think and simply said:

"Countess, I've trusted you all along and have never had a reason to be disappointed. So, let's agree that I might be prepared to go along."

"Great!"

"Well, that leaves one important question: are there personal risks to me or my family if I take the assignment."

Countess Renate was impressed, because this was the one question she knew was the most challenging. She explained that there were

always certain risks. However, she added that Sir Martin's role could easily be behind the scenes, in the sense that nobody would need to know that he was involved, other than her client. She concluded:

"I can totally vouch for the client. More to the point, if anything they'd be protecting you. But I feel that, if you agree, our next step should be to manage to introduce you to one of the representatives of my client."

"Would that require me to travel?"

"I don't think so for the next go around, but there will be travel involved afterwards."

"Deal!"

■ ■ ■ ■ ■

Countess Renate immediately called David in Tel Aviv. She wanted to share the good news with him, which she stated as:

"I can offer you an investment banking resource."

"Really?"

"Yes. We know him very well. He has spent all his life in the financial world, at home, which for him is the United Kingdom, or abroad, principally in Asia, with a short stint in the U.S."

"You say you know him very well; he is one of you associates?"

"David you know I don't typically discuss this, particularly this early in an assignment. But, I can tell you that you should trust him as if he was, whether he is or is not."

"I get it. Sorry; an automatic reaction on my part. Does he know the full story?"

"Not yet. He knows the general outline and the challenge we will all be facing. He understands it and I suspect that he will be able to help you enormously."

"That sounds wonderful, Countess. Is there a hitch?"

"Well, not really, but there's an issue, nevertheless."

"How serious?"

"Well, as you know, our experts do not look for the limelight. Most of them would prefer to stay in the shadows, and this is true whether they are just resources of ours or true members of our network. However, the gentleman in question here is very well known, particularly but not solely in the international finance field."

"Do we have to create a fake name for him?"

"I don't think it would help. If he simply serves as an advisor to *Mossad*, I have no issue with you knowing his name, even his biography if that helps. But it should not go beyond a tight group around you."

"Should not be a problem. But let's be clear, how well-known is well-known?"

"First, he was knighted for his services to England in his field of activity. So, his name is on a list which is not terribly long if you see what I mean . . ."

"I'm not sure I do?"

"We wouldn't want anyone to blurt out his name by accident."

"Our people are used to that. Can he physically be with us at any point in time?"

Countess Renate knew she had to push further:

"Sure. Most people would not recognize his face. However, assume with me that he is brought into a place that is under enemy surveillance—by the way, here I mean a place where there may be pictures taken. Assume that and someone might pick his face up in the crowd."

"So, it's not his name that could be an issue; it's that he could be recognized?"

"Yes and no. The enemy would have no trouble knowing who he is given his name. But that's not all. We should also avoid having him appear in public. One thing I haven't mentioned yet, but which has its place here: beware of facial recognition software. I can't believe

someone would be looking for him, but I want no part of the risk someone could find out he is helping."

"OK. I get it. Let me ask a last question."

"Shoot."

"Compared to the people to whom you've introduced us in the past, what makes him special?"

"Truly, not much. He's as outstanding in his field as all others, but not more than anyone. The issue is his political visibility in the U.K. There could be embarrassment to him if he was known to be helping us."

"That's clear then. We bring him in if he agrees, but all his work will be with *Mossad* people and possibly with Nathan. While Nathan is not *Mossad*, he's as good as if he were given the kind of work he does. By the way, how is he in day-to-day dealings?"

"An angel, someone with great class and a high degree of sensitivity, and an absolutely top mind hidden in a humble body."

David pushed further:

"He doesn't know about us, right?"

"Not yet. Actually, I would suggest that our next step would be for us to meet him in London. I suspect he will want to avoid his house and any place where he is well-known, and that extends to his gentleman's club. However, we can easily book a conference room in a hotel near Hyde Park and that should work for everyone."

David was ready to accept, though a couple of further questions were on his mind. He asked Countess Renate:

"When do you want to organize the meeting?"

"I'll have to talk to him and come back to you. Any date that doesn't work for you?"

"No. Quite flexible. Also, I'd like Mark to be in the loop; is that going to be a problem?"

"Can't imagine why, but this might be as far into your organization as he would agree to go."

"Thanks a lot. I'll be waiting for your call."
"Cheers."

CHAPTER.19

TEL AVIV AND BEERSHEBA, ISRAEL, SINGAPORE, ST. PETERSBURG, RUSSIA, AND SOMEWHERE IN THE AUSTRIAN ALPS

Oleg who was reading in the living room of his penthouse which doubled up as his office was only half surprised when he saw the name of the caller on his cell phone which had just vibrated.

"Mark! Anything new? What can I do for you?"

"To be sure, I don't know. But I just received a phone call which made me worry. I could not wait to warn you."

"Worry. Warn me. What are you talking about?"

■ ■ ■ ■ ■

Having learned that Yuri had discovered a couple of "incidents," as he had called them, made the whole team accelerate the execution of the next phase in their plan to work themselves into the Russian cyber space. While Hai Chock and Nathan were still confident that the exact source of the virus could not be pinpointed, the risk had just gone substantially up that the proverbial finger would eventually point to Oleg. Oleg's behavior on the call when the group discovered the problem had been totally "normal." He did exactly what the CEO

of Visla should have done and said exactly what he should have said. In short, there was no indication that he was somehow colluding with Yuri against Israel. At the same time, in all honesty, there was no indication either that Oleg was falling over himself to help Israel; this was totally expected as he really did not know what role, if any, Israel had played with respect to these "incidents." Though the group was not ready to give a blank check to Oleg and assume that he was above board, the odds seemed to be gradually shifting in his favor: Oleg might well be for real. He might not be a plant after all . . .

The idea which had been bantered about earlier within the cyber team and *Mossad* came back to the fore, though in a somewhat different form. The notion that Oleg might "discover" an Israeli company that appeared to be far more technologically advanced than his own firm in Russia resurfaced. At the outset, one of the goals behind the idea was that it would allow Oleg to recover some more of his fortune still stuck in Russia. He would have to be convinced that it made sense for Visla Cybersecurity to buy for cash the company he had "discovered". Doing so, money would have to flow from Russia to some named account, which could then be made available to Oleg. The other goal remained just as obvious: any weakness, be it financial or otherwise, injected into Visla would hinder Russian work on cyber warfare.

The new iteration on the theme was somewhat more mischievous in that Oleg would be introduced to the Israeli company as a firm which had just seemingly developed a revolutionary way of scanning for viruses. That new approach had allowed it to identify some virus which may have been contained in a document. That document would be the article which had been forwarded to Oleg.

■ ■ ■ ■ ■

Mark replied to Oleg's question, explaining the new development: "Wong Hai Chock, you remember, one of our cyber consultants?"

"Yes, I remember him, nice man. Quite knowledgeable too."

"Well, he says that he may have discovered that there may after all have been a virus in the attachment that contained the article I sent to you last week."

Oleg was obviously not happy, but, though Mark could not know or see it, he was also greatly relieved. Mark's use of words like "worry" and "warning" had led him to anticipate the worst news. His own biggest worry indeed was that Yushin, and his crowd would discover where he was hiding and would proceed to send assassins to "deal with him and his family." Perversely anything short of that might even have felt like "good news" to him. Focusing on Mark's "announcement," he still said:

"Come on. I don't understand. You swept the document; we swept the document, and nobody found anything. Now you tell me someone found something. Is that correct? More importantly, how could that be?"

"Afraid so. I don't need to tell you that I am stumped too. Don't know how it could have happened."

"Didn't your friend Hai Chock do the sweeping for you?"

"Absolutely. He did. He did it with his most advanced virus scanning software."

"So?"

"Well, he just told us that he was recently working with a small but rapidly growing Israeli cybersecurity startup. They mentioned something about some new virus they had just discovered."

Oleg definitely perked up, asking:

"Wait, you don't discover a new virus just like that. You discover it because you've developed a new way to scan, or you've added new viruses in the library against which the text you are scanning is compared."

"Absolutely right. You do know your stuff, Oleg. That's the point. They have a different way of building their virus library. Long story short, they tested the document, on a bit of a hunch. And guess what?"

"They found a virus!"

"Exactly. Not any kind of virus. They found the one they had just discovered scanning other documents at their disposal."

Oleg mechanically had to ask:

"Where does that virus come from?"

"Hai chock hasn't told me. Maybe he even doesn't know himself."

Oleg shrugged and asked the obvious next question:

"What should we do?"

"I think the best thing would be for you, Hai Chock and me to get onto a zoom conference call and have the two of you discuss it. At the very least, Hai Chock would determine how they could get them to test your computer . . ."

"Who's them?"

"The small Israeli company I just mentioned."

Oleg seemed to be thinking hard. At first, the idea that someone might come even close to his computer made no sense. He simply would not let it happen. So, he replied:

"I'm really not comfortable giving some unknown entity access to my computer . . ."

"How else would we find out if it is infected? You don't expect the Israeli company to give us the scanning software, do you?"

Oleg again seemed to be thinking before replying:

"Tell you what. I'd be prepared to work with Hai Chock, but not with some unknown entity. After all, you are telling me he works for you. Could that be done?"

"We've got to ask him."

Oleg looked a bit relieved and simply said:

"That would be great. As I think of it, you may have to test my wife's laptop too as we have sent each other emails, principally documents that we found on the web that could interest the other."

"Let me call Hai Chock and see if he can get on a conference call."

"Will the time zones work. By the way, where is he actually located?"

Mark was initially surprised by the question. It rekindled in his mind the worry that Oleg was not totally clean, as he thought: *just the question a spy would ask*. Mark still elected not to focus on his renewed concern. He could of course not disclose where Hai Chock lived, so he came up with a reply that could satisfy Oleg:

"Don't know where he normally is. He's constantly on the move. Come to think of it, it's a good question. Where is he?"

■ ■ ■ ■ ■

Nathan, Mark, and Hai Chock were hard at work planning their next move. They knew that they still had to convince Oleg to let his computer be swept. They suspected that the specter of having unwittingly potentially infected a whole slew of computers both at Visla Cybersecurity and more broadly among its clients would be sufficient. At the same time, there was no question for *Mossad* of giving up an advantage it had cunningly secured: access to a whole variety of Russian networks.

The video conference which Mark and his tech duo held focused on three primary questions. The first dealt with the need to eliminate the virus/worm from Oleg's computer. The issue with that first virus/worm combination is that it contained what Hai Chock estimated to be the bleeding edge in terms of sophistication. He did not want to share any of the more hidden dimensions of his viruses. Having it out of the computer allowed him to leave it up to others to work on the second phase without risking his secrets being uncovered. In practice,

this first phase simply required him to insert an instruction for the first virus to disintegrate.

The second was the craftiest of the three, it involved the execution of what had just been discussed. The team needed a virus to be detected on both Oleg's computer and eventually on the servers that had been infected. The solution was not terribly difficult on a theoretical level, but its implementation required precise coordination. The first phase would already have removed the original virus/worm combination. The work consequently only involved the insertion of another virus which, lacking the special hiding features created by Hai Chock would easily be identifiable by a classic virus scan software. The third phase involved inserting anew a mildly modified version of the initial virus/worm combination without anyone appreciating it was happening.

Once that process completed, the team would have kept access to the computers, servers, and networks they had penetrated, all the while having been able to "show off" the "know how" of a new Israeli cybersecurity venture, which would have found a virus which all other software programs had not detected. The team, meaning here Nathan and Hai Chock, quickly went to work and created a process which could achieve all their goals.

In their next conference call, the team showed the "finished product" to Mark, complete with a series of graphs and diagrams that explained what should be happening each step of the way. Mark was suitably impressed, but the practical individual that he was really wanted to know how they were going to proceed *in practice*. Hai Chock replied:

"That's where the rubber meets the road, doesn't it?"

"And?"

"Well, we need to find a way to control Oleg's computer."

Mark asked:

"Do you need for me to ask Oleg to let me have the computer? And by the way, if yes, how much time do you need?"

"The main advantage of having the computer away from Oleg is that it allows us the room for error."

Mark was frowning. Nathan explained:

"We are pretty sure we know what to do. In truth, we have already conducted a dry run."

"Dry run?"

"Yes, we infected a laptop with the original virus/worm combination. We then went through the process we've agreed and then checked the outcome."

"And?"

Hai Chock beat Nathan to the conclusion with some pride:

"Just as the doctor ordered. The old was gone. The new was inserted and discovered in the scan. It was removed and a new one similar but not totally analogous to the first was at work."

He paused for a second and offered Mark the opportunity to follow the process on a real time with a real computer, adding:

"The only thing is that we wouldn't want that laptop to be connected to the *Mossad* network. Shouldn't happen, but there is always a risk of a leak into the system and that would be an absolute no-no there."

"You can say that again. By the way, I think it might well be a good idea to demonstrate your work to David and me. I think you've got it right, but the risk associated with failure is too much for me to make the decision on my own.

■ ■ ■ ■

The session with Mark and David when Hai Chock and Nathan demonstrated their plan went just as expected. Countess Renate was on the video conference as well, though she had to apologize that her video was not working. Mark immediately understood that she felt there was no need for Nathan to be privy to anything more than he needed; and he did not need to know her physical appearance. So, a

disfunction in the video link was the easy excuse. Mark had to bring David and Renate into the details of the plan first, because he had not until then thought that level of granularity was needed. In the end, David, after having heard the plan and seen it executed, only said:

"This looks excellent, gentlemen."

The female voice on the phone added:

"This goes for me too. Well done."

■ ■ ■ ■ ■

As he had told Mark at the outset, Oleg was not prepared to allow his computer out of his sight, although Mark had modified the earlier offer: the scan was going to be run by Hai Chock and not by the Israeli company that had discovered the new approach to virus identification. His objection was deceptively simple:

"Mark, you know that I trust you. But let's be honest with each other. I know that you trust me but do it up to a point. You once told me that I would behave exactly as I do if I were a plant and not a real fugitive. Right?"

"Can't debate that."

"So, please, do not expect me to trust you any more than you trust me. I am totally prepared to have you guys work on the computer, but I want to be in the room. I want to be in a place where I can see what is happening on the screen. Fair?"

Mark could only reply:

"Again, Oleg, I can't argue with that."

Mark and Oleg therefore agreed that they would meet at *Mossad* headquarters two days hence. Mark wanted to have to time to warn Hai Chock of Oleg's requirement so that Hai Chock could organize his work in a manner that would allow him to do what he needed to do and so that Oleg could be satisfied that he was not being set up. Hai Chock as well as Nathan knew indeed very well that the screen of a computer can display both all the instructions that are given to

it as well as only those which the operator wants to be seen. This was important because the speed at which these instruction would appear and run through would be such that very few people, if any could really read and understand them. But, there was no point taking a risk. What if, for instance, Oleg had surreptitiously installed some video camera which could record what was happening on the screen? For instance, discreetly, on the lapel of his blazer . . . If that, it would be child's play, afterward, to replay the video on a frame-by-frame basis if needed and as such to know exactly what had happened.

Right on schedule, Oleg was brought by chauffeured car to *Mossad*'s headquarters and escorted to a conference room, actually located on the floor where David's office was. David made it a point to come and greet him, thanking him for his flexibility. Mark and Hai Chock had decided that Nathan would be connected by phone into an earpiece which was only available to Hai Chock. In short, he could participate in the process and follow the work which Hai Chock was carrying out; however, at the same time, Oleg would still not know of his existence.

Hai Chock was connected via a video conference. He had looked into the possibility of flying to Tel Aviv for the occasion but was quickly scared away by the inconvenience and the waste of time. There is no non-stop flight between Singapore and Tel Aviv, and the quickest flights require one stop and take almost a day and a half, usually stopping in Dubai. Other flights transit through western Europe, which looks like a crazy way to get from one point to the other.

After the usual banter, Hai Chock asked permission to take remote control of Oleg's laptop computer. Oleg agreed but repeated his requirement that he be able to follow on the screen whatever was happening. Hai Chock simply replied:

"I'll do better than that. I'll tell you what I am about to do, and you will be able to follow the process."

Oleg smiled and thanked him. Hai Chock proceeded to explain that he was going first to connect to Oleg's computer via Wi-Fi and ensure that the laptop's screen showed all the action. Of course, he and Nathan had worked on the sequence so that a couple of the secret steps they were taking could be carried out while they were doing something else, with the work taking place behind the scenes and accordingly unseen on the screen. This is precisely what was happening during the so-called connection phase when instructions were sent to Oleg's laptop to erase the virus/worm they had originally inserted into Oleg's computer via the corrupted document. He replaced it with another virus lacking the special hiding features he had created; this would ensure that the new virus could easily be picked up by a classic virus scan software. A few seconds later, he triumphantly declared:

"Well, that was not so hard, was it?"

Hai Chock could see Oleg nodding on the video screen. He then announced:

"The next step is easy. Let me run this new virus-scan software and see whether we do or don't pick up a virus. By the way, I should add that the company has given me the ability to connect to its library in a remote manner, but I do not have access to it, nor can I see what's in it."

He paused for a few seconds, to let the software do its job. Suddenly he exclaimed:

"Ta-Da! Here we are. What virus is this?"

Oleg's face simultaneously betrayed satisfaction and some fear. He was happy to see that the software could detect the virus but did not like the fact that his company's own virus-scan software had missed it. He asked:

"What so special with this new tool?"

Hai Chock had had plenty of opportunities to rehearse the reply to that question with Nathan:

"Well, theoretically it's deceptively simple. The real challenge is in the execution. Let me try to explain. As I am sure you know, antivirus software scans incoming files or code that is part of the traffic into or out of your computer or network as the case may be. The key to their work is that companies which provide the software have extensive databases of already known viruses, worms, malware, trojans and all the rest. So, comparing the code in the traffic into or out of the computer to those stored in the database, it will detect and flag anything that is suspect and will if instructed to do so remove the danger."

He paused to take a breath and continued:

"The idea is to use artificial intelligence to anticipate what sort of mutations could be carried out to transform a virus, that is already known for instance, into a new one. As an aside, that's how hackers work: they start with something that worked and has just been detected and modify it to avoid detection. So, on the surface, it should not be rocket science."

He paused again and could see on his screen that Oleg was furiously nodding. He concluded:

"In theory, with all the tools developed by what we all call "Big Data," anticipating mutations should not be rocket science. However, as I'm sure you know, Oleg, life is more complicated than that. The one company that developed this new antivirus software has found a way to focus their mutation analysis such that it is both faster and more likely to catch mutations."

"Will they catch everything?"

"Of course not. Everything in Big Data relies on the probability Law of Large Numbers. They'll catch many if not most. Still, you're bound to get outliers that escape through the cracks. But that's nothing new. This software simply makes the cracks a hell of a lot smaller."

Oleg could only say:

"This is brilliant."

Hai Chock announced that he was then instructing the software to remove the offending virus. Unsaid and undetectable on the screen, he was able simultaneously to insert a mildly modified version of the initial virus/worm combination. This was to ensure that the entry into the systems they had already gained would not be lost. Any email with an attachment which Oleg would henceforth send to Yuri, or his network would be corrupted and infect anew the network with that new virus. The old one, when it had not been erased from certain computers or networks, would simply keep existing until it was eventually discovered and destroyed. Oleg could only add:

"I need to get my hands on this software. Can you guys help?"

CHAPTER.20

TEL AVIV, ISRAEL

Though the trip normally takes about five hours and despite there being around ten flights daily, *Mossad* had sent a jet to pick up Sir Martin at the London City Airport to fly him to Palmachim Air Base. The major issue that entered into the decision was the need to keep Sir Martin's trip as discreet as possible; nobody needed to know that he was travelling to Tel Aviv. Countess Renate had organized to fly in at about the same time so that she could take Sir Martin with her to the hotel which had been booked for them, the Sheraton Hotel on Hayarkon street. *Mossad* had specified in the reservation that they wished the rooms to face the Mediterranean, so that they could see the exclusive Greco Beach, with two of Tel Aviv's public beaches to the north and the south, Gordon Beach and Frishman Beach.

Sir Martin and Countess Renate were expected to have a quiet evening together probably involving watching the sunset while enjoying dinner at the renowned Surfside Seaview restaurant of the hotel. It was also expected that they needed that dinner both to relax and to prepare the next day's work. Though absolutely not required, Renate had planned to dress up for dinner, as she knew that Sir Martin would hardly ever have dinner without wearing a tie, at least

in a public place. After a good night's rest, they would be driven the short distance to *Mossad* headquarters, on Aluf Meir Amit Boulevard the next morning. Before retiring to her bed, Countess Renate would unquestionably feel sorry for her husband, Captain Frederik, who, as always, would find himself sleeping at the base, in the bedroom that was arranged at the back of the plane. Though explaining why Countess Renate rarely planned meetings that required her to stay in a hotel, this had never succeeded in becoming anything other than the unpleasant part of their normal routine.

At Palmachim Air Base, Countess Renate and Sir Martin met in the hall near the tarmac reserved for official or specially authorized private jets, where a chauffeur was waiting for them. Countess Renate smiled and greeted her guest:

"Sir Martin, delighted to see you. Hope the trip was pleasant."

"Quite pleased to indeed, Countess. You told me that we could use some time together to discuss the assignment."

"I sure did, but, as you know, I never have any such conversation in a public place, and to me a car, even if it is sent by *Mossad* and probably driven by a *Katsa,* the name by which a *Mossad* agent is typically called, is a public place. Let's have our debrief in the hotel. I know *Mossad* booked suites for both of us at my request. We can meet in either place."

She paused and with a smile and a wink in her right eye she added:

"Though this might look like an improper invitation in other circumstances, I'm sure we both know that everything here is above board."

She stopped again and corrected herself:

"At least as far as the two of us are concerned."

They spent the rest of the half hour car ride talking of anything but business. It was Sir Martin's first visit to Tel Aviv, and he was quite impressed the moment the car started driving along the beach:

"Almost looks like we're here on holiday, wouldn't you say?" Renate simply smiled.

■ ■ ■ ■ ■

The next morning, they met again at the Surfside Seaview restaurant, where the hotel is proud of the lavish buffet breakfast which they serve daily. The extensive choice and variety of the offerings were unfortunately somewhat wasted on Countess Renate and Sir Martin, as they both chose a simple healthy continental option, comprising fruit juice, granola parfaits with yogurt and a hot beverage, coffee with skimmed milk for Countess Renate and Darjeeling tea for Sir Martin.

The trip to Mossad headquarters took a bit longer than one might expect given the short distance owing to the numerous jams for which Tel Aviv has unfortunately become renowned. They were ushered into a small conference room adjacent to David Heller's office. He was there at the door to greet them; Countess Renate introduced Sir Martin to him and to Mark Levi who had joined them. After having invited them into his office, David motioned Renate and Sir Martin to a seat on the cream leather sofa which allowed his guests to gaze at the sea in the distance through the window. Mark and he took their places on armchairs set at either end of the coffee table set in front of the sofa. David's assistant, Joan, quickly took drink orders and the conversation started in earnest when they were served with a normal complement of small Middle Eastern pastries. David welcomed both Countess Renate and Sir Martin and ceded the floor to Mark whom he introduced as the person directly in charge of the project. Mark repeated David's thanks:

"Thank you both very much for taking the time to make this trip."

Countess Renate and Sir Martin smiled and let Mark continue:

"I'm sure Countess Renate has briefed you, Sir Martin . . ."

He smiled and nodded. Mark went on:

"We need help to execute a plan which involves selling a fictitious company to a Russian cybersecurity outfit. We expect to receive somewhere in the neighborhood of $1 billion!"

He let the seriousness of the situation penetrate the audience and offered a menu of the issues which he could not address on his own. He started with the basic reality that *Mossad* did not employ any investment banker, though they could probably seek advice in Tel Aviv. Sir Martin interrupted:

"If I may and please forgive me for interrupting but can you summarize the genesis of the idea, in your own words? I would like to make certain I understand all the various nuances."

Mark was happy to comply with the request. He prefaced his presentation with the expected warning:

"Everything I'm about to tell you is top-secret. I don't need to add that it will be good for all of us to assume that, when we are together, we are discussing matters that cannot go any further."

Countess Renate chimed in:

"Goes without saying Mark, but I understand why you had to say it."

"Wonderful."

Mark started his story with the need to help a Russian fugitive Oligarch escape from the probable wrath of the Kremlin. He made it clear that, until he did leave Russia, the individual had not done anything wrong or even treacherous. His point was that the situation in Russia was becoming quite dire, with the President requiring absolute, total loyalty. He further indicated that such loyalty could not often be demonstrated and fears on the part of the President that such and such oligarch was not sufficiently loyal had led a number of them to meet an untimely death. Mark cautioned his audience that there were still reasonable doubts as to whether the individual was a real fugitive or a plant, but simply conceded that *Mossad* had

decided to proceed as if he was for real, avoiding however to give him anything of value. He also explained that the goal there was not for Israel to attack Russia, but rather to gain better control over the communications between Russia and their clients in the Middle East. Skipping over unnecessary detail he came to the heart of the matter:

"We were pretty successful inserting a virus into certain Russian computer networks but did not manage to get all the information we wanted. At the same time, we felt we ought to help our "friend" recover as much of his wealth as possible from Russia. Our computer geniuses came up with an elegant solution which achieved both goals in one fell swoop: we invented a fictitious company with a special ability to detect and destroy viruses, we demonstrated its capabilities to Oleg, the Russian oligarch, and his reaction was exactly what we expected: he wants to buy it."

"I'm not sure I understand here. You say he wants to buy it, by which I assume you mean he wants his company to buy it. And yet he probably knows that he will no longer have access to the company at some point. Isn't this the case?"

"Extremely perceptive, Sir Martin. Yes and no. There is one detail I omitted which makes everything clearer. To convince him of the value of the algorithm, we claimed that his own computer and those of many in his company in St. Petersburg were bugged. He knew at the same time that his company had scanned everything for viruses and had found nothing. We suspect that he worries that this lapse could either destroy his company, incite a greater anger against him or even both."

"What I understand here, Mark, is that his mind is still not clearly in the right spot. He still doesn't know on which side he is . . ."

"Maybe, but not quite. I suspect that he knows he wants to flee because he doesn't trust the current head of the Kremlin. On the other hand, I would not be surprised if he harbored some hope that Yushin somehow will disappear, potentially opening for him some

way to return. Further, he surely knows whether he is for real or a spy; the problem is that we don't and couldn't ask as we couldn't trust the reply. You follow?"

"I do. I do. But it surely is messy."

"You said it, Sir Martin."

"So, what do we need to do?"

Mark replied:

"Well, we need to go through whatever process is needed to produce whatever documentation which a privately-held company ready to sell itself would have."

Sir Martin seemed to be thinking of the various possibilities:

"Hmm. Exactly what Countess Renate had said."

Countess Renate interrupted:

"Sir Martin, what if the company was not considering to sell itself. Would your answer be any different?"

Sir Martin batted away Renate's question arguing that most of the documents he was going to discuss would be required and produced in the normal course of doing business. He continued with a brief discussion of what the process normally would be in such circumstances. He started at the very beginning, noting:

"Companies which have decided they are ready to look for a merger partner or even an initial public offering know or soon find out that they must be able to offer at least three years of financial results, good, bad, or indifferent, together with any supporting documentation. Again, whether a company does or doesn't plan on seeking some transaction, these documents would still be there; the difference is that a company that plans to sell itself tends to spend some time "cleaning up" its operations to ensure it appears in its best possible but true light to potential suitors."

Sir Martin paused to take a sip of the cup of tea in front of him and continued:

"Note that the documents in question would extend beyond the mere financial information. They would need to have appropriate audit statements, probably income tax returns if applicable, legal papers, minutes of past board meetings, together with any material which they would have been expected to need in their marketing and client servicing efforts . . ."

Sir Martin would have continued had he not been politely interrupted by David:

"Thank you, Sir Martin, but what about a hypothetical case where the company has both public and government customers? I mean what if the company, which it probably would if it was real, has us, *Mossad*, as customers? We surely would not want any of that disclosed . . ."

"Probably not indeed, David. Let me think. In truth, this should not be a major issue. After all, particularly in the technology area, many start-ups are in part funded by governments or at least with the help of governments or their agencies. I saw a case once where the company simply divided its business into two parts, which he called public and top-secret. The CEO did not guarantee that the top-secret part of the company would remain after a sale. He offered to use what we call "best efforts," and to have any resulting sale to the top-secret customer be paid in part as incentive to the current owners after the sale . . ."

Mark asked:

"While this makes a lot of sense in general, given the fact that the company doesn't exist, I suspect that this avenue is not feasible for us here. Wouldn't you agree, Sir Martin?"

"Absolutely. Given the circumstances, I think that you're not really talking of selling the company as a whole. You probably mean that it would just be selling its intellectual property and its book of public business if any of it is deemed to be recurrent. I suspect that

also means that the buyer might have the right to try and hire the personnel it wishes to employ."

He paused and added with a wry smile:

"As you know, people are very important assets, but no one can be forced to work for someone he or she does not want to."

Mark could not agree more, but the follow-on question became crucial:

"Makes a lot of sense. But this may be where we need the most help. How does one construct anything in this context?"

"I don't want to presume anything, but I have a strong connection with a chap here who runs a private equity firm. He specializes in high technology ventures, many of them were started either by former employees of the Israeli Defense Forces or with the crucial cooperation of the Ministry of Defense."

He paused and explained that he had an idea which would make the whole effort considerably simpler if it could prove doable. He did mention in passing that he has been privileged to be allowed to invest in the funds managed by this private equity firm and had been delighted by the results. He suggested that his next step should be to meet with the friend and discuss the question in a very roundabout way. Turning to David, he asked:

"Would it be possible for you to run a check on this friend, just to certify that, as a foreigner and an investor, I haven't gotten myself into the wrong kind of association?"

"Absolutely. We would not be able to tell you anything if it is just a conjecture or some form of hearsay, for the obvious privacy reasons, but we can of course find out if there is any reason not to do business with him. More to the point, depending upon his personal background, it may even be possible to bring him closer to the center of the effort, though I might prefer not to: the fewer people in the loop the fewer the chances of an unfortunate leak."

Countess Renate interrupted:

"This sounds like we are moving in the right direction. I need to take care of a couple of things. First, I need to debrief with Sir Martin and get a sense of the resources the project will require and for how long. Second, I need to agree with you David on our contract. I should add that I am not going to lose any sleep over any of this . . ."

She paused and added:

"Sir Martin, would you be able to stay here for a while?"

"I can probably commit to being here until the weekend. After that, I may have to have a conversation with "she who must be obeyed" as we say in London . . ."

Countess smiled and replied jokingly:

"And I'm sure you do not mean Her Majesty the Queen!"

CHAPTER.21

TEL AVIV, ISRAEL

Sir Martin took a chauffeured car from the hotel to the offices of his friend Shlomo Elalouf, the CEO of one of the top two venture capital firms in Tel Aviv. Shlomo, originally a medical doctor from France, returned to Israel, the country of his birth, when he realized the potential to invest in technology startups back in Israel. He had indeed understood that many bright individuals, male and female, working in the engineering field, had developed intriguing new technologies or solutions while in the army *and* were looking for opportunities to transform these ideas into rewarding financial ventures. Interestingly, the firm which he founded not only invested in proven businesses with at least some serious operating history but also helped incubate newer ventures. Walking into his modern offices, one could for instance see a room where a half a dozen budding entrepreneurs were polishing ideas with a view, eventually to go from the project stage to reality, with the potential to be funded by the venture capital clients of the firm.

Sir Martin rode the elevator to the top floor of the mid-rise building and was greeted by a receptionist in what looked like an "all glass" environment. Light indeed seems to be coming out of

everywhere despite the fact that there was no window in the room. She told Shlomo's assistant that his guest had arrived, and Shlomo immediately came to welcome Sir Martin:

"Sir Martin so nice to see you. It's your first time in our offices here, isn't it?"

"Indeed, it is, Shlomo. Truthfully, it's the first time in Tel Aviv or Israel for that matter. Quite impressive I should add."

"Not sure if you mean Israel, Tel Aviv, or our humble offices. Anyway, would you like a tour, or should we walk directly to my office?"

"Why don't we look around on our way to your office. We'll do a real tour afterwards if that's acceptable."

As they walked toward the back of the building, where Shlomo's office was right next to a large glass-walled conference room, they passed by the "incubator"—the rectangular seven hundred square foot room where potential new ideas were being sharpened. Shlomo introduced the leaders of each team of two or three people and let them describe their work in a minute or less. Sir Martin realized that this had to be a routine part of visits to Shlomo's office, as each of the teams had their "elevator talk" ready and polished. As they were reaching Shlomo's office, his assistant enquired as to what beverage she could bring. Sir Martin chose plain sparkling water, while Shlomo stuck to coffee.

"What can I do for you, Sir Martin. Your email said that you had an issue on which you might need some help?"

"Quite. Quite. Before I say anything, I need to hear you confirm that you understand that whatever we discuss cannot go any further than you. We are talking top-secret Israeli matters."

"Understood. You know you can trust me. This is a business where you get to make a first impression anew every day. You can never rest on your laurels."

"I knew you would. Excellent."

Sir Martin brushed an outline of the challenge which was before him. In short, as he explained, he needed to develop the due diligence material which a three-year-old venture would have to present to anyone interested in acquiring them. Shlomo initially missed the point. He asked:

"With your experience, I'm sure you know what needs to be produced, right?"

"Well, I probably do, but the problem we have is that this is a trap."

"A trap? Not sure I understand, Sir Martin. So unlike you."

"Well, you're one step ahead of me. When I was told it was a trap, I was sure I did not understand too. Anyway, seriously, yes, it is a trap. The company does not exist, and the buyer will not get anything for his money."

"Wait a minute here; that's illegal. Isn't it?"

"Absolutely. In most cases . . . Let me try to tell you a bit more without crossing into information that I cannot share."

Sir Martin went on to explain that the potential buyer was a Russian group which, in a typical form of British understatement was "not on the side of the good guys." He added:

"I cannot tell you why, but the sale of a "fake company" to them is a way of getting the rightful owner his share of ownership which he could not otherwise access."

"Can you tell me about the business in which this company is supposed to operate?"

"Cybersecurity."

"Oh My! I think I am beginning to understand. Is there official Israeli involvement?"

"Yes, and the answer to the obvious next question as to whether it is top secret is yes as well, as we allowed at the outset."

"I see. I see."

Shlomo paused for almost a minute as he was thinking of how he could proceed. He asked:

"Is there any risk that anyone could trace anything to this firm?"

"You mean your firm I assume."

Seeing Shlomo nod, Sir Martin continued:

"No. Neither to you I should add. I only really need to help them procure the materials which will eventually be produced within the secret service. I received their commitment that your name, or mine for that matter would never come out."

"You trust them?"

"Absolutely. We are talking of the very top of the organization. Their word is their bond. They know that leaks can kill!"

Shlomo resumed his quiet thinking process. Sir Martin who had met Shlomo in London a few times was not surprised. He knew that he was a careful type, who would never skip any step in his decision-making process, very much as a physician who works to reach a diagnosis. As a matter of fact, Sir Martin believed that this was the reason Shlomo had been so successful in his business. Venture capitalists that have contacts are not legions, but there are quite a number of them. What differentiates the grain from the chaff is this ability to maintain discipline in the analysis, to rein in any passion so that decisions are rational rather than emotional and to take whatever time is needed to make that decision.

As he was patiently waiting, Sir Martin reminded himself of a few instances of what investors call "bubble environments" where venture capitalists with insufficient rigor and intellectual discipline embarked on wild goose chases, literally throwing money at ventures which should never have been funded if their premises had been analyzed carefully enough. Sir Martin knew of many people who regretted certain investments frequently because they had moved too fast. In reality, he often said that a tell-tale sign that a deal is to be avoided is too strong of a push by the sponsor of the deal to make a

quick decision. Creating a false sense that the window of opportunity is narrow is a tool commonly used by sellers who need to pressure their clients. Sir Martin had learned over time and was happy to have observed it in Shlomo that it is better to let go of something that looks good but may need more work than to jump in to avoid missing the train. Smiling, Sir Martin often said to his friends that he could not count the number of times when he had missed a good deal, adding:

"The key is that I have only been fooled very few times. So, I got fewer winners than others, but precious few total wipeouts."

■ ■ ■ ■ ■

Sir Martin had requested a meeting with Mark and David to bring them up to date on progress he had made. In short, he was happy to report that he had found a way to simplify the otherwise tedious challenge of preparing a full deck of due-diligence documents in the absence of real data to back it up. He prefaced his short presentation with a warning however:

"My friend who will remain nameless to all but you two is willing to help. That's the good news. On the other hand, he will want to receive official assurances from the Israeli government that he and his company will not only be held harmless against any form of legal challenge but also that his role in this matter will be secret and remain classified for the foreseeable future."

Mark asked:

"Why would he worry?"

"He's afraid he is going to be a party to a massive case of forgery."

"Understand. Is there more?"

"Yes, the common currency in the venture capital business is integrity and having the right contacts. Anything that can shake people's confidence in you is a death sentence."

Mark nodded and replied:

"No problem. However, note that I view this whole exercise as a two-part game. The first part involves some fabrication of materials. The second is the use we make of that material."

He paused and immediately corrected himself:

"Let me take the "some" out. We're talking of a fabrication. That's granted. However, and to us here at *Mossad* this is key: nobody should know what we are doing with the deck. In practice, I would argue that *Mossad* is fabricating the deck while The Shadow Experts with some outside help are helping us by providing data that we could use. The key word here is "could." Neither you, not Countess Renate or anyone else should feel responsible for the output or what we do with it."

Mark paused again. It was clear to him at the time that something had to be revisited. Suddenly, the proverbial lightbulb went on:

"Come to think of it, I should probably rephrase my definition of the two parts of the project. The first involves procuring everything needed. The second has to do with the fabrication and the use we make of the deck we created. Does this help?"

"It does Mark. It does. I'm sure you know I'm over that hurdle. I think that the really helpful thing that you just said is that you take full responsibility for the fabrication itself."

"Absolutely. In practice, one of the things we'll be asking you, Sir Martin, is to ensure first that nobody can trace anything to anyone and second that everything still makes sense. And let me note, and your friend should know it, that we do not know who he is and are not about to ask you."

Sir Martin looked satisfied, though he knew very well that David had run a check on Shlomo at his request. Mark's use of the pronoun "we" might have been warranted, but though it covered any member of his team who would use the data and the formats, it could not extend to David. David came into the conversation and asked:

"What do we need to do in the short term to help you?"

Sir Martin thought for a little while and replied:

"I think I need to have another short session with my contact. With the benefit of hindsight, I should have made it clear that his name and that of his firm have not and do not need to come out. He is only supposed to help me source data and information. For all I know, any of that could just as easily have come for overseas. There is no need for an Israeli connection . . ."

Mark interrupted:

"Provided we get the numbers in both Shekels and Dollars . . ."

"Goes without saying. But let's face it there are plenty of Israeli companies that have to maintain accounts in two currencies. Think of all the subsidiaries of non-Israeli companies."

Mark noted:

"Correct."

Then he added:

"Don't want to be the devil's advocate, but could your friend be worried that Tel Aviv is not a huge city and its financial community not terribly large either?"

"I see where you're going, Mark. That's what I meant when I mentioned him wanting to safeguard his reputation. Beyond David, no one needs to know who he or his company are. I can easily have him, or his team remove any mark pointing to him or his company."

David nodded:

"Works for me."

Sir Martin was hesitating asking the last question, but went ahead anyway:

"Would you be prepared to give me your assurances in writing that you would hold my source harmless and would keep its identity classified top-secret?"

"Not a problem. Countess Renate might want that document sent to her. Why don't you discuss it with her and let me know. I suspect

we're talking of an email and nothing more. I don't want anything like this in our records . . ."

■ ■ ■ ■ ■

Sir Martin's second visit to Shlomo Elalouf's office was considerably more relaxed than the first. He was able to report to Shlomo the contents of his conversation with his counterparts and to show him an appropriately censured email message making it clear that he was protected: his name should never, ever come out. Shlomo agreed that he would therefore be able to help Sir Martin. They needed to work together to identify the "donor" that would provide the framework for the creation—rather the fabrication—of the due diligence deck. Shlomo still had to ask:

"You have all you need on the product or service front, right?"

"Yes, the client has a pre-packaged routine which demonstrates the huge power of the software they developed."

"Then, it's good. However, let me note that, in this business, a demonstration is very important, but usually not enough. I can only encourage you to ask your client to create some marketing documentation. I can provide examples if that helps . . ."

Deep down, it is probably sure that all actors in this mini drama fully appreciated that they were playing somewhat of a game. Shlomo was not supposed to know that *Mossad* was Sir Martin's client, only that the client was the Israeli government. However, if not *Mossad*, who? David and Mark knew very well that the number of well-respected venture capitalists with a worldwide reputation could probably be counted on the fingers of a single hand. Countess Renate knew *Mossad* well enough that they would most likely never be found out on this particular project, and even if something were to come out, steps would be taken such that nobody would be allowed to dig into it. Everyone was in a position where there was some measure of uncertainty left. The classical "what if?" case, which though unlikely

could backfire. After all, all the players knew that a hoax was going to be perpetrated. A real cynic might even argue that the target of the hoax might create unexpected risks if the victim attempted revenge . . .

CHAPTER.22

TEL AVIV, ISRAEL, AND HERAKLION, CRETE

Meanwhile, Oleg had had to schedule his next conference call with Yuri. They had admittedly allowed the call that should have taken place the prior week to be skipped: after all they had been going back and forth on the recent virus problems and they had certainly spoken enough to each other. With a solution in sight for the virus problem, Oleg wanted to talk to Yuri to discuss the success that he had experienced with the unknown virus scan software and the idea he had had. When Oleg visited Mark's office to discuss his plans, Mark's recommendation remained steadfast:

"You shouldn't be there in person."

"I wasn't planning on flying to Crete."

He paused for a second and added:

"By the way, when we last talked I had asked Anton to sail near Matala, on the southern coast of Crete."

"I remember that."

"Well, I had to ask him to change, thankfully before he had passed abeam the west end of the island."

"Why?"

"Simply, because the closest airport to Matala is Heraklion, the capital of the island. It's located on the north coast. So, it was much easier anyway for Anton to sail directly off the coast near Heraklion. Indeed, he told me that he would anchor near Día island, six miles offshore and due north of Heraklion."

Mark was quietly fuming internally, as all the precautions he and David had arranged were off the southern coast of the Island. Still, neither did he show it, nor did he say anything, as Oleg was not supposed to know about the protection. He simply excused himself for a minute, knocked on David's door and gave him a quick summary. David replied:

"Don't worry. I'll let Gael Orbach know immediately. They should have plenty of time to reorganize themselves. I'll call you if he says this poses a problem."

Mark returned to his office and resumed his conversation with Oleg. He had not talked for more than a minute or so when his phone rang. Noting that it was David, he picked it up, thinking *Oleg may not speak Hebrew, but we should still be careful. You never know.* David's message was short and sweet:

"No problem except that the submarine must stay in deeper waters off Palekastro, at the eastern tip of Crete Island. It's about a hundred miles away from Heraklion. There, depths are in excess of 6,000 feet, halfway between the islands of Crete and Karpathos. All other equipment, including the Orcas can get discreetly closer to the *Volga*."

■ ■ ■ ■ ■

Anton was not surprised when the helicopter approached the *Volga* asking via radio for permission to land on the deck. Oleg had told him that he was planning a conference call which would use his office in the yacht as the background. He had simply added:

"We're going to follow the same routine as we did in Mallorca."

The surprise came when he saw the helicopter land. For a start, it seemed bigger than the one that was chartered the last time: the tail rotor definitely protruded over the bow of the ship. While the prior time, the helicopter really could not have carried more than four people including the pilot, two of them squished behind the pilot, this one clearly could contain more: he saw six people, dressed in commando clothing, all in black, getting off the helicopter. More ominously, they carried weapons. He ran from the bridge where he normally would have been to the heliport and asked the one who was running at the front of the group:

"What is this?"

The leader of the group simply replied:

"We are here to protect you and your ship."

"Protect us from what?"

"Don't you remember what happened in Mallorca?"

"What does that have to do with this?"

"Same scenario, except that, this time, we are prepared. Nobody will come onboard."

Anton was beginning to figure things out but was still not clear in his mind. So, he asked:

"What do you mean?"

"Remember, in Mallorca, pirates were able to come onboard. You managed to control them very well, but we fear that this time they may be less prepared to "forgive you" if they do not find what they are looking for."

"What are they looking for?"

"It is not a what; it's a who: Oleg Nichakov."

All of a sudden, Anton realized that the yacht was really just a pawn in a substantially larger dispute. He asked:

"Can I call Mr. Nichakov?"

"You can, but I wouldn't. As we speak he is on a conference call and will probably not be able to take your call. Further, he doesn't

know we're protecting him. Finally, assuming that his phone is bugged, you'd be telling the pirates that he isn't onboard."

The *Katsa* leader had hardly enough time to finish the sentence when things heated up. Anton who had wanted to reply, simply did not have the time. First, one of the *Mossad* agents still on the bow near the helicopter pad, on the portside of the boat, noticed a Zodiac approaching at a fast speed toward the yacht. The Zodiac had ostensibly been hiding in one of the creeks of Dia Island, less than two miles away from where the *Volga* was anchored, off Heraklion. She was larger than the prior one, and the agent thought there was another boat coming at them from the same general direction, though somewhat further east than the first Zodiac. The leader spoke a single command into the microphone he had hanging from his neck:

"Hold your fire. I don't want anyone to come onboard. But I want to learn more about who they are. Take your positions. Everyone but Cristian to the port side. Cristian keep watch on the starboard side."

Anton understood then and there that the yacht was about to be under attack. He asked the leader of the *Mossad* team:

"What do you want us to do?"

Before the leader could reply, Anton was surprised to see one of his sailors run toward the Katsa leader.

"Cristian, what are you doing here?"

Cristian responded:

"Permission to talk to the leader of the commando."

Anton did not have the time to reply. The leader of the commando turned toward Cristian and recognized him from the pictures that had been provided. He motioned to the helicopter pilot to bring something. A high-powered rifle appeared and was handed to Cristian. Anton asked:

"Should I call the harbor police?"

"No need. We have already done it. By the way, no word to anyone about Cristian. Understood?"

Almost mechanically, Anton replied:

"Understood."

But then, turning toward Cristian, he added:

"But wait; who are you?"

Cristian laconically and with a wink in his right eye replied:

"Trust me. You don't want to know. Just believe that we're on the same side and everything will work out fine."

A man on the starboard side spoke in his microphone:

"Two police boat approaching to starboard."

The leader replied:

"Just as planned. Cristian, go to the lower stern deck and be ready to help the police come onboard."

Turning to Anton, he added:

"Could one or two of your men help Cristian with the police?"

"Sure."

The two pirate boats were getting quite close to the port side of the *Volga*. They did not know that a number of rifles were pointed at them. One of the *Mossad* men, on the lower stern deck shot in the direction of the leading Zodiac, which understood that they were not totally unexpected. The Zodiac continued in the direction of the *Volga*, ostensibly to try to board the ship via the lowest deck accessible from the side. The *Mossad* agent on the lower stern deck sent a warning:

"Zodiac approaching mid-ship, near the portside lifeboat."

The *Volga* indeed carried two lifeboats one on either side of the ship. They were lodged in elongated box-like cavities on the lowest deck, just above the waterline. In case of emergency, people onboard would climb into them after which the lifeboat is moved away from the side of the ship and lowered down to the water. The cavity in which these boats can be located is one of the easiest points of surreptitious entry into a yacht as it can be reached from the outside

and then, once in, the pirates can reach the lowest deck and from there the rest of the vessel.

Two *Mossad* agents converged onto the point where the pirates planned to board the ship but kept their distance. On the main deck, another agent had also moved in position so that he could shoot as soon as the order was given. When planning the action, Mark had been particularly careful to select the agents based on their linguistic capabilities. He wanted Russian-speakers so that they could hear and more importantly understand whatever was being said by the crew. This turned out to be particularly helpful.

While the first police boat had docked to the *Volga* and all but one officer were onboard, the other police zodiac was slowly moving around the stern of the yacht. Cristian indicated to the police that pirates were attempting to come onboard on the portside of the yacht. The captain of the first police boat motioned to his colleague on the other vessel to move slowly around the stern. He was rightfully warning him against the risk of being shot at by the pirate.

Meanwhile, the agents allowed the first of the pirates to set foot near the ledge of the lifeboat anchoring position. He was surprised to hear a voice, probably no further than fifteen feet from him, say:

"Put your weapon on the floor and come slowly onboard."

The pirate hesitated and did not see the agent on the top deck fire a couple of shots, right behind the Zodiac. The intention was not to kill or disable the zodiac, but to intimidate the intruders. The pirate that had tried to come onboard yelled out:

"Igor didn't warn us."

He then climbed right down the boarding ladder and let himself slide into the Zodiac which went straight into reverse to try and escape. The second police boat closed in on it. It was followed by the first police boat which had been dispatched after it, despite having left its officers onboard the Volga. A shot from the *Volga* hit one of the outboard motors of the pirate Zodiac, which immediately stopped.

A second shot hit the inflatable tube on the portside. Ostensibly, the Zodiac was not of a type using ArmorFlate, the first bulletproof system Zodiac developed for inflatable boats for the military. It did not deflate completely as the tubes comprise several individual inflatable cavities precisely to avoid this kind of accident. Nonetheless, the pirates knew that they could not resist.

The second police boat was by then right behind the pirates' Zodiac and blocked it. The first police boat was closing in as well. The pirates instinctively raised their hands and motioned that they were giving up. The second police boat docked alongside the pirates' boats. A police officer boarded the Zodiac, confiscated all the weapons and passed them to a colleague that was still on the police boat. A couple of his colleagues were standing on the rigid bottom of the Zodiac aiming their weapons toward the pirates.

After they were disarmed, the pirates were asked to sit on the bottom of their boat. One of the police officers took over the control of the outboard engines. With one police boat leading the way and the other right behind the Zodiac, the pirates were brought to Heraklion harbor where they were properly arrested and taken into custody. They would have to face the music in Greece.

■ ■ ■ ■ ■

"Oleg, do you know anyone by the name of Igor?"

Mark's question to Oleg resonated like a handgun shot. He had gone to see Oleg at what they simply called "the penthouse" to brief him on what had happened while he was on the conference call with Yuri. Mark had not waited for Oleg to be aware of the full story before he asked the question. Oleg simply replied:

"Igor? Do you know how many Igor's there are in St. Petersburg alone?"

"OK, bad question. Let me tell you a story and give you some context. You'll understand my question better then."

Mark proceeded to tell Oleg that he had anticipated that whoever had sought to kidnap him off the coast of Mallorca would try again, this time off the coast of Crete. He had therefore decided to take all sorts of precautions. First, he had sent a contingent of *Mossad* agents, of *Katsas*, to help. They had used the helicopter which was assumed to bring Oleg onboard the Volga and had taken positions around the boat. He had also warned the Greek police, offering if needed to put them in touch with the Spanish police in Mallorca, an offer which they had as it turned out accepted. The police had sent two speedboats which had remained semi-anchored about two miles from the Volga to avoid scaring the pirates away. Mark indeed explained:

"We hoped to be able to get some intelligence from the pirates. So, obviously, we would not let them get onboard and do any damage, but we hoped to learn something from them . . ."

Oleg interrupted. He had understood, or at least thought he had understood. He asked:

"So, you were able to catch them and one of them dropped the name of Igor during questioning."

"Close but no cigar. We did not catch them, but we ambushed one of them. He cursed Igor before letting himself drop back into the pirates' vessel."

"Same, same. Wait, I think I understand your question better. However, my answer remains the same. I wouldn't know where to start."

"Well, let me help you. Are there any people named Igor in Visla Cybersecurity?"

"You bet. More than that, I'm sure there's more than one. Let me see, for a start, you've got our Chief Financial Officer, Igor Zatopek."

Mark interrupted:

"What about him?"

"I've known him for quite a while. In truth, he was with Yuri and me when I founded the company. Better yet, as I told you, Yuri and I were FIS agents then; remember?"

"Sure do."

"Well, so was Igor."

"Is he still with FIS?"

"No. He told us he left at the same time Yuri and I both did."

"Could he have lied?"

"Your guess is as good as mine."

Mark changed tack and asked:

"Does he own any of the company?"

"Yes. 10%. Yuri owns 15% of the company."

"Any special political activity on Igor's part?"

"None that I know of. He's just like the small cadre of people around me. We all know that we have to stay on the good side of the regime, but I don't know of any of us being more involved than . . ."

He suddenly stopped and said:

"Well, come to think of it, wait a minute. Wait a minute. Igor is probably a bit closer to the government than either Yuri or myself. He's been involved in local St. Petersburg politics. Nothing nefarious though. He just wanted to be plugged both at the local and the national level. Plus, the clout of local politics made it easier he said when getting financing was tough earlier on . . ."

Mark replied:

"Makes sense. Any other Igor?"

"I can think of at least another two straight off the bat. One is in Moscow as a government liaison with a crucial role in terms of getting us government contracts. The other one, in St. Petersburg, but he is a youngish software engineer. I really don't know much about him other than his name."

"Is it something you can discuss with Yuri?"

"Sure. But I'm not going to talk about Igor Zatopek. I'm first going to ask him to investigate the other two. I won't even tell him that someone heard the name "Igor.""

"Why?"

"Well, technically, he and Igor Zatopek are peers. I don't want to place one ahead of the other. I don't want Yuri to start to suspect Igor unless everything we have points to him. Too dangerous. Plus, it could leak upwards if you see what I mean."

"Not sure I do . . ."

Oleg explained that there could be a risk that Igor would finger Yuri to the Kremlin and expose him to an attack on his life, dejectedly adding:

"They might not have gotten me yet, but they would get Yuri. Don't want to create that risk for him. Not fair unless we are absolutely sure."

Mark reluctantly agreed.

CHAPTER.23

TEL AVIV AND BEERSHEBA, ISRAEL, ST. PETERSBURG, RUSSIA, AND SINGAPORE

Meanwhile, Oleg had had to schedule his next conference call with Yuri. It went as planned. It was chiefly focused on a conversation on the virus which had crept into the system. Oleg took Yuri through the steps which had been taken with respect to his own computer. He was careful not to disclose either where he really was or where the solution to his problem had come from. He could easily see Mark from the corner of his eye, with the mission to create instability or static on the line if he was about to say something he should not have.

Yuri's reaction to the diagnosis was the same as that which Oleg had had at the time: complete disbelief. In fact, his was even stronger. As the person in charge of the technology, he could not accept that he would have missed something so powerful. Oleg repeated, in his own words, what he had been told:

"The problem is that viruses can be mutated by their creators, in very much the same way as human viruses do except those also do it on their own, as a part of their survival strategy. Do we have that contingency in our systems?"

"Wait a second here. Do you mean that whoever it is that has that technology has a way of anticipating potential changes and then include both known viruses and potential variants in the database library against which they compare all lines of code?"

"I guess that's what I'm saying, but you're already ahead of me."

Yuri remained silent as he was deep in thoughts for a few seconds. He then said:

"Do you know how they do it?"

"Really I don't. But they gave me the headline: they are using artificial intelligence to anticipate what sort of mutations could be carried out to transform a virus that is already known. In point of fact, they added, as an aside, that this was exactly the process that hackers use: they start with something that worked and has just been detected and modify it to avoid detection."

He paused for a second and then said:

"On the surface, it shouldn't be rocket science."

"On the surface maybe, my friend. But in practice, I sure wouldn't know how to do it as we speak. Is there any way you could get me into a demonstration?"

Oleg replied that he was sure something could be arranged, though he noted:

"Are you thinking what I am thinking?"

"Probably, yes, if you are thinking we should either steal the technology or buy the company."

"I see. Remember, if these guys are smart enough to develop something like this, I would assume they would be smart enough to hide the key elements of their technology."

"Worth a try anyway. But if we can't steal it, we've got to buy it. Is it for sale?"

"At this point, I don't know. Let me offer this. I can contact the person who helped me clean my computer and ask if they could clean yours as well."

"Would you be using the *Volga* to do that? I could always fly there if you tell me where "there" is. I think you told me you're off the coast of Crete, correct?"

"Absolutely."

Mark was making a sign with this thumb drawn across his throat. Oleg understood that he should not go any further on that topic. Mark still passed him a paper offering for the session to take place by remote control. Oleg offered that option to Yuri who replied that he was not fond of letting anyone into his computer, adding however:

"but might make an exception in this case if it was the only way."

They agreed that Yuri would find a way to make himself available when the computer specialist was available himself.

■ ■ ■ ■ ■

Right afterwards, Mark contacted Hai Chock and Nathan to tell them about both the opportunity and the obvious risk. Hai Chock was totally non-plussed:

"Remember, we took care of Oleg's computer right in front of his eyes and he saw nothing. I would suggest following exactly the same process with Yuri's computer."

Nathan added:

"Actually, I thought of one way of hiding more behind the scenes while we do what looks like innocuous stuff on the surface."

Hai Chock exclaimed:

"Wonderful. Can we discuss it offline first?"

"Sure."

■ ■ ■ ■ ■

While on a video conference call, Oleg introduced to Yuri a gentleman whom he called Jim Ng, the "pseudonym" Hai Chock used when the other party was not a client of The Shadow Experts, directly or indirectly. Jim greeted Yuri and confirmed that he wanted him to

have a look into his computer, to check for some virus which had so far not been detected. Yuri replied:

"That's exactly correct."

Jim started to explain that the process would entirely be through the Cloud. He would first connect via Wi-Fi to Yuri's computer. Yuri asked:

"Will I be able to follow everything on the screen while you're working?"

"You sure will. Hopefully you can read quickly, as the process works at high speed."

Seemingly non-plussed Yuri replied:

"No problem. I'm used to that."

Hai Chock, aka Jim Ng, smiled broadly, as did Nathan, though Nathan could not be seen by anyone; he was connected to Hai Chock through a different line which allowed him to hear and more importantly to see the screen of Yuri's computer. They were both thinking exactly the same thing: *sure you do!* Having secured Yuri's agreement and gotten him to provide the necessary access and permission, Hai Chock went to work, with Nathan there as an advisor to help Hai Chock if there was any problem. First, Hai Chock remotely connected to Yuri computer and during that initial phase, sent instructions to Yuri's computer to erase the virus/worm they had originally inserted. At the same time, he replaced it with another lacking the special hiding features created by Hai Chock.

This completed, Hai Chock indicated that he was going to run the special virus-scan software. He prefaced his comment:

"One thing you should know, Yuri. I have no control over what the scan does. I've used it and am satisfied it does what it is supposed to do. However, and unfortunately I cannot see everything that it does. For one thing, I can't see inside the virus library."

Again, Yuri calmly replied:

"That's par for the course. I understand."

"Glad you do. So, here we go."

Yuri's screen was showing the typical data any computer would show when being checked for virus: number of files scanned, number of abnormalities detected and elapsed time. Before the program had run its course, Yuri exclaimed:

"Oh Shit!"

He had just seen a message appear on the screen: it clearly demonstrated that at least one abnormal file had been detected. He knew very well that he had run his own antivirus software a few minutes before he had taken the call from Oleg, and that it had not detected any virus at that time. He asked:

"Jim, are you sure?"

Oleg interrupted before Jim aka Hai Chock could reply and simply said:

"I hate to tell you so, Yuri, but I did tell you so my friend."

"This is just crazy. More than crazy, it makes no sense. Jim how do you do it?"

"Well, truth is Yuri that I don't know myself. We bought the virus scan software from a company in Israel of all places . . ."

Yuri interrupted:

"Israel?"

"Absolutely. It's easy to get a rundown of their program. I've already done so. I've checked it line by line. It's bog-standard virus detection software. What's different is the reference database, the one thing to which I have no access."

"But you bought the program, didn't you?"

"Yes, but as most of the best providers, they do not release the database. They allow you to connect to it while doing a scan, but that's about it. Think of it this way: I own the actual virus-scan program and the program has access to the virus database, but it isn't on my server; it remains on theirs and I can't see anything within it. Protects them and gives them an opportunity to keep charging access fees . . ."

Hai Chock paused for a second and added:

"To be fully honest with you, my guess is that looking inside the database wouldn't tell me much. The key is how they update it. And that, I'm sure, is a different program to which no one but them has access.

"I see. But do you understand how they do it?"

"I do and I don't. Conceptually, it's simple. They say they use artificial intelligence, and I can believe it. That's the easy part, as you know you can hide lots of things behind the artificial intelligence moniker; it's so broad you could drive a truck through it. I believe that what they call artificial intelligence is simply a process that looks at prior variations in the bugs, you know the viruses worms and assorted trojans. I bet that the process uses probabilities to guess which variations are most likely to follow one another. Can't deny that the concept is quite smart; wish I had thought of it myself! The hard part is how they use the concept, what parameters they've put in it and even how they've structured their algorithms. Without that, I can't replicate what they're doing."

He paused for a second and added:

"That's why I ended up buying it!"

Yuri was ostensibly disappointed, though Mark noted that he seemed quite impressed by Jim, aka Hai Chock. Mark himself thought that Hai Chock had outdone himself. He thought he had been *beyond believable*. Yuri asked Jim whether he was done with his computer. Jim replied:

"Just about. Let me do a minimum of clean-up."

With that, he proceeded to insert a mildly modified version of the initial virus/worm combination without anyone appreciating it was happening.

Yuri asked:

"Oleg, can we speak as soon as possible? This is both a wonderful opportunity and a major threat."

"No problem. I'll call you right back without our friends on the line. It'll be just a cell phone call."

■ ■ ■ ■ ■

Within minutes, Oleg called Yuri back, with his guardian angel, Mark, still by his side. Yuri was in a high state of excitement:

"This is big, very big!"

"I know my friend, I know. Tell me something I don't know."

"I'm sure you realize it, but my point is that it's big in two ways."

"You're ahead of me. Two ways?"

"Yes. Obviously there is the commercial potential. That be great for us. Imagine: we would get to resell something to all our customers. But I worry about the negative piece of it too."

Oleg did not understand where Yuri was going. He simply asked: "What?"

"Well, remember the virus which they detected. It has to have come from the document which you had sent me."

"Is that the only way? After all, I also opened documents that came from you or more broadly the company. So, the entry point into our system could be absolutely anywhere."

Yuri was taken aback, while Mark was smiling interiorly at having suggested that comeback to Oleg. Initially, Yuri had assumed that Oleg was the guilty party. After all, Yuri had told him of what he called "incidents" after he had downloaded the document sent by Oleg. Still, Mark first did not want to add to the cloud under which Oleg might be within his company. More importantly, he wanted to avoid the "easy solution" which Yuri was probably contemplating: buying the software and accordingly cleaning their computers, and possibly afterwards simply point the finger at Oleg. Given the number of computers that could be infected, there was no chance that Hai Chock would have the time or even the energy to repeat the one-on-one exercise he had carried out on Oleg and Yuri's computers. As it

turned out, he had called Hai Chock to find out whether he could scan all the Visla Cybersecurity computers and servers in one fell swoop. His reply had been unfortunately quite clear:

"Somewhere between hard and impossible."

He had explained that the challenge was not in the scanning which was routine. It was in removing the original virus, inserting a new one that would come out on the scan, removing it after the scan and re-inserting another one which would maintain the control *Mossad* had gained on the internal systems of Visla Cybersecurity. He then added:

"The closest we can get to it would be to offer to scan their computers and remove the offending virus. I'm the only one that can do it since the virus they have in there is my really special variety. However, we would lose access to all the computers we've cleaned that way. A lot of work getting in for nothing."

Mark looked puzzled and then blurted out:

"Wait a minute. Maybe not after all. Think of it. We would still have the two top guys running infected computers. Also, we would have the clients of Visla Cybersecurity that were infected still with the bug on their systems. We would lose something in the short term, but within a while, probably not as long as we think, these guys would have reinfected one another."

"Mark, you're brilliant. You're right. It would work. More than that, it could serve as the ultimate incentive for them to want to buy the company . . ."

CHAPTER.24

TEL AVIV, ISRAEL, AND ST. PETERSBURG, RUSSIA

Oleg had to talk to Yuri after what he had learned from Mark about the attack on the *Volga* offshore Heraklion. In truth, his reply to Mark that he was more prepared to suspect anyone named Igor, inside or outside the company before considering his own Chief Financial officer was not a put on. Instinctively, he was simply not prepared to suspect Igor Zatopek. More than that, had the pirates yelled the name Yuri rather than Igor, he would have been equally unwilling to suspect his close associate. To him, until proven otherwise, they both were trusted lieutenants with whom he had journeyed for quite some time; they may not have made as much money as he, but they surely had been handsomely rewarded.

In the case in point with Mark's comment with respect to Igor, the only thing he knew was that he had been working alongside him for quite some time. Igor was one of the only two executives in the firm, besides Yuri, that had equity. He had been a friend, a counselor and a gifted finance executive. Oleg knew that Igor had served very well when Visla had needed financing with a weak balance sheet on which to fall back. Igor had managed to find financing at reasonable rates. Curiously for someone like Oleg who was usually quite perceptive, it

never entered his mind that Igor's apparent skills were something that might suggest contacts in places that had a vested interest in Visla succeeding. In other words, had Igor been a plant himself, one of his roles would probably have been to help the powers that be nurture their cybersecurity jewel until it could run on its own two legs.

Oleg could not deny and therefore accepted the fact that there had to be someone who wanted him either out of the way or simply dead. As a matter of fact, the two attacks on the Volga when he was supposed to have been there would make it incredibly difficult for him not to see himself as a target. After all, this was nothing but the extension of the concerns and then fears that had led him first to create his "twin" Dimitri, second to establish his family outside of Russia and third, more recently, to ask for help from *Mossad*. More to the point, had he totally rejected the notion that anyone was after him, it seems pretty clear that Mark and David would have to have concluded Oleg was a plant or a spy. You cannot deny the evidence when it's staring you in the face.

Deep in Oleg's mind, he knew the real problem he had to face was in Moscow. It was caused by his lackadaisical support for President Yushin. He had never come out against him, but whether it was what he saw as predatory enrichment by certain oligarchs or more recently excessive ruthlessness against domestic opponents, he had not been able to convince himself to sing out loud the praises of the regime. At times, he had regretted not being more visible and ardent a supporter. His difficulties did not have to do with the President at the outset. After all, that's what had made him rich, even if admittedly he had managed to get richer under the presidency of Boris Yeltsin than more recently. There was no question in his mind that the value of his company was certainly in no small measure linked to the support provided by the Kremlin to it. He owed it some degree of gratitude.

However, though he was ready to suspect anyone in Moscow, or possibly in the St. Petersburg area, if they were under Kremlin orders,

he could not take the step that would have put his two colleagues in that same category. Nobody had taken the time or the effort to explain to him that his knowledge of Kremlin tactics involving inserting spies in the management of companies about which they wanted to know everything ought to have made him conclude that someone near to him, or at least near enough to him had to be a spy. After all, how else would the authorities ensure that they could count on his loyalty or that they would know quickly enough as and when he became dissatisfied and ready to shift to the political opposition? Everybody knew that Moscow had experienced quite a bit of trouble with a couple of Oligarchs; they had started to compete against President Yushin. Therefore, Moscow wanted to have all the notice they could. Someone up there must have thought *let's catch it when it is still a grenade and before it becomes an atomic bomb*, whether that applied to Oleg or any of his peers. And Oleg's apparent naivety was all the more surprising that he and his two colleagues had indeed started as employees of the FIS. In the end, there was no psychoanalyst to help him address this blind spot and he would have to live with it, even if it could at any moment explode in his face.

■ ■ ■ ■

Oleg's email to Yuri conveyed a sense of urgency. They needed to speak quite soon. That urgency was not lost on Yuri. He called as soon as he received the email and did not even bother to try to go for a video-conference call. In retrospect, the fact that he did not request a video conference call was probably a good thing; Oleg did not have a "plan B" with respect to what would appear as a background on a video conference call. He had simply not even considered the possibility.

Oleg picked up the phone on the first ring:

"Oleg here."

"Hey, it's me, Yuri. You said we needed to talk. More than that, you seemed to say between the lines that it was very urgent. So, what's going on?"

The issue which Oleg wanted to discuss with Yuri was the attack on the *Volga* and the subsequent events. Oleg had not finished his sentence announcing that Russian-speaking pirates had again tried to attack the *Volga*, that Yuri interrupted:

"What are you talking about?"

Oleg calmly replied:

"Remember Mallorca"

"I do, so?"

"Well, same with quite a bit more firepower."

Oleg was convinced: Yuri was surely telling the truth when he said that he had no idea what had happened. Whether he was or was not involved in the planning of the attack, as Mark had suggested was a possibility, it was a fact that nobody in St. Petersburg had received a call from the yacht. The first person whom Anton had called was Oleg, and Oleg had told him not to talk about it to anyone else, arguing that he had everything under control. He could not see the doubtful look on Anton's face as he said that, but Anton was a good soldier. He stuck to his orders. At the same time, there was no way that anyone among the pirates had had a chance to call their masters with details: they had all been taken into custody in Greece and would surely spend at least a night there, and maybe a lot more. Oleg noted Yuri's surprise and thought that he needed to report it to Mark.

After all, one could have imagined one of the sailors being in the employ of the attackers. That sailor would not have been captured by the Greek police and he would have been able to call his master. The fact that no one had called Russia suggested that the *Volga* crew was generally loyal to Anton and to Oleg. The only one in the lot whose loyalty might have been doubtful was Cristian, given what Anton had

witnessed offshore Heraklion. In that case, Anton could not possibly have doubted that Cristian was loyal to Oleg. After all his job was to protect Anton and to inform on anything occurring on the yacht. A cynic would note that once he received Oleg's email, the only thing which Yuri could know was that Oleg was definitely not kidnaped, but he could not know much more.

Oleg skipped a few of the details, including the fact that *Mossad* had organized stronger defenses on the Volga, as well as the direct early protection by Greek harbor police. Mark had made it clear to him that his personal safety was critically dependent upon making sure that no one outside of Israel should know how he was being protected. Any indication he gave that some protection was available would inevitably lead to him being traced, and eventually captured.

Oleg stunned Yuri when he came to the punch line:

"The Greek police told Anton that at least a couple of the pirates that had been arrested had referred to their boss as Igor. Now, as you know, it's not as if Igor is an uncommon name."

He paused for a few seconds. Yuri did not offer any other reaction than a real surprise, which, whether he was onboard with Oleg or against him, did not need any theatrical skill: he was either surprised that there had been an attack, or he was surprised that Oleg had escaped. Oleg continued:

"I immediately thought of the two employees we have who bear Igor as a first name. You know, the young software engineer on your team and our senior marketer in Moscow."

Yuri was surprised that Oleg did not mention Igor Zatopek and said so:

"Any reason you're not mentioning Igor Zatopek?"

"Yes. Just like I wouldn't suspect you if the pirates had revealed that their boss's name was "Yuri." You and I have known Igor for so long. The three of us are a team. I can't believe he would be involved

in anything like that. I can't imagine either of you in such a plot . . . Am I crazy? Should I suspect Igor Zatopek?"

Yuri did not reply directly, though he nodded, which Oleg could not see on a regular phone line. He was stuck either way. Again, if he was a part of the plot it would not be smart to encourage Oleg to dig too close to home. On the other hand, if he was not, he shared Oleg's feeling for Igor. However, he immediately picked up on the two potential problem individuals whom Oleg had identified. He asked:

"I assume that you want this quite close to the vest, right?"

"Absolutely. Come to think of it, I would prefer it if Igor Zatopek did not know about it."

"Why? You still have some doubt, right?"

"Well, as I said, I cannot imagine he is involved in that. But if he is, I don't want him to know that we have that piece of information. Don't you agree?"

"Well, you know, Oleg, I really don't have a view. I'm a software guy and I couldn't do Igor's job. I don't want Igor's job. Admittedly, I wouldn't mind having his share of the business, but I want it above board, if you see what I mean."

"But you're not answering my question . . ."

"I know. I can't appear to be shooting at a colleague. On the other hand, I've got to say that I cannot shake a fear that he might be involved. To tell you the truth, I would suspect myself if the name revealed had been "Yuri." Just precaution. You never know. And if your life is on the line, you can't assume anything. Am I making more sense?"

"Totally my friend, totally. That's why I trust you."

Yuri sensed that the conversation on the *Volga* attack was coming to an end, and there was another topic on his mind. He surprised Oleg:

"Oleg, while I've got you on the phone, where are you with respect to the purchase of the Israeli cybersecurity company?"

Yuri did not want to let go on what he saw as a great opportunity which could simultaneously remove a major weakness and create a boatload of new business potential. In response to Yuri's direct question, Oleg had to admit that he had not made a lot of progress. In truth, he sorely needed to have a talk with Mark and his colleagues to find out what the next steps were. He knew what was involved in any merger or acquisition, but there was a serious complicating factor in the present case. From his point of view, it was clear that he wanted to buy the company, though he fully understood the challenge involved in a Russian company buying an Israeli firm at the present time. Russia was definitely not "the flavor of the month" in many business circles. He shared his hesitations with Yuri who pushed all the harder, going as far as saying:

"Whatever the business is worth, we should be prepared to pay twice that to get it."

"Twice?"

"Call it a premium for unpopularity. Think about it. I am guessing that the seller may feel they're betraying someone or even their own country. But the truth is that people are still quite sensitive to what the Americans like to call the "almighty dollar." Offering twice what a seller could get in the market might allow us to bypass any form of competitive bidding. You agree?"

"Totally understand, Yuri. But we still need to go through due diligence . . ."

"I know, but just between you and me, I've done a good part of that due diligence the other day when they fixed my computer. I had intentionally run my computer through a virus scan literally in the few minutes before you called. It had come out totally clear. Then, they connect to my computer, run their software and bingo a virus appears. I don't need much more to be convinced . . ."

He paused for a second and then added:

"Hold it. There could be one and only one trap."

"A trap?"

"Yes. What if they introduced the virus as they were connecting to my computer?"

"Wouldn't you have seen it?"

"Should have but could have missed it."

"I can see that. What does that mean?"

Honestly, it changes next to nothing. The scenario I just brushed is a one in a million. Let's just keep our eyes open. We may need another demonstration. Would you mind having a conversation with Igor on the issue? I know we don't have the cash we would need to pay for the acquisition. Further, I would bet a fair chunk of money that the seller would not accept shares in Visla Cybersecurity in exchange for their stock."

"Are you talking of having Igor secure some form of financing?"

"Right on. Do you think that the seller, if he is willing to sell, would accept any stock in Visla Cybersecurity?"

"I see what you mean. Most likely not!"

"Right, so I'm pretty sure that this would have to be a cash deal. And we both know that Visla is not cash rich. How much did we have in cash the last time we looked?"

"A couple hundred million dollars, at most. Plus, some receivables. But we also have bills to pay. So, I agree. But that's really for Igor to deal with, right?"

"Absolutely."

Oleg was not through sharing his worries with Yuri:

"Now let me add one thing that could complicate matters further: I am not even sure that the cash deal would be totally above board."

"What do you mean?"

"Taxes are not cheap in Israel. Having some money paid in Switzerland, for instance, might very well be a part of the package. Plus, the seller might in fact not even be a full-time Israeli resident . . ."

"Understood."

■ ■ ■ ■ ■

"Hey, Mark. Oleg here."

"What can I do for you, sir?"

Oleg explained to Mark that he wanted to go forward on the potential purchase of the company behind the virus scan software. Mark was elated but replied that he would first need to contact the potential seller. Still, to confirm that he knew what Oleg felt he needed, he thought he had to ask:

"What do you need at this point?"

Oleg, who had bought other businesses during his career, knew the theoretical answer, but replied:

"Isn't it first a question of knowing whether the owner is prepared to sell?"

"Goes without saying. But remember that I don't even know if the company is totally operational. I know they've sold some software and I'm sure they've done plenty of consulting. But beyond that, I don't know."

Oleg matter-of-factly asked:

"Wouldn't they have financials?"

"They probably do, if only because I am sure they must have paid taxes. However, some of what they do might qualify for tax-exempt income status . . ."

"Tax-exempt?"

Mark explained:

"Yes, for instance stuff they do for the government."

"I see. Well, can you try to find out what financials would be available, any banking document, and things like that?"

"Sure can. Let me talk to David and come back to you in a few days . . ."

"Any chance you can get it done faster?"

"I can certainly find out if there is any interest in selling quite rapidly. However, everything else, including getting documents ready will likely take some time."

"Can't see why."

Mark took Oleg through the whole of his logic. He really needed time to organize himself and he had to convince Oleg that things would have to fall into place at their own speed:

"As I said earlier, I'm sure they have done business with the government. And I'm sure too that any of that ought to be taken out of the totals. So, either they can give us pretty high-level summary documents, or they'll need to get their accountants to get cracking on creating pro forma audited financial statements separating what business could be sold from the business that could not be in the deal."

"I see. From my point of view, summary documents would initially be enough, though I'm sure Igor would ask for more detail. At the same time, I would like to meet the man or woman behind the company and its technology as soon as possible."

"Understood. Leave it with me."

■ ■ ■ ■ ■

Mark walked into David's office with a decidedly satisfied look on his face. His first sentence summarized it:

"Oleg has taken the bait."

David raised his eyebrows. Mark took his statement a bit further:

"And from what I understand, so has Yuri."

"Excellent news my friend. Now what?"

Mark explained that was where the real work began. He needed, as he put it, "to prep" Nathan Sharon so that he could become Dr. Adam Schlossberg, the founder of the company and owner of its intellectual property. He also explained that he needed to put Sir Martin to work with a team of Mossad agents to create the track

record he felt he needed, together with the kind of legal, financial and business documents which a three-year-old company should have. That's when he mentioned:

"That's going to take some time. The first step here is to get Sir Martin to start the process with his source."

He paused and added:

"Though this may be a bit premature, I need to talk to Countess Renate about opening a bank account for the shell company we'll create as the ultimate owner of the company. We don't want the money to come to Israel, as it really does not belong here . . ."

"Totally agree. But I wouldn't worry about that step until you have all the others under control. This has got to be the simplest one. After all, remember, Countess Renate has an associate, as she calls the members of her team, who heads up a bank in Austria."

"Good point. Thank you, sir.

CHAPTER.25

TEL AVIV, ISRAEL, AND SOMEWHERE IN THE AUSTRIAN ALPS

Sir Martin wanted to share with David and Mark the draft of the first set of financial accounts that had been produced for the company they decided to call Avigdor Cyber Experts. Avigdor is the Hebrew word for Protector, which they had all agreed conveyed both what the company was purported to be doing and what they would like it to be doing if it really existed. The idea of using the word "Experts" in the name was meant to convey that the company was not only developing software tools for sale, but also that it was staffed by engineers who could offer their expertise on a consulting basis. The company was based in Tel Aviv, at an address that was but a mailbox routinely used by *Mossad*. The documents did not require a physical address other than a Post Office box, of which *Mossad* had plenty at its disposal. Everyone had agreed that there was no point providing more information than absolutely necessary.

This first round only focused on the three main accounting reports which all companies have to generate and provide, annual income statement, annual balance sheet and annual statement of flow of funds. Later on, there would be a need to develop additional

elements for the due diligence package, including three years of tax returns and auditing certificates, a corporate brochure describing the company and its products and services—this would need to be replicated on the Web to offer an Internet Page for Avigdor—and some basic product literature. More complicated, but also later on, the annual statements would have to be broken down into quarterly intervals, as is customary in Israel. Sir Martin had convinced Mark and David, as well as Countess Renate—they were the only four in the loop for that detailed work—that the rest would be considerably easier. More to the point, he had argued:

"Imagine that the buyer pushes back against the financials, there's no point spending the time and money working on the rest."

David had replied:

"Excellent idea, Sir Martin, but I would add another contingency. We need to discuss what our price is going to be and on what basis it is determined. They might push back on that as well."

"Totally agree. However, there might be some room to maneuver or negotiate with respect to the price. On the other hand, there is no room to move with respect to the historical financials. They do or don't exist, and they do or don't tally up."

Mark interrupted:

"True, with one caveat. We had agreed that we would say that the financials have broken out whatever is related to work which Avigdor is doing on behalf of the Israeli government. This gives us some wiggle room, claiming that we are just reclassifying various entries."

"I understand the logic but would caution you against it. My advice would be to be prepared to "disclose" a bit more on the government business, but not mix that up with the financials. I would suggest that we argue that the financials we offer are the only real ones, and that business with the government occurs outside of that format. Say the government gets its services for free, but also provides some measure

of financing, the whole being set so that there is no income impact and consequently no tax liability."

He paused for a second and then added, almost as an afterthought:

"Any money which the government provides would have to come into the company's accounts. It's easier to claim that the costs incurred by the company are directly billed to the government and thus do not ever come into Avigdor's accounts."

Countess Renate interrupted:

"You know better than we do, Sir Martin. So, I'm sure we'll be ready to follow your lead. Can we look at the first draft you want to show us?"

■ ■ ■ ■ ■

Sir Martin had agreed with his friend, Shlomo Elalouf, to use the actual accounts of a real company at the appropriate stage of maturity. They had combed together a universe of possible candidates, focusing primarily on companies involved more or less directly in software development. They were likely to have the same general cost structure as that which would be expected for Avigdor, as well as revenues combining one-time sale and "subscription revenues." Pointing to one set of accounts he had dug up for Sir Martin, Shlomo Elalouf had commented:

"This one seems quite interesting, Sir Martin. Actually, I know that it went on to be a darling of equity markets, first here in Tel Aviv and then in the U.S."

"What do you think it should sell for, if the record you have here was as of today?"

"As you know, it always depends on the mood of markets. In the current liquidity-driven market, I am sure that it would be valued over $750 million. At the same time, tech stocks have been hit quite seriously in the last three months. So, in a market where sentiment does not provide a tail wind, I don't know . . . maybe $500 million."

"That's great. This gives us wiggle room to put a premium on top of that price to account for the scarcity factor and the apparent strong desire the potential buyer has to own the company. Let me use these. As you know, nobody will recognize anything when we're done with it, and more importantly, you will not hear of it as well. Officially, I'm gonna develop a case study. Agreed?"

"Sounds believable. Glad to have been of help."

■ ■ ■ ■ ■

Sir Martin then took the three sets of reports to *Mossad* where a group specialized in fabricating fake documents. Their activity ranged quite widely, as it went from the creation of identity papers for individuals, complete with passports comprising a travel history with appropriate entry and exit immigration stamps, to the task at hand which involved creating a company and a record for that company from nothing or in this case next to nothing. Luckily, the "models" which Sir Martin and his friend had chosen included data in both Israeli Shekels and U.S. Dollars. This would avoid requiring the *Mossad* "artists" as they often called themselves to have to go back and look for the exact exchange rates that ought to be used in each of the last three years.

However, while the model documents had all the data and even the appropriate accounting notes already written, they would need to create a different set, reflecting first, of course, the different name and second and more specifically the variation in services and products. Particularly, this was the time when some mention would need to be made of both the fact that the accounts did not include revenues from government contracts and the management practice of having the government pay all the various costs directly to anyone who had a claim related to the contract.

Sir Martin explained that he had devised a simple construct which would keep everything clean: he imagined that Avigdor had

created a separate company, same ownership, but no relationship between the two. That company would be the one paying the costs incurred for the supposed project. For instance, Avigdor employees would also receive compensation from that company to the extent that was required by the nature of the work. At the same time, that company would receive payments from the government. In the end, that company was designed to operate on a strict zero net cash flow and net income.

David asked why Sir Martin had felt the need to create such an apparently complicated design. He simply replied:

"Remember David we are dealing in fantasy. None of this exists in reality. The scheme which I propose appears complex, but it is relatively easy to explain, and more importantly, it is plausible. I should add that, paradoxically, the more complex the scheme, the more challenging it should be for the buyer to poke holes in the accounts; complexity is a great excuse."

"I see. You put the complexity upfront so that downstream everything looks quite simple."

"Exactly."

Sir Martin paused and mused:

"In effect, if negotiations eventually made it a requirement that some information should be provided on that new company, it would not be hard, a few days at most, for anyone to create relevant and believable financials."

"Excellent."

Countess Renate observed:

"As you know, Gentlemen, I received the draft documents by email earlier, just like you, David and Mark. I looked at them with all the care of which I am capable and must say that I cannot distinguish them from real ones. Sir Martin, did you need to take any short-cut?"

"No. Absolutely not. We simply took the numbers we found in what I like to call the models and multiplied every entry by a factor

of one and a quarter. That is meant to ensure that even if Oleg or Yuri had seen the financials of the company behind the scheme, they would not recognize them."

He paused for a second and continued:

"I know that the so-called fixed ratio I used could be pierced if someone had both sets of documents at their fingertips. After all, since all numbers are multiplied by the same factor, it goes without saying that any financial ratio that is calculated will be exactly the same as those of the donor company. My friend, the venture capitalist, assures me that the documents used when the company went public covered a period that was different, as the model accounts I used were in fact provided to investors in the last private financing; they call it the last private round. Nobody ever saw them. So, I think whatever risk we run is minimal."

David could only agree:

"This looks absolutely great."

With his customary humility, Sir Martin replied:

"I can take credit for the idea and the sourcing, but those who did a tremendous job are your own people, David."

■ ■ ■ ■ ■

David and Mark agreed that a first next step, even before introducing Oleg to the CEO of Avigdor, would be for them to have a conversation with Oleg. They would invite him to come to *Mossad* headquarters and would show him the financials. At that time, they would have Sir Martin on a conference phone line, though he would practically be seated in an office a few doors away. His voice would definitely be disguised, though they decided they should do nothing with the British accent. After all, changing an accent electronically would be considerably more complex than just altering the tone of the voice, and it was really not needed. The idea being that he would be introduced as the potential seller's investment banker, who,

conveniently, was located in London. He would as such be able to comment on financial matters which were definitely foreign to David or Mark, but would, as had been agreed at the outset, remain totally invisible and hence unknown from Oleg's standpoint.

Oleg was excited when he walked in David's conference room. He was somewhat surprised when he heard David introduce Archibald Cormie as the investment banker. He asked for the spelling of the name, which David was happy to provide. He then asked why the gentleman was not at the table. Archibald, aka Sir Martin, simply replied that he was based in the U.K. and would only fly to Tel Aviv if his client needed him. Mischievously, he added:

"Contrary to what I hear is often done by accountants and consultants, I hate to bill time that is not really needed by our client."

Sir Martin, aka Archibald Cormie, allowed himself s quick laugh. Oleg was not finished with his preliminary questions. He asked:

"I had understood that the owner of this company was not terribly interested in selling. Now you tell me that he already has an investment banker. I'm confused."

Sir Martin replied:

"I understand your confusion. My mistake, really. In fact, your information is correct. I have not heard him indicate a desire to sell. The owner has asked me for some help. My mission, or should I say my current project, is not to help him sell the company. His current focus is on raising some more money. We are looking for debt with equity warrants, because he feels he does not want to dilute his ownership any more than needed."

"So, his balance sheet is stretched?"

Sir Martin invited everyone to look at the financial data that was in a folder in front of them. He added that these documents were for the time being totally confidential. Everyone would be expected to leave them in the folder on the table. Oleg understood that this was mostly directed toward him but was not surprised as this is perfectly

normal practice in similar circumstances. After all, why would *Mossad* officers want to keep these documents? Sir Martin took this a step further and asked that everyone keep what they were going to see to themselves. Oleg asked:

"As I'm sure you know, I would want my Chief Financial Officer to study these before agreeing to anything. Am I prohibited from doing this?"

"Oleg, may I call you Oleg?"

"Sure."

"Thank you, you may call me Archibald. In my mind, this first meeting should serve as an indication of interest. I was prepared to show you the data, because as I said a minute ago Dr. Schlossberg . . ."

He paused and corrected himself:

"I'm sorry, Dr. Schlossberg is the name of the owner."

Oleg asked for the spelling of the name, and Sir Martin revealed that his first name was Adam. Sir Martin continued:

"Dr. Schlossberg is looking for financing. So, though I do not know that he has even considered selling some or all of Avigdor, I felt it would be worth our while and yours to have this brief conversation. You look at the information which is in front of you and then tell me, with no legal engagement on your part, other than your gentleman's word, whether you are interested or not and, if you are interested, how you would value the company. Does this make sense?"

"You are. You are. Can you tell me a bit more about the company? I just stumbled on this note to the financial statement which discusses government contracts. What is that?"

Sir Martin was smiling broadly, though nobody could see him. So far, Oleg had fallen directly into the trap that was laid out for him. Sir Martin explained that the genesis of the company was in a university laboratory. Dr. Schlossberg had been working as a PhD candidate and had shown a great deal of promise. He explained that Israel had

a number of programs combining the private and the public sector when it came to advanced technology. He added:

"From what I know, Israel understands that the only way they can retain their smartest and most entrepreneurial people is to give them the same chance at fame and fortune as they would get if they were in the U.S. or a few other advanced countries."

Oleg noted that he understood and that this was quite a smart policy. With his usual humility, Sir Martin, who was increasingly enjoying the role he was playing replied:

"Totally agree, though I can't take any credit for any of it."

Sir Martin explained that the government had a model which they used in circumstances like these. In short, they initially pay the researcher until he or she could find the first external customer. Then, a joint venture would be established where the new company would contribute resources for the work required by the government, on the basis that all services are provided at cost. Oleg interrupted:

"At cost? How does he ever make money?"

"Well, that's where the private activity comes in. The inventor's company retains the right to all intellectual property."

"Wait, this does not look reasonable from the point of view of the government . . ."

"It actually is if you appreciate two important elements. The first is that the government is incubating a number of potential companies. It does not know up front which will make it, and which won't, but that's no different than any other venture capitalist. Secondly, the government also takes a 25% ownership in the new company. When you bring it all together, I'd say these are quite cheap options which the government is buying."

Oleg sat back in his chair. He truly admired the way Israel was organized and thought: *. . . that's why these guys are so advanced in cyber technology. They have to focus on the area to protect themselves; they allow their smartest people opportunities to find the right solutions;*

and they retain some ownership of those that succeed. Somebody should write a book about that.

Sir Martin was well aware that the last several minutes had drifted away from the central preoccupation of *Mossad*. He certainly knew that the goal of the meeting was not to make the Israeli government look good in Oleg's eyes. On the one hand, that part of the conversation, which was more or less true in practice though Sir Martin had dispensed with a number of nuances, was necessary to gain credibility, assuming, as he did that Oleg had at least some familiarity with it. It had demonstrated that the scenario they had constructed was believable and, to a point convincing. But, they were still no nearer hearing Oleg formulate an offer for the company. So, he asked point blank:

"Oleg, sorry to be so direct, but as an investment banker my principal concern is my client. I'm sure you'll understand. Is this something in which you would be interested?"

"As I said earlier, Archibald, I will not make a final decision without my financial guy having reviewed the finances and my technology guy having reviewed the technology. But, on the surface, this looks quite interesting."

"Glad to hear it. Let's take this further, if you were interested in buying the company, how would you go about valuing it?"

"Well, that's what difficult without Igor in the room . . ."

"Igor?"

"Sorry, Igor Zatopek, my CFO."

"I see."

"Let me turn the tables around, Archibald. How would you value this company?"

"Just like you, Oleg, it's impossible for me to go there without Dr. Schlossberg next to me. But, assuming that this year's profits will be up another 50%, which I'm told is quite probable, I think that in the

U.S. market I would most likely not price an initial public offering under $1 billion. But again, please take this as a guess."

Oleg scratched his throat but, to the surprise of David and Mark, did not seem to blink. He simply said:

"I suspect you're in the ballpark, though tech stocks have not done terribly well in the last few months, pretty much anywhere in the world."

"I'll grant you that. On the other hand, my experience suggests that private market valuations for good companies have not budged nearly as much as public market pricing."

"That's what I hear as well."

David and Mark were marveling at the exchange they were witnessing. They were as usual quite impressed by the work of Countess Renate's associates or near-associates as they did not know whether Sir Martin was or was not a member of The Shadow Experts.

CHAPTER.26

TEL AVIV, ISRAEL, ST. PETERSBURG, RUSSIA, SINGAPORE, AND SOMEWHERE IN THE AUSTRIAN ALPS

The Russian due diligence was running its course. Each of the three major Visla protagonists, Oleg, Yuri, and Igor had individually looked at the various aspects of the potential acquisition and were still seemingly quite keen to proceed. The next step clearly was having at least Oleg and Yuri, and even possibly Igor, meet the man behind the company, Dr. Adam Schlossberg, aka Nathan Sharon. The Russian trio had not initially asked for the meeting to be in St. Petersburg, which did not surprise Mark, as he would surely not have expected Oleg to agree to fly back to Russia. Mark decided to ask David's advice. He walked into his office early in the morning and was delighted to accept the cup of coffee that was offered to him.

David and Mark discussed the three most obvious alternatives: Russia, most likely St. Petersburg, the *Volga* or Tel Aviv. Russia was quickly ruled as out of the question: the risk to Oleg was way too high for the benefit he might gain. Feeling responsible for his safety, David said that he could not see himself sending him back to the wolves.

They debated the possibility of using the *Volga* but kept bumping against the same obstacle: they did not know how quickly whoever had already tried three times to kidnap Oleg could marshal their forces. They agreed that the risk was too high, and the only way to mitigate that risk would be to have a very tight *Mossad* or Israeli Navy escort, neither of which were desirable nor feasible, unless the meeting took place in international waters.

■ ■ ■ ■ ■

The waters bordering any country are divided into three distinct zones: the territorial sea which extends 12 miles from the shore; the contiguous zone with extends another 12 miles beyond the territorial waters; and the exclusive economic zone which extends 176 miles beyond the contiguous zone. While the *Volga* could be in any country's exclusive economic zone and not be subject to the law of that country, there would still be a need for helicopters to ferry all different parties at least 24 miles out to sea.

■ ■ ■ ■ ■

Mark came to the obvious conclusion:

"Using the *Volga* would involve way too many roundtrips for the trouble to make sense."

The advantage of Tel Aviv was indeed overwhelming. *Mossad* could argue it had virtually full control over the situation, particularly as Oleg could easily have "officially" hired a bodyguard or two. Nobody needed to know that these were *Mossad* agents. David added:

"Not to mention that Tel Aviv is a natural location given where Avigdor is supposed to be located."

The decision behind them, they then proceeded on planning the meeting so that it would take place in what might be a regular office and still allow *Mossad* to control the environment. Finding an office space which would be simultaneously big enough and not too big was

not difficult. *Mossad* controlled enough space within Tel Aviv and its immediate suburbs that they had plenty of choice. They selected a building which was easy to secure, all the while otherwise totally innocuous. The office was supposed to be the Tel Aviv office of Avigdor, though most of their engineers were supposed to work from the Technology Park, near Ben Gurion University of the Negev. Mark commissioned a graphics designer to create a corporate Logo which would be displayed behind the receptionist. All the personnel staffing the office worked for *Mossad*, and all were given a briefing on what they were supposed to do and say and a clear set of instructions as to what they were not supposed to discuss.

■ ■ ■ ■ ■

A while earlier, after he had spoken with Archibald Cormie, aka Sir Martin, Oleg organized a phone conference call with Yuri, who insisted that Igor should be brought into the picture. Oleg had agreed to having him in the meeting and had asked Yuri to be sure to brief him. Oleg opened the meeting:

"My friends, I got my first chance to look at the financials of the company which is of interest to us. By the way, I know its name at present: Avigdor Cyber Experts."

Igor was totally in character when he asked:

"What did you find out?"

Oleg deadpanned:

"Well, I can tell you one of two things and they'd both be correct. First, I could say that I found out a lot. They gave me all the time I needed to look at the financials, three years' worth of financials . . ."

"Balance sheet, statement of profit and loss and cash flows?"

"Exactly. I was told that they had been audited but was not shown the audit certificate."

Igor kept leading the questions:

"Why?"

Oleg replied:

"They're playing it quite close to the vest. They said I could check the website, and I did. Very little information of any interest is available. Believe it or not they don't disclose their Board of Directors."

Igor could only ask:

"That doesn't pass the smell test, does it, Oleg?"

"Well, my friend, that's where things get a bit complicated. I learned that the company is still private. I was told by their investment banker . . ."

"Investment banker?"

"Yes, Igor. They have an investment banker because they are working on a first round of external financing, private debt with equity warrants, I'm told."

Igor simply nodded, but his body language, if Oleg could have seen it, was definitely not very supportive. Oleg continued:

"As I was saying, their investment banker says that they are neither looking to sell, nor do they want more equity capital. They want to avoid dilution. Their statement of profit and losses helps understand the situation: they are in a positive cash flow situation, though not by a lot."

"How can that be?"

"I asked. The answer which was half given . . ."

"Half given?"

"Yes, more of a suggestion that an outright statement, Igor. They have contracts with the Israeli government. There is a note to the financial statements that explains how that relationship works, but I suspect you could drive a massive truck through it. In short, I bet you that they have been subsidized by the government. As I understand the scheme, the government effectively awards them contracts in a way that, practically though that's not the stated purpose, help cover a good part of the overheads. By the way, I also found out that the Israeli government owns 25% of the company."

Igor said almost triumphantly:

"Now we are getting somewhere."

Oleg replied:

"True enough. But what this means is that whatever data we get will by nature be limited. They've clearly told me that whatever was taking place with the government would stay in Israel and remain secret."

Igor had to ask:

"Why don't we simply give up?"

That was the point when Yuri thought he needed to take over a large part of the discussion:

"As I told you, Igor, their intellectual property is simply beyond what we now know. It could certainly help us develop a much more powerful virus scan service. We could leapfrog ourselves, so to speak."

He paused for a second and continued:

"However, the other day, I had a thought. Sorry Oleg; didn't call you with it. I figured we would talk about it when the time was ripe. I guess this is now!"

Oleg simply replied to Yuri that it was not a problem. Their main goal, in his eyes, was still to get to the right conclusion. Yuri continued:

"This intellectual property and more specifically the ability to anticipate virus mutations through artificial intelligence could also help us on the offensive side. We all know that the government wants to use cyberspace as a fighting ground. Imagine what we could do if we're ahead of the game with virus creation . . ."

Oleg thought for a few seconds and decided that he should reply, but not give his exact feelings. To him, cyber warfare was not a pleasant thought, nor something in which he wanted to be known as the offense. He liked to play defense but did not feel that he wanted to be among those who made it more powerful. He simply said:

"Interesting thought, Yuri. Where are you with respect to the technology?"

"The only thing I've seen is the demonstration and I was blown away."

Igor asked:

"Could there be a trap in there?"

Yuri replied:

"Sure. There can always be traps. But, I did not see anything untoward as they were working with my computer. Oleg, do you think you could ask them to do another demonstration but this time with Igor's computer?"

Igor jumped up:

"What's wrong with my computer?"

Yuri matter-of-factly replied:

"Nothing other than the fact that there is a virus in it and that our software and any other commercial software I've tried hasn't been able find it."

"How long have you known that?"

"Not much more than a week to ten days . . ."

"Come on guys. Why didn't you bring me into the loop?"

Oleg decided to take care of the reply:

"Quite simply because all our computers and servers and also those of a few of our customers are infected. Still, with our role and position in the market, do you really want to go public without having a solution? I brought Yuri into the loop simply because of his position as our technology guru. I didn't feel you needed to know."

Igor mumbled a few words but quickly realized that Yuri and Oleg had done exactly what they needed to do. Oleg asked:

"What do you guys need to support going to the next step?"

Igor replied:

"Do you mean what due diligence do we need to do, or what do we need to do before we start our due diligence?"

Oleg snapped back:

"The latter. By the way, let us not assume anything as we speak. We may not be able to keep going. They may not be willing to sell to us."

He was going to continue when Yuri interrupted:

"I'd like us to keep digging to find out how we can get access to the intellectual property. After all, owning the company would be great, but having the intellectual property is really what we're after . . ."

■ ■ ■ ■ ■

"Welcome to Avigdor, gentlemen."

With these words, Dr. Adam Schlossberg, aka Nathan Sharon, was welcoming Oleg Nichakov, Yuri Vassiliev, and Igor Zatopek to the office which *Mossad* had created for the non-existent company. A charming receptionist was sitting behind a counter with a blueish glass partition behind her; on that partition was the logo of the company; Mark and his team had not tried to be overly creative: it simply had the full name of the company in both English and Hebrew characters. The text in Hebrew was shorter than in English and was read from right to left. The space left free under "Avigdor" was filled by a symbol representing the Eye of Horus. Originally found in Egyptian mythology, the symbol includes a stylized eye, an eyebrow, a dark line extending behind the right corner of the eye and a line extending diagonally below and toward the rear of the eye, ending in a curl. Ancient Egyptian religion associated well-being, healing and, more importantly protection with the symbol: it fit perfectly with the name Avigdor and more importantly the purported purpose of Avigdor. The Russian group was quite impressed when Dr. Schlossberg explained the connection between the logo and the purpose and mission of the company.

The Russian trio was shown to the conference room, with three of the four walls made of glass. Confidentiality could be ensured at the flip of a switch. The glass which was normally fully translucid would then cloud up and prevent anyone inside from seeing outside, and vice versa. Adam introduced the people that were with him to Yuri and Igor:

"I'm sure you know Oleg Nichakov who does not need any introduction. On my right is Mark my bodyguard and personal secretary. I do not go anywhere without him."

He paused and pointing to the speakers on the table, he added:

"We have two people on the phone with me. Archibald Cormie, my investment banker, and Tony Ho, my right-hand technology man."

Mark discreetly tapped Nathan's foot to let him know that Yuri was looking at him intently. Adam picked up the hint and asked point blank:

"Anything wrong, Yuri?"

"No. No, nothing. It's just that I feel as if I know you. Your face looks familiar. Have we met before?"

Adam did not miss a beat:

"Could very well be. I attend as many conferences as I can. Maybe our paths crossed once or twice. If we did and I did not recognize you please allow me to apologize. I am not gifted with a great memory for faces."

With that, his face broke into a charming smile. Yuri smiled right back.

■ ■ ■ ■ ■

Prior to the meeting, Mark and his colleagues at *Mossad* had made sure that Nathan would wear a disguise that would make him at best hard to recognize if not unrecognizable. The first, and simplest change involved him growing a beard. By the time of the meeting, it had grown fully and framed his mouth, whose lips had

been slightly enlarged with the cosmetic developed by the agency. It was a mix of Botox-like substance and fat filler which was meant to accentuate certain features of the face to help agents look as different as they could without having permanent cosmetic surgery. The effect of the drug usually lasted no longer than two weeks, and, when applied to zones which absorbed the fat faster, as little as a week. While Nathan used the substance to make his lips fuller, other agents could use it to alter the shape of their chin. Though Nathan would not normally wear glasses, Mark had also provided him with black-rimmed hexagonal glasses.

Mark had also organized for Hai Chock, aka Tony Ho, to be on standby so that, if needed, he could demonstrate his prowess with Igor's computer. Mark had anticipated that it might well become a necessary exercise when any request by Yuri or Igor to have access to the intellectual property, or to the company's software engineers would be politely declined. Being known as Jim Ng to Oleg, Hai Chock had to use a different pseudonym: Tony Ho. He would be using a "voice box" on his telephone so that Oleg could not recognize the voice of Jim Ng, with which he was familiar. Together with Countess Renate, the group had agreed that Tony Ho would be introduced as an employee of the company rather than as a consultant. They had decided that Nathan would position himself as the "genial inventor" who recognized he needed some assistance from another super-software specialist. They would argue that Tony Ho, aka Jim Ng, aka Hai Chock, would be presented as a software programming genius.

Sir Martin, aka Archibald Cormie would also be on the line to answer any detailed questions on the documents and the financials of Avigdor. Next to him would sit another *Mossad* agent who had first worked in the finance industry. He would be positioned as the current banker to the company. Unbeknownst to the Russian delegation, including Oleg, all the individuals on the line would be seated in another office nearby and would have access to a video of

the main conference room. They, on the other hand, could not be seen by the Russian delegation. Countess Renate and David would "attend" the conference as well, in a totally silent mode on their parts, though they too would have access to the video feed.

CHAPTER.27

TEL AVIV, ISRAEL, ST. PETERSBURG, RUSSIA, SINGAPORE, AND SOMEWHERE IN THE AUSTRIAN ALPS

Adam, aka Nathan, opened the meeting with a proposal:

"Igor, you are the only one who had not seen the software at work, correct?"

"Yes."

"Would you like my colleague, Tony, to demonstrate it on your computer?"

"Demonstrate what?"

Adam asked Igor to switch his laptop on, which he immediately did. He then suggested that he connect to the wi-fi system. He asked him to look for a network called "AvigdorGuest" and, once he had found him, told him to use the password "SpecialTest." Once done, Adam asked again:

"Now, Igor, do you have a virus scan software on your laptop?"

"Sure."

"Well, may I invite you to have it scan your computer right away?"

Igor did not look surprised when the results of the test came out: "No virus on this computer."

Adam smiled and said:

"Excellent."

He added:

"Now, would you mind allowing Tony to connect to your computer remotely?"

Igor initially hesitated. Though not himself a technology expert, he knew that many things can be done to a computer remotely, and in the words of a famous U.S. college football coach, Woody Hayes, two out of three of them are bad. He explicitly asked Yuri for his advice; it came straight back—he was safe. So, though with a definite lack of enthusiasm, Igor replied:

"Go right ahead . . . I guess."

People in the room could clearly see that Igor did not seem to be enjoying the exercise, but he was in a position where he could not refuse. Tony, aka Hai Chock, connected to Igor's computer. This is when Yuri sprung his surprise on Tony. He said:

"I hope you will not take it the wrong way, but I thought that there could be a sleight of hand in there."

He was being careful not to come out directly with his concerns and doing so to risk alienating the potential seller. He continued:

"Is there a way that you could slow down the speed at which everything appears on the screen? I want to follow more carefully what happens when you connect to Igor's computer."

Hai Chock immediately understood that Yuri had imagined one of their tricks: the insertion of a virus into the computer as he was erasing the first all the while pretending to be connecting. Thankfully, both he and Nathan had anticipated this contingency. He replied:

"Well, I'm not sure I can slow down a processor inside the computer. But we can do better than that. Tell you what. Why don't you all see if you can take a video of the screen. You will then be able to replay it at a much slower speed and read every line of code as it appears."

Yuri beamed when Dr. Schlossberg replied to Tony that it should not be a problem. While connecting, Tony, aka Hai Chock, managed to carry out exactly the same steps as earlier though they did not all appear on the screen. Accordingly, while connecting, he removed the original virus he had placed and replaced it with a less stealthy variant. Adam asked Igor again:

"Would you mind re-running your virus scan."

"Why?"

Tony replied on the conference phone line:

"Just to confirm that my connection did not infect your computer."

Slightly exasperated but in no position to decline, Igor went ahead. The outcome of the test was the same: no virus. Tony, aka Hai Chock, then explained that he was going to run the special virus-scan software. He went ahead with his scan. Igor's face betrayed complete disbelief when the verdict came in: a message appeared on the screen that showed that at least one abnormal file had been detected. Tony then offered to eliminate the virus, a request which Igor could not turn down. He took advantage of the operation to reinsert a variant of the earlier virus which Igor had no means of picking up, in that following exactly the same routine he and Nathan had used for Oleg and Yuri.

If anything, the technical demonstration served to close any discussion as to the value of Avigdor's intellectual property. Yuri's minor objection fell by the wayside, and he became a vocal open supporter of the technology. More important for Mark, and David, was the fact that nobody noticed anything untoward in the presentation of the supposed virus scan. David had expressed some concern with the fact that Hai Chock was going to have to take on a third "personality." In particular, with the conversations held in English, he was concerned that two of the three software experts, the third being Adam, aka Nathan, had a detectable Chinese accent. Mark had

argued that technology specialists would spend more time focused on the software than on anything else and had been proven correct.

Oleg started the negotiations in earnest when he asked Adam:

"As you know, Dr. Schlossberg, we are here to discuss the potential acquisition of your company. Before going any further, it begs a crucial question: are you willing to sell the company to us?"

Adam took his time to reply, listening to coaching by Sir Martin. He replied:

"To be honest, I have not yet made up my mind. There are several issues which would need to be brought out in the open."

Oleg asked:

"Would you mind helping us understand them?"

"No problem. However, I need you and your colleagues to understand that a couple of thoughts may appear aggressive vis-à-vis Russia. It is not my intention to offend. Still, we cannot ignore the elephant in the room."

He paused and seeing Oleg and his colleagues nod, he continued:

"The most important issue relates to the buyer, or should I say the potential buyer, being Russian. In the current geopolitical environment, this is definitely not a plus."

Oleg replied:

"Can't fault you for that."

Oleg did not notice that both Yuri and Igor seemed a bit surprised that he would have capitulated so quickly on that one. Neither felt that there was any mileage pushing back against the obvious challenge. Oleg offered that there had to be a way around the problem. Adam continued:

"Let me give you what I'll call the second headline. We do quite a bit of business with the Israeli government. I can't imagine the government maintaining the relationship if we were sold."

Sir Martin whispered in his ear that he should remember how the financials were presented. Adam added:

"In reality, as you know, the pro-forma financials exclude the government business. So, you would have to determine whether you would be prepared to let certain employees continue to work for the Israeli government, and in effect partially outside of Avigdor . . ."

Oleg had to ask:

"Would that include you or Tony Ho whom you presented as your right-hand man?"

"Could!"

Yuri jumped into the fray and simply argued:

"Gentleman, to me this is the hardest issue. I cannot imagine having a subsidiary which would be outside of our control in certain areas. How could that work?"

Sir Martin gave Nathan another thought. Adam asked:

"Why do you want to own the whole company? Why not simply ask for a license to the software?"

■ ■ ■ ■

Mark had rehearsed that phase of the conversation with Countess Renate, David, Nathan and Sir Martin. They had agreed that they should try and get as much money as they could from Visla Cybersecurity, all the while remembering that they were doing it for two different purposes. First, they wanted to weaken its financial condition to slow its ability to keep helping Russian allies in the Middle East. Second, they wanted to help Oleg, who was not in the loop, to get as much money as possible from his financial assets still in Russia. They would have liked to generate close to $1 billion but had agreed that they might have to be satisfied with less.

■ ■ ■ ■

Yuri was again the first to react:

"That could in fact be a much more attractive scenario, Adam. How could that work?"

Nathan waited until Sir Martin had finished giving him the hints he needed and then said:

"Well, from our point of view, the only issue is that a standard license agreement would not be feasible?"

Igor asked:

"Why?"

"Again, I do not want to offend you Igor but the idea that we would receive both an initial payment and then a royalty flow makes little sense. No offense again, but how could we verify the basis on which the royalties would be calculated?"

Igor with a mock smile on his face conceded:

"You're not pulling your punches, are you."

He paused for a second a seemingly reluctantly added:

"But we understand."

Yuri added:

"I don't know how Oleg and Igor would react, but I would be willing to consider a single upfront payment. However, would that give us access to the artificial intelligence element?"

Prompted by Sir Martin, Nathan replied:

"Could be. I suspect that we would first sell the software and then offer to train one or several of your engineers on what you call the artificial intelligence part of it. Remember, this is a second process that helps populate the virus database with the variants most likely to come up."

Yuri asked further:

"So, initially, your software would come without the database..."

"Yes. But there would be a commitment to help you build our process into your own database as soon as you have started using the software. I assume you already have such a database, correct?"

Yuri immediately replied:

"We sure do."

He then asked if Igor, Oleg, and he could use a nearby conference room to discuss the matter among themselves.

■ ■ ■ ■ ■

While Oleg and his team were discussing the new development, Mark, Nathan and Hai Chock stayed in the original conference room, allowing those whose phone lines had been muted to speak. David was the first to ask a question:

"Nathan and Hai Chock, how would your idea work in practice?"

Hai Chock who was more used to these kinds of geopolitical maneuvers than Nathan suggested:

"Quite simple in reality. First, we create a simple virus scan program. That's very easy as there are plenty of them in the public domain. Second, we connect that software to a virus database, which again is not hard as they exist in the public domain. I would suggest making sure that it does not include the virus we have put into their systems, but aside from that, we're talking a couple of day's work, not more."

David continued:

"Now, what about the training you're offering?"

Sir Martin cut into the conversation:

"Gentlemen, I suspect you should assume that they're either going to ask for more than simple training on your so-called artificial intelligence or won't offer anywhere near what you want to get?"

Mark asked:

"What does that mean?"

Sir Martin simply replied:

"Commitment to training . . ."

Mark deadpanned:

"A promise, right?"

Sir Martin agreed.

Countess Renate threw a major curve ball in the conversation:

"Should you not tell Oleg what there is for him to gain in this?"

David replied that he and Mark had considered that option and, initially at least, decided against it because they wanted to make sure Oleg would behave exactly as his colleagues were used to seeing him behave. Countess Renate conceded, but asked further:

"But how can he be expected to react naturally when he is currently trying to extricate himself from Russia?"

"Excellent point, Countess. Our bet is that the current Russian environment might very well evolve to the extent that he might be prepared to consider a return to the homeland at some point."

Countess Renate seemed to "buy" Mark's logic. David surprisingly pushed Mark a bit further:

"Given what we have planned for Oleg, does it really make sense?"

"On the surface no, but he doesn't know, does he?"

CHAPTER.28

TEL AVIV, ISRAEL, ST. PETERSBURG, RUSSIA, SINGAPORE, SOMEWHERE IN THE AUSTRIAN ALPS AND RHODES, GREECE

When the Russian trio returned to the main conference room, they appeared to be all smiles. Oleg summarized their conclusions:

"We are prepared to agree to buy a license with a unique upfront payment. You would commit to provide us with training on the artificial intelligence dimension of your invention immediately."

Adam, aka Nathan, replied:

"This sounds totally reasonable. Next, have you discussed the nature of the offer you are prepared to extend?"

Igor took the lead:

"We have discussed it. However, we wanted to have a better sense of your expectations before finalizing our offer."

Adam, listening carefully to the coaching in his ear by Sir Martin, replied:

"Let me set a few parameters first. Clearly, the purchase has to be for cash, in U.S. Dollars or Shekels, though I suspect that U.S. Dollars would be simpler for you. Also, I would prefer the payment to be made offshore. I am not sure I want Israeli authorities to know

that a license has been granted to a Russian company. So better for the funds not to transit through Israel. Finally, I believe that the price we should eventually agree on should relate to the current value of the company. After all, this is our most precious resource. When you have it, there will only be two firms that have access to it: you and us. Since we would agree to provide both the software and training, I think the bidding should start at something above 50% of the current value of Avigdor."

Igor opened and closed his mouth a couple of times. As he had previously when taking to Oleg, Yuri had warned the group in their small separate conference that the price would probably be steep. Igor did not expect Adam to be so direct. He still had to reply:

"How do you value the company?"

Adam was listening to Sir Martin who offered to reply in his stead. He was all too happy to accept the offer:

"Archibald Cormie here, Gentlemen; I am the merchant banking advisor to Dr. Schlossberg. I believe that you have the financials, which should serve as the basis for your valuation. Of course, I have a view based on experience, but we feel that you also should develop your own view. Let's face it, there have been enough transactions in the space for anyone to be able to develop some reasonable range."

Igor countered:

"I have not been as active in the initial public offering space as you have been, but, nevertheless, it seems to me that Avigdor would probably be valued around $250 million. Would you disagree?"

"Different people come to different views. Still, I would have to tell you that, speaking for our client for a moment, I don't believe he would entertain a transaction in the price range you mention. Frankly, my estimates would have likely started at a level at least three times higher than the value you mention."

Archibald, aka Sir Martin, paused for effect and then added:

"Does it mean that we are too far away from each other for this conversation to proceed?"

Igor was looking around the room to look for a sign from Yuri and Oleg. Whatever they had agreed among the three of them must have allowed him to continue the negotiation, as he replied:

"We are indeed far away, at the outset, but we could close the gap, assuming you're willing to entertain a counteroffer."

He paused for a second and asked:

"I'm pretty sure that we could not reach anywhere near the figure you mention, but is there any wiggle room on your side, Archibald?"

Archibald simply replied:

"I don't believe that this is the time or the place for us to conduct direct negotiations, but I'm encouraged if you agree we should continue. Could you give us an indication of how you would go from the valuation of the company to the price you'd be prepared to pay for the perpetual right to use the software subject to some minimum training requirement?"

▪▪■▪▪

After the negotiations had gone back and forth, with each new round requiring some additional piece of information, the parties settled on a $350 million price tag, unfortunately quite a fair bit away from the $1 billion Mark had initially envisaged. Countess Renate organized for her associate Hans Koerig, the Head of the Globale PrivatBank in Vienna, to open an account that could receive the funds and then disburse them.

▪▪■▪▪

Oleg had decided to organize a party onboard the *Volga* to celebrate with the appropriate flourish the purchase of the technology from Avigdor Cyber Experts by Visla Cybersecurity. He had invited a number of people who knew him in his capacity of founder of

Visla Cybersecurity, mostly from Moscow or St. Petersburg. He had also invited the key executives from the company, starting with Yuri Vassiliev but extending to Vladimir Kroshenko, the head of security, and Igor Zakopek, the Chief Financial Officer. The guest list was of course limited by the capacity of the ship, though no one was expecting to spend the night. Oleg had also invited Mark and David to attend, though only Mark proved to be available. Finally, Nathan, still in his heavy disguise posing as Dr. Adam Schlosberg was also on the guest list, as one would of course expect.

The guests had boarded at Mandraki, the main harbor of Rhodes, the largest among the famous Dodecanese Islands in the Aegean Sea. In antiquity, Rhodes was the island where the Colossus of Rhodes was standing, reputedly as tall as today's Statue of Liberty in New York City. A couple of statues of deer, named Elefos and Elafina, stand at present where the famously weak feet of the Colossus were. The harbor is protected from the sea, which can at times be somewhat rough, by walls originally erected to protect the city from invaders. Today, the castle of Saint Nicholaos, named after the patron saint of seamen, can still be seen dominating the landscape, though its role has evolved from that of a formidable defender of the city to a mere lighthouse.

The plan was to navigate around a part of the island, whose coastline approximates 120 nautical miles. They were going to sail about twenty miles to the east of the entrance of the harbor and then turnaround and come back. The ship would not be cruising anywhere near full speed, if only so that the ride provided to the guests would be as comfortable as possible. They knew that whatever speed was selected had to depend on the weather conditions on the day, sea swell, wind direction and wind speed among others. After all, guests were to be able to sip cocktails and eat a fancy dinner without having the *Volga* being tossed about because of too high a speed given difficult seas. Anton had been instructed to set the route and select

the U-turn point so that the cruise would last a bit less than four hours.

■ ■ ■ ■ ■

Somewhat before that celebratory cruise could take place in Rhodes, Mark and David had to take care that everything was organized as well as could be and down to the smallest detail. They both knew that this could be the culminating point of this project. Meeting in David's office a week ahead of the scheduled date, David first congratulated Mark on a well-run execution of the whole plan. The latest developments had served to convince all and sundry that Oleg was for real: he was not a plant. He was a true oligarch who was afraid of the Russian regime and was prepared to leave some of his wealth behind in order to save his life. Mark had at some point told Oleg that the measures he had taken after his marriage to Irina had led to a long period of suspicion on *Mossad*'s part, though it proved to have been an excellent precaution from Oleg's point of view. Oleg conceded that he could see how the suspicion could arise and lamented that there was nothing he could possibly do about it, other than play along in as forthright a way as he could. He added:

"Any effort to try and convince you otherwise early on would likely have made matters worse."

Mark surprised him with his reply:

"When did you start playing chess?"

"Quite young. Quite young. I still do by the way, but I mostly play on the computer; neither Irina nor either of the children play the game at this point. Frankly, this has helped me pass the time during this forced exile."

He was of course referring to the current situation where he was prisoner in the golden prison which his penthouse in Tel Aviv constituted.

David asked Mark the crucial question:

"What is your plan if something goes awry during the *Volga* cruise?

Mark replied that there were not one, but two plans, which, he conceded with a wry smile, were named at a time when he was clearly lacking imagination or at least inspiration: Plan A and Plan B. David smiled back and added:

"You might live to bless the time you made that simple choice. First, you're unlikely ever to confuse them or forget the name, and second you can bark it quite quickly if needed. Nobody would necessarily guess what is about to happen."

Mark expanded on his plans. He started with the premise that the key issue had to be some harm being inflicted on Oleg. He added:

"Frankly, I would be totally baffled if nobody tried anything. This could well be their last chance, particularly since they think they have gotten everything they needed or wanted."

David simply replied:

"Agreed."

Mark then made the point that the major difference between the two plans therefore involved the nature of the danger faced by Oleg. Plan A was designed to deal with real danger in the moment: it required immediate protection to be deployed whatever the consequences. Plan B would respond to the identification of something that could quickly develop into a dangerous situation, though the danger was not imminent: it would allow some more time, though, as he said:

"We're taking minutes, not hours."

He added:

"And that is good because Plan B requires more resources to be marshalled, both onboard and in the immediate vicinity of the *Volga*."

He went on to explain in a great deal of detail the various components of the plans, which though relatively straightforward did require Israel to provide quite a high level of protection. The major complicating factor was that Israel's protection would have to remain

invisible to anyone. Ostensibly, it should remain invisible to the guests onboard the Volga: whoever was going to do something would not act, if they suspected anything. Mark would therefore have missed at least this opportunity to complete the mission as both he and David understood it. Importantly as well, though, the protection was being provided within Greek territorial waters; hence, whatever was happening should not be visible to the Greek authorities. *Mossad* was not about to take the risk of a diplomatic incident!

■ ■ ■ ■ ■

The cruise had started with a small, but beautiful bang, literally. Oleg had organized a small fireworks display to be fired from the seawall next to Saint Nicholaos castle, as soon as the yacht had gone past the harbor markers and the low wake zone that is the norm within the channel. The yacht was still sailing slowly, and all passengers had been invited to congregate on the port side of the vessel as the cruise was going to start with the vessel sailing toward the east. The yacht had mildly accelerated but was still not sailing any faster than 5 knots. Only once the fireworks were over could everyone feel the yacht picking up some speed as guests were ushered to the reception suite on the main deck. A string quartet had been set to perform at the top of the copper and bronze staircase that led from the reception suite on the main deck to its continuation on the promenade deck just above. It created a sort of two-story atrium and had a crystal chandelier hanging in its middle. The string quartet was playing classical music with a few traditional Russian folk songs in-between. An appetizer buffet had been set up to allow guest to munch on delicacies, including Russian caviar, while sipping their favorite drinks, be they vodka, champagne, ouzo, or any other form of hard liquor.

The plan was to move everyone to the main dining room where a fancy dinner would be served about an hour after the start of the

cocktail party. By the time the dinner finished, liquors would be offered anew in the reception suites, with petit fours and chocolates for those who still had room to eat anything. A dance floor was available for those guests who felt like dancing, at which point the instructions to the string quartet were to play solely folk music to which people could dance.

■ ■ ■ ■ ■

Cristian who was still serving onboard suddenly stopped dead in his steps. He was looking at one of the guests who was chatting with Igor Zakopek. Initially, he could not believe his eyes, but the more he looked, trying not to be seen to be staring, the more he became convinced he had seen the face of the guest earlier. His immediate reaction was to seek Mark among the still relatively small crowd. As he was looking for Mark, he maintained as carefully as he could, a demeanor which would fit a guest who enjoys speaking with other guests.

A "flash of lightning" hit him as he saw Mark from the corner of his eye. He had just managed to put if not a name at least an identity on the guest speaking to Igor Zatopek. He thought *the guy speaking to Igor is the guy I pistol-whipped onboard in Marbella.* The sailor had clearly been released from prison as expected and rejoined his master as quickly as he could. Mark was a bit surprised that his master would have used him again, but he assumed that the leader of the pirates had stuck with the initial explanation that the sailor must have lost his balance and hit his head against something onboard, probably a piece of furniture.

Cristian shared his "discovery" with Mark, who simply replied:

"Plan B in fifteen minutes. In the meantime, follow Oleg like a shadow. On my end, I'll do the same, but first I need to set in motion everything that should occur beyond the yacht through David. Nobody saw Mark make a quick phone call to David who smiled

when he heard: "Plan B in fifteen minutes." David had a number of pieces he needed to coordinate. Mark, on his end, only needed to wait, watch over Oleg and a couple of minutes before the onset of Plan B to lead Oleg to the terrace on the lower stern deck.

■ ■ ■ ■ ■

Guests were surprised when they heard the sound of voices which seemed certainly not to be in agreement. Harsh words were being said, and voices were operating at maximum volume. They recognized one of them as being Oleg's. Very soon thereafter, they heard another voice joining the other two. Those who knew him recognized Anton's. As people were congregating on the part of the main deck overlooking the lower stern deck, they could clearly see that a dispute was underway. A man was holding a gun and pointing it at Oleg. Anton was trying to come to Oleg's help but was kept at bay by the constant menace of the gun.

Eventually, a shot was fired. Oleg, who was close to the gunwale when he was hit, fell on it. The shooter who had come quite close to him pushed him overboard. Anton immediately rushed toward the man. He did not have a gun at the ready, but he was planning on overpowering him. As Anton approached the man, he side stepped to his right; Anton's momentum sent him falling on the gunwale as well. The man shot him in the back and pushed his body overboard.

As guests were trying to intervene and security closed in on the man who shot Oleg and Anton, he jumped overboard too. In a matter of two minutes, all the action that was taking place on the lower stern deck had been replaced by an eerie void, only broken by voices screaming a variety of instructions which nobody heard or noticed. After he had instructed his second in command to place an emergency call to the harbor police, the first mate had ordered the engines of the Volga to be turned to idle and the propellors to neutral. The yacht was moving increasingly slowly. The first mate

asked both engines to be thrown into reverse for ten seconds to bring the vessel to a complete stop. Several crewmembers congregated on the back terrace and on the side of the boat using both fixed and mobile projectors to scan the surface of the water. The water was clear enough that the light from the projectors penetrated probably ten feet or so into the water, allowing some ability to look for anything floating immediately below the surface. The crew moved around the stern of the boat to look on the other side of the yacht, thinking that the one individual they were sure was alive and well when he jumped into the water could very well have decided to swim away from the scene. Though the sea was relatively calm, the search did not reveal anything as to the whereabouts of the assassin or the two victims.

The man who had shot the two Russians had chosen not to surface. He had slipped on a self-contained underwater breathing device, comprising two mini compressed gas cylinders and a mouthpiece. While most people believe that the device is just a movie prop which has no ability to work in practice, *Mossad* had managed to make it work, though in fairness the reservoirs provided hardly more than ten minutes of breathing assistance, if that. As the crew of the *Volga* had surmised, he had swum underwater in the direction of the shore, as the two people he had pushed overboard had fallen away from shore, on the port side of the yacht. He was met a couple of hundred meters away by a Zodiac semi-inflatable boat which was sailing without any light. The motor was kept operating at relatively low speed to minimize any sound that could be heard from that direction. The shooter was provided assistance climbing onboard and the Zodiac sailed away still without the engine's revs exceeding 3,000 rpm, again to control its noise. It actually sped up as soon as the captain was convinced that nobody could hear the engine noise with enough strength to be able to gauge the direction from which the noise came. He was also careful to avoid a couple of projectors he could see coming toward the *Volga* in the distance; he thought and

was correct in his assessment that they belonged to police boats which the first mate would have called.

Nobody knows for sure, but there is a very good chance that nobody on board the *Volga* saw that part of the action.

The two people who had been "killed" and pushed overboard thankfully "resuscitated" as soon as they hit the water. Nobody knew that the gun which the assassin had been using was loaded with blanks, the "bullets" being nothing more than a small cartridge of animal blood mixed with ketchup. They too had been provided with the same underwater breathing device as the wood-be assassin. They both pressed on a small button on their belts as they had been instructed to do. It triggered a small light which was only visible from below; consequently, anyone watching from the Volga could still not see anything in the water, all the more so as the ship was still sailing away, albeit quite slowly, from the spot where it had been at the time of the accident.

Two underwater scooters were in the immediate vicinity. They had shadowed the *Volga* as soon as Plan B had been ordered into action. They closed in on Oleg and Anton. They motioned each of them to join them astride the scooters, where they had the opportunity to trade their emergency breathing device for a full scuba-grade oxygen apparatus. It provided them with both the mouthpiece and a full-face mask, substantially enhancing their comfort. Oleg and Anton noticed that they were not going anywhere closer to the surface, but actually were diving; that was in keeping with the scenario which had been painted to them. Soon, however, they saw a big, massive grey hull which they immediately recognized to be the belly of the submarine they had been told to expect. The two sailors driving the scooters guided them to the entry to the air lock. The two scooters floated in with their four passengers. Oleg and Anton could see that the two men who piloted the scooters were equipped with wet suits and full, two-tank breathing apparatus. They, on the other hand, were still in

their street clothes, which were totally soaked and stuck to their skin in places. They were given towels and escorted to meet captain Ayel, who commanded the *INS Storm*. He welcomed them onboard, but immediately said:

"I'm sorry that we can't patch you to *Mossad* headquarters and David Heller quite yet. For us to be able to initiate that conversation, we would need to surface, and we can't do this for as long as we are in Greek territorial waters. We'll send a message by sonar. The message will be picked up by one of our surface ships and Colonel Heller will be informed as soon as possible."

He paused and then added:

"I suspect you need a shower and dry clothes. I hope you won't mind wearing an Israeli Navy work uniform, as that's all we have onboard. I'm sure we'll find a couple that fit you."

He let go a healthy laugh. Oleg asked:

"What's the plan? Where are we going?"

"At this point, the plan is to stay submerged for a while. There is a fast surface ship which is tracking us. The plan is to transfer you onto it as soon as feasible. He will navigate much faster than we and should get you to Tel Aviv in a day or so. Do any of you gentlemen have family?"

Anton replied first:

"Unfortunately, not—though here it might be fortunately not."

Oleg simply said:

"As Oleg Nichakov I don't, but under my other name, I do."

"Could anyone from the yacht or outside of our colleagues inform them of the accident?"

"No. Nobody knows of their existence or their whereabouts."

■ ■ ■ ■ ■

Back on the Volga, Mark and Nathan, aka Adam Schlossberg, were congregating with the other guests and what was left of the

crew. The first mate who had brought the ship to a virtual complete stop continued to scan the water surface on the port side, with the help of two large search lights. The ship was less than a half hour away from the entrance to the harbor, if that. So, they did not have to wait long before two police boats appeared in the distance and soon had reached the yacht. One of them moored to the stern of the Volga near the swimming platform using a rope. The gate in the stern gunwale had been opened by a crewmember allowing two uniformed policemen to come onboard. They asked first to talk to the first mate. He gave them a list of all the guests together with a roster of the crew. The police dutifully matched everyone who was still on the boat to either of the lists. That is when the news came out that Oleg and Anton were indeed missing, as was one of the sailors, the one named Cristian. The first mate exclaimed:

"Could that all be part of a ploy since the beginning?"

The most senior police officer picked up on the comment and asked the first mate to explain what he meant. He went through the full story of a sailor "falling sick" in Marbella, of Cristian offering his services and staying onboard because the doctors who had treated the sailor had recommended that he should take some rest. The first mate had to look for the crew records but was eventually able to provide the registered home address of the "sick sailor."

When it was Mark's turn to be interviewed, he explained that he was the bodyguard of Dr. Adam Schlossberg whose company's sale of a license to the late Mr. Nichakov's firm was the reason for the party. The conversation with Dr. Schlossberg lasted a while longer, though he of course confirmed all that Mark had said. While the police officers were interrogating the guests and crew onboard, the other boat went to search for any trace of one or two survivors if the gun shots had not been sufficient to kill them. They eventually called off the search, took down its coordinates and organized for the effort

to be restarted as soon as it was morning. The search and rescue mission had unfortunately turned into a search and retrieve recovery

■ ■ ■ ■ ■

Mark and Nathan, aka Adam, together were allowed to leave the *Volga* as she docked at Rhodes harbor, just as was the case for most of the guests. Everyone had been asked to provide proofs of identity, which most people had with them. Those who had not come on board with sufficient proof were escorted by the police back to the place where they had said their papers were. Most often they were taken to a hotel and from time to time to a rental home. Mark and Nathan had been quite careful before coming onboard and knowing how things might turn out to have the papers provided to them by *Mossad*. Their passports were still Israeli, as Nathan, aka Adam, made no secret of the fact that he was an Israeli businessman.

Mark's plan provided that a jet would be awaiting Nathan and him at Diagoras International Airport, which is located in the northwest top corner of Rhodes Island, north of the village of Paradeisi, less than ten miles from Rodos, the capital. They took a taxi to the Lindo Blue, probably the best luxury hotel on the island, where Oleg had booked rooms for two nights for his guests. They asked the taxi to wait and went to retrieve their belongings in their rooms. From there, they took the same taxi directly to the airport. The taxi driver was surprised as there were no scheduled flight that late in the evening. He quieted down when Mark simply said that the plane was not run by a commercial airline: it was private. The driver actually quickly had the opportunity to verify the statement Mark made as he was directed to a small twinjet that was sitting on the tarmac. Mark and Nathan climbed onto the plane, greeted the pilots and the crew and sat back for a short snooze. Before falling asleep, Mark could be seen sending what appeared to be an urgent message.

An hour and a half later, they landed on Palmachim Air Base where a *Mossad* car was awaiting them. The car first dropped Nathan at a *Mossad* apartment very near headquarters, and then took Mark home, where his wife Minoo and sons Cyrus and Simon were both sound asleep. Minoo and Mark had indeed chosen to name their first son after Minoo's father, and the second after Simon Rabinowitz, the head of the *Disruption* unit of *Mossad* when Minoo was extracted from Iran[6] and eventually met with Mark. He made every effort to slip into bed without waking Minoo up but was only marginally successful. She realized that he had come back and was briefly surprised that he was early, as he had told her he expected to spend the night in Rhodes. She went straight back to sleep, as Simon was still a baby and liable to wake up at any moment looking for a feeding.

---

[6] By the same author, see "Operation Kovesh," Barringer Publishing 2020.

CHAPTER.29

TEL AVIV, ISRAEL AND RHODES, GREECE

Oleg and Anton, who had both gone to sleep aboard *INS Storm*, the Israeli submarine, were suddenly awakened by Captain Ayel, who said:

"Sorry, Gentlemen, but there has been a small change in plan . . ."

Oleg's heart skipped a beat. Initially, the operation had followed a course which he expected, though he had only been made aware of the details that concerned him. Mark had indeed previewed the upcoming operation in a sufficient amount of detail that would satisfy Oleg and convinced him to go along, all the while leaving aside anything that could lead to a security breach. He remembered how David's simple observation had startled him and caused him to "lose it" for a short while.

■ ■ ■ ■ ■

Indeed, less than a week earlier, therefore well before the onset of the celebratory cruise, Mark and David had visited Oleg's office, in the Tel Aviv penthouse. The official point of the visit was to discuss the next steps in the operation designed to allow him to escape the Russian bear. Oleg was in a jovial mood as he motioned David and

Mark into his office. After all, he was delighted that a deal had been struck that allowed Visla Cybersecurity to purchase a license from Avigdor Cyber Experts. He was ready to celebrate and had in fact had glasses set on the coffee table in front of the sofa. He was going to offer Vodka or any other "adult beverage" his guests would desire. The deal clearly had not closed yet and would not for a short while; however, from Oleg's standpoint, the sale had taken place, which had been his principal focus in the most recent past. *Mossad* still had a number of surprises for him.

David started the conversation with what in most circumstances would have to have been a real downer:

"Oleg, I have some bad news for you."

"How bad?"

Without hesitation, David simply replied:

"Terminal!"

Oleg jumped up from his armchair on the right side of the sofa:

"Terminal? What the hell do you mean?"

Without losing an ounce of his calm David replied:

"Oleg Nichakov must die."

At that point, Oleg really "lost it," as his voice went up at least an octave and its volume ten decibels:

"Wait a second. Wait a bloody second. Nobody told me about that when we first met. Come on, what is going on? Not fair guys. I fulfilled my share of the bargain, didn't I?"

David quickly realized that the trick he was playing on Oleg had gone about as far as it should. He smiled broadly as he simply replied:

"Come on; calm down my friend. It's simple. You see. Oleg must die so that Dimitri and his family can live undisturbed!"

Oleg's face initially displayed total disbelief. It was almost as if his mind was processing each word alone as it came out of David's mouth, sequentially and by itself. His face started to light up as his

mind as reached the comment about Dimitri. Mark did not have much of an effort to get him over the "finish line" as he explained:

"What David is saying is that unless Oleg dies, and his body is never found, Dimitri will never have the freedom to live in the open, together with Irina and the children. It would be a terrible life: fugitives forever."

He paused for a second, smiled and continued:

"Think of it, if we can make Oleg disappear, then whoever is after him will no longer have any target. They won't have a need to kill someone that's dead"

Oleg started to smile and finally almost reluctantly conceded:

"Ingenuous, but a bit of a hard pill at first . . ."

David kept smiling as Mark concluded:

"We know, Oleg. We know. But we didn't know how to break it to you more gently."

He paused for a second and added:

"Still, come to think of it . . ."

Oleg was finally relaxing. He had regained his more normal composure. Mark and David then started to take him through the plan Mark had formulated. Mark explained:

"Now, the plan is complex and requires a certain number of steps to be carried out, and more to the point carried out in the right order, so that Dimitri and his family can live in peace."

He paused and noting that Oleg was currently paying close attention, he started with the first step:

"Oleg needs to dispose of as much of his assets as possible and do it in a way that is as discreet as possible."

Oleg clearly looked as if he did not understand. His mind was racing as he was thinking that he would not know how to do that. He simply said:

"But how? Anything I do would be obvious. Don't you think? What am I missing?"

David calmly replied that he was not sure Oleg's conclusion was correct. With a broad smile on his face, he asked:

"Think of the purchase of the license from Avigdor. How much of your estimated fortune does the price represent?"

"Well, let me think."

Mark could clearly see that Oleg was running through a series of computations in his head. He encouraged him to think out loud. Oleg noted that the question was not simple as he had already shifted quite a bit of his wealth to Dimitri through a number of offshore entities, which Dimitri eventually controlled. Mark realized that he had asked the question the wrong way. He rephrased his question:

"Let's leave Dimitri and his share of the wealth alone for the time being. Think of what is still in Oleg's name. Oleg seemed to breathe a sigh of relief and said:

"That's quite a bit simpler. Oleg really owns three main assets. The first is my share of Visla Cybersecurity, the second is the *Volga* and all that goes with it, and the third is my personal home in St. Petersburg with all its furnishing. Though of course a lot of that ownership is through corporate entities . . . to manage risks. I do also own some financial assets, but the total is limited, principally checking and saving accounts."

"OK, excellent. Whatever that total is, how much of that is the monies to be received from the sale of Avigdor?"

Oleg was again hesitating: it was taking him some time to think of the purchase by Visla of the license from Avigdor as something he owned. He eventually blurted out:

"About 40%. I guess, but I still don't understand why that number means anything."

David remarked:

"Good. Excellent."

Mark surprised Oleg with his next question:

"Now, how would you react if I told you that Visla Cybersecurity had bought a hoax?"

"A hoax? What do you mean? Avigdor is a hoax? No way, I saw what its software did, and our team did a lot of due diligence. Come on . . ."

"Absolutely. Avigdor only exists on paper. And it has no miracle software."

Oleg was again totally confused:

"Hold it? What does that mean for me?"

He paused and with a distinctly worried look on his face he added:

"The money that Visla Cybersecurity borrowed to pay for Avigdor will have to be repaid. Do you simply mean that I should not worry about it because I would be dead? But wait, why are you asking me to count the funds we're about to receive as assets of mine? I'm lost guys. Completely lost . . ."

Seeing that Mark and David were still smiling, Oleg was starting to doubt his own intellect. He asked:

"What's going on here? What am I missing. Can't believe you would have swindled me."

He stopped speaking again, as if he was checking his own logic. Then he asked:

"Come on. Somebody got swindled. Right? Am I losing my mind?"

David still the image of total calm replied:

"No, my friend. You're not. Your logic is impeccable. You're not losing anything as it turns out. You will receive the funds that Visla sends. The real losers, those who were swindled using your own words are those who own the balance of Visla Cybersecurity."

"How do you figure that?"

"Simply. The funds which are going to be received in exchange for the shares in Avigdor at closing will be made available to Dimitri when he asks. After closing, obviously."

Oleg first broke into a weak laugh. He looked as if he was beginning to understand. He said:

"You sold a hoax to Visla in exchange for money which you will make available to Dimitri. Right?"

"Right my friend."

Oleg's laugh turned into a heartier laugh:

"You thieves! Wicked thieves . . ."

He paused as if he wanted to pinch himself to be sure he was not dreaming. Then he added with a wonderful smile:

"Wicked thieves, but wonderful people."

Oleg was getting up to go to the liquor cabinet to get some vodka to celebrate, but Mark brought him back to reality:

"Let's hold off on the vodka. There quite a bit of work we still need to do. Is there any other asset which you could sell?"

Oleg looked quite pensive. Mark noted:

"Remember, whatever is not sold before Oleg dies will be lost forever."

Oleg's smile vanished. He immediately understood what Mark was saying, but the situation still looked too awkward for him to rejoice openly about his death. He mechanically replied:

"Well, I guess I can't do anything about Visla, so that leaves the *Volga* and the house in St. Petersburg. As I said, there are also a few balances in various bank accounts, but, as you know, most has been in Dimitri's name for a while."

He paused and almost casually added:

"Wait a minute. Why not simply have Oleg sell to Dimitri and be done with it?"

Mark immediately replied:

"Oh, That's exactly the solution I would avoid. I would strongly advise against any transaction involving Dimitri. I think it would be too transparent if Dimitri simply kept on where Oleg left off."

Oleg thought for a second and replied:

"Glad you said that; what was I thinking? So, I guess that I really cannot sell much without drawing attention. The house in St. Petersburg is worth a fair amount, but why would Oleg be selling it? The rest of Visla Cybersecurity is also off limits: Oleg couldn't sell it without drawing a lot of attention. The *Volga*?"

David replied:

"In general, I can't fault your logic. But I don't agree with the ultimate conclusion. There are things you can sell. The key is that whatever you do sell, must have a closing not later than the date when the money from the sale of Avigdor is received. And that's because that's the date when Visla will discover that they were sold a hoax."

Oleg was raking his brains to come up with a solution. He had gone from the fear of being killed, to the satisfaction of knowing he would live, but might have to do so with a lot less money, to one now trying to minimize the money he might have to leave on the table. His first thought was:

"I could sell the *Volga*, close the sale quite quickly if I find a buyer, which should not be too hard, demand is quite high for yachts at present. I could charter it from the new owner if I needed it."

He paused and added:

"If I did that, I would sell it with the crew subject to the crew agreeing obviously, but I would want Anton to remain with me."

"Shouldn't be a problem. Start looking for a buyer. And, if Dimitri still wants to have a yacht, I'd suggest you start looking for one that's already built. There's bound to be something on offer in the second-hand market."

David noted:

"Makes sense. Need to be quite discreet though. This is a small world and people could talk."

Oleg replied:

"Oleg is not buying the new yacht, Dimitri is . . ."

David smiled and reminded Oleg:

"You want to create as big a distance between these two people as possible. I know it's tedious, but I would use two yacht brokers, one for the sale of the Volga and the other for the purchase of whatever you need to replace her."

Mark, concerned that they were going too deep into secondary matters, interrupted David in his reply:

"Any other asset that can be sold?"

"I'd love to be able to get back some of the furniture, artwork and personal stuff out of the house in St. Petersburg, but I have no idea how to do that."

"We can help you with a temporary location to which you could move that stuff. You'd have to organize the move."

"Let me see. Maybe I even could sell the house quickly probably at discount, get moved out and at the same time hire a broker to look for a new apartment for me."

Oleg was again moving from trying to recover some wealth to not wanting to leave anything on the table. Mark simply said:

"Makes sense, but you don't have much time. Could you leave a power of attorney to someone?"

"I already have my personal lawyer. He will take instructions on the telephone."

"How would he react if he learns of your death before everything is done?

"He is one of the only ones who knows about my distant past. I'll create a fake uncle or something. We have a code we have agreed to use if ever I needed his help in a situation like this one. I'll send him a note with an address in Kiev . . ."

"We can help with that too."

■ ■ ■ ■ ■

The next topic of conversation was more difficult but needed to be planned down to the smallest necessary detail. At the same

time, Mark and David did not want to cover anything that was not necessary, for instance who was going to do what to whom, if the "whom" was not Oleg. They needed to ensure that he would behave in as natural a manner as possible up until the very last moment. The next major challenge indeed was the need to organize Oleg's demise. They agreed that they had little or no control over where and when the enemy, if there was one, would try to assassinate or kidnap Oleg. To Oleg, the latter option was equivalent to an assassination, which, in his mind, would inevitably result from being in the hands of the regime as he called them.

David started to take Oleg through what he meant to be a series of logical steps to try to clarify where he saw the greatest risks. The first question was obvious, though Oleg displayed some clear discomfort:

"Who could possibly be against you within Visla Cybersecurity?"

"I don't know. I've told you that I don't believe Yuri is against me. Lord, we have known each other for long enough. But anybody below him could well be a plant. As I think I also told you, that plant does not need to be a high-level executive. Remember the story in "The Hunt for Red October;" one of the traitors was a junior cook on the submarine from memory."

"Understood. The way I take your reply is that we should keep an eye on everyone except Yuri."

". . . and Igor?"

Mark beat David to the reply:

"I remember your logic and we can buy it, though we must keep an open mind. Anything came out on the people we call the two junior people named Igor?"

"No. Both look as clean as can be."

Oleg paused for a second and sadly added:

"I guess it must mean that Igor Zatopek has to remain a suspect . . . I can't get myself to say it, but I should probably have him as a primary suspect if your analysis holds."

Mark let that one pass, feeling sorry for Oleg, but knowing that there was precious little he could do about the situation, at least until further developments had taken place. He switched back to the discussion of the plan:

"Given that we believe the enemy doesn't know where you are, and that the two attacks we have seen so far have been around the *Volga*, I would suggest that the simplest would be to organize a party on the yacht. Say, what about a party on the *Volga* to celebrate the closing the Avigdor purchase?"

Oleg perked up and became visibly excited. Mark and David marveled at Oleg's apparent ability to shift from one mood to another, at times virtual opposites. Was he a great actor? What if because of the dual life he had been living ever since he had created Dimitri, his alter ego? Was it a simple psychic defense mechanism? He exclaimed:

"Sure. In truth, it would be in keeping with what would normally be done. We've done it whenever we had a big milestone. Typically, we had organized for the *Volga* to be in the Baltic Sea, because that's a natural for a company based in St. Petersburg; our celebratory cruises would leave from and return to what we call the "Great Port of St. Petersburg." It's a major seaport and covers nearly sixty-five square miles. Anyway. I'm getting lost in detail, but given the time of the year, my usual travel schedules, and where the ship currently is, we could imagine the party in the Mediterranean."

He was clearly thinking out loud when he added:

"So, if the cruise is not based in St. Petersburg, guests would likely expect me to charter a plane to bring them to the airport nearest the chosen harbor."

He paused again:

"Actually, the harbor we pick has to be near an airport. Otherwise, the logistics become way too complex. Also, since the *Volga* doesn't have sufficient staterooms, I'm guessing we'd have to book hotel rooms for the guests. Didn't have to worry about that in St. Petersburg, as

most people would simply drive home at the end of the cruise. The hotel has to be top class for sure. May have a few stay onboard where we actually organize this celebratory cruise."

David came back and simply replied:

"This sounds like a reasonable scenario. Now, Mark will take you through more detail, but you don't need me here."

David stood up and was walking in the direction of the door when Oleg asked:

"Can your plan include Anton as well? I don't want him left behind. Nobody knows we're family, but he knows a lot about me. In fact, he knows too much about me. He's the only person who knows that Oleg and Dimitri are one and the same . . . Even my lawyer, the one I mentioned earlier; he knows of my past but does not know about Dimitri!"

David breathed a visible sigh of relief and replied:

"I'm glad you're not asking us to get rid of him because we don't get involved in these kinds of things. But since that's not the request, I'm sure Mark can plan for that contingency. While I think of it; can the first mate really run the *Volga* without Anton?"

"Sure. That's his job. He doesn't know everything particularly with respect to all administrative matters, but he knows everything he needs to know from an operational or navigational point of view."

"Excellent."

■ ■ ■ ■ ■

Oleg was still asking himself why the plans had changed as he had just been told by Captain Ayel. Nonetheless, he did not get much of a chance to delay the unfolding of Mark's plan or find out more about why the plan was changing. The *INS Storm* surfaced. Oleg was increasingly confused: this was still exactly on plan. The submarine was supposed to surface and to have him and Anton transfer to a faster surface boat. So, what had changed? It was not yet dawn,

though there were signs that the sun was pointing its early rays in the East. Oleg and Anton were escorted up the sail of the submarine from which they would climb onto the top of the vessel.

When there, Oleg who was expecting the sound of the engine of a fast boat was surprised to hear the definite sound of a helicopter approaching. Captain Ayel seemed to anticipate it, turning to Oleg, he said:

"That's the change. We're going to heli-lift you back to Tel Aviv. This is even faster than a fast boat and Colonel Heller felt that speed was of the essence."

Oleg felt decidedly reassured on the one hand, but, on the other, wondered where the helicopter would land. Captain Ayel replied:

"Oh, the chopper won't land. We'll use a hoist on the helicopter to lift you up, one at a time, while the aircraft hovers over the submarine. You shouldn't be afraid, though the wind may lead to some apparent swinging. The hoist is an electric drive system that winds a cable around a drum. By the way, there's a braking system, a double system as it turns out. So, if something should jam, you won't go free falling into the water."

"Why did they change the plan?"

"As I said a minute ago, the only thing I heard is that our confreres at *Mossad* believed you should be brought to Tel Aviv sooner rather than later. Oh, I've also been told to let you know that special guards have been dispatched to your penthouse, just in case . . ."

Oleg would have liked to continue the conversation, but there was no time. He was ready to be lifted up into the Eurocopter X3, the fastest helicopter in the world. It could reach a top speed of more than two hundred and fifty miles per hour, as it was equipped with a central rotor with two additional propellers one on each side of the aircraft. Anton followed a few minutes later. The copter then turned around and flew back directly to Tel Aviv, as *Mossad* headquarters had a heliport. On its way to rendezvous with the submarine, the

helicopter had made a small detour: it had landed on the heliport of an Israeli Navy tanker that was in the general vicinity. It filled up with fuel to ensure that it would have more than enough for the return flight even if there should be a snag or two.

When Oleg and Anton, somewhat clumsily dressed as Israeli naval officers arrived in Tel Aviv, they were given the bags that contained their wet clothes and brought down right away to David's office. He was already standing there with Mark who looked like he definitely ought to have had more sleep. Mark immediately said to Oleg:

"Oleg, my friend, I have unpleasant news for you?"

Oleg suddenly took a step back:

"Nothing had happened to Irina or the children, right?"

"No. Everybody is safe. That's not the news."

"What is it then?"

"Well, it has to do with the tip I got on the *Volga*; you know the tip which started the whole Plan B as we called it . . ."

"Yes. So?"

"Well, you'll remember that I didn't give you the details then. I just told you that both I and another *Katsa* had seen something that we felt was quite dangerous. I told you that I had seen the man whom I thought was the one I pistol-whipped in Marbella . . ."

"I remember that." Who was the man talking to?"

"Your CFO, Igor Zatopek!"

Oleg slumped in the armchair on which he was already seating. Mark added:

"I know this is a real downer for you. But two of us did see Igor speak to someone who had intruded onto the Volga thinking you were there. So, to me, the conclusion is hard to avoid: Igor was therefore definitely in on the plan to have you kidnaped and brought back to Russia . . ."

For the first time, Oleg had to face the realization that Igor was indeed a traitor to him. He mumbled:

"That's terrible. Igor, I trusted him."

Mark felt sorry for Igor, but he added:

"Steel yourself my friend . . . The worst is yet to come."

Oleg straightened up. He did not know what to expect but appeared to be getting ready against almost anything. Mark continued:

"However, after you and Anton were shot, I kept mingling with those guests that were not in shock."

"And?"

"Well, it turns out that Igor and Yuri seemed like the best friends in the world. They certainly did not seem upset by your apparent demise. Unless drinking vodka, joking heartily, and laughing more and more loudly as we were sailing toward the harbor is the way you all mourn the death of friends . . ."

Oleg appeared dumbfounded. He sat down on the closest armchair, and simply began to cry.

EPILOGUE

TEL AVIV, ISRAEL

It is never easy for anyone to tell a story in which he has participated. As a matter of fact, my boss, General Simon Rabinowitz, had to remind me that he was himself once compelled to write about a story in similar circumstances. So, if he did it when he had to, it would be real hard for me not to do it in my turn.

I should of course start with profuse thanks to all those who were kind enough to share with me details or developments that I did not witness firsthand. My deputy, Mark Levi, has to be first on that list, but there are many others, in fact too many to name them all here. I am sure they know how much I appreciated the help they provided.

The first development for me to report since the episode has ended is that the Greek authorities eventually declared that Oleg Nichakov and Anton Chernenko were both lost at sea and presumed dead. They said that though it is unlikely that they were eventually eaten by sharks which though plentiful in the Aegean Sea are usually harmless to humans, nobody seemed to be concerned with locating their bodies. Considering what we know, that can only be seen as a good thing! They would not find anything and would be wasting resources.

The various transactions which Oleg had organized prior to his apparent untimely demise eventually closed on time, even though there were a few difficulties with respect to the house in St. Petersburg. His lawyer there, however, did exactly as instructed and I am glad to report that the personal items and furnishing which Oleg wanted were eventually delivered to Dimitri's house in Zurich. When the delivery was announced, I asked Mark to fly with an associate to the warehouse in Geneva where it was supposed initially to be stored to sweep everything. I wanted to make absolutely sure that there was no bug which might have been slipped in there. I was worried about a bug which would allow the geolocation of the goods at some point, which eventually would allow the FIS to go check, discreetly at first, who the new owner was. That proved to be a welcome intuition: there were indeed a number of tracking devices. Oleg's belief that he was under surveillance was definitely correct.

Now, whoever planted these bugs may conclude that they ought to look into who might eventually pick up the delivery from Geneva; they will be stumped. Knowing of the effort to track the belongings and fearing that we may have missed one or another bug, we organized for them to be carried around for a while. Whoever was attempting to put a trace on them will have had an opportunity to travel around the world. Actually, we even organized to have different teams of *Katsas* inspect the shipment in several of these "interim stops" as we call them. I hate to admit to it, but we did find a couple of bugs that had escaped earlier detection at our first two stops. Since then, nothing. So, I know that Dimitri was disappointed that he will not have some of his cherished belongings as rapidly as he expected. However, presently he has them and he is quite relieved to know that either they cannot be tracked or that any tracker will have given up.

In the end, Dimitri has been able to continue his "new" life with Irina and the children with minimum disruption, though he certainly left some of his fortune "on the table" in Russia. Between the residences

he already had prior to his decision to take refuge outside of Russia and the new yacht which he was able to purchase, entrusting the captainship to Anton, his life is certainly nearly as comfortable as it was before. We have been told that the yacht was quite comparable to the *Volga*, though a few interior improvements were needed to cater to the need for something like the "family quarters" which had been designed into the *Volga*. The yacht being more modern, the heliport is duly at the back of the vessel rather than at the front, and it is located on the highest deck, at the back of the flybridge.

Dimitri does not have to worry about protecting his life from the Russian regime. I hear that he has been contemplating a series of corporate ventures. This does not surprise me as I cannot imagine him simply retiring from active life and focusing solely on golf and his family. I am pretty sure we will find him doing something of interest sometime in the future.

Nathan has returned to his laboratory, which, quite frankly, he was not all that keen to leave in the first place. We have been told that he used the substantial reward he received for his services in this effort in part to invest further in The Advanced Technology Park; it seems quite in keeping with what we knew of him that he would share some of his bounty with his colleagues. I am sure, though, that he has not shared with them anything about how he came upon it. Yet, there are rumors that at the prompting of Wong Hai Chock he may have had advanced conversations with Countess Renate. As always, we will never know whether he had become a member of the Shadow Experts, until we hire Countess Renate on another project and that project requires the help of someone with Nathan's profile.

Though we certainly did not wish to attack Russia directly, we still let Hai Chock and Nathan unleash a last wave of viruses into the Russian system, using the Visla Cybersecurity Company as their entry portal. Our prime targets, the communications between Russia and its "clients" in the Middle East were certainly impaired and we have heard

rumors that a few of them are doubting Russia's ability to help them. That's the good news. The bad news is that these former Russian clients are turning to China: from Charybdis to Scilla; from bad to equally bad if not worse! Hai Chock and Nathan's attacks caused havoc across a wide swath of the Russian defense establishment, at a time when it was already stretched by the war they had started in Ukraine. Of course, there was no official announcement that any sort of problem had arisen, but our eyes and ears on the ground confirmed that a few missiles were unintentionally fired, and communications interrupted between domestic headquarters and various units overseas.

Unfortunately, the story which I just felt I needed to tell did not finish too well for certain people. The realization that Avigdor was as it turned out a hoax, and that some substantial monies had been paid into an overseas account for effectively nothing was the proverbial drop that led the vase to overflow. We are convinced that it was the one problem which led to the arrest of Yuri Vassiliev. While this suggested that Yuri may not have been as "guilty" as we had anticipated, it did confirm our hypothesis that Igor Zakopek was most likely the most senior of the Foreign Intelligence Service agents planted in the late Oleg Nichakov's company. We have not heard what happened to Yuri and will await any news on that front with keen interest. Any sign that he escaped a drastic punishment would strongly point to the fact that he too was a senior Foreign Intelligence Service agent. However, in the current environment where suspicion runs rampant within the regime, he may still end up paying with his life, even if he was not totally "clean" as we believed and reported to Dimitri.

Signed: D.H.

Printed in the USA
CPSIA information can be obtained
at www.ICGtesting.com
JSHW060353220124
55764JS00006B/20